by BERNARD B. FALL

THE VIET-MINH REGIME

LE VIET-MINH

STREET WITHOUT JOY

THE TWO VIET-NAMS

THE VIET-NAM READER (*co-author*)

VIET-NAM WITNESS

HELL IN A VERY SMALL PLACE

Last Reflections
On a War

BERNARD B. FALL

Last Reflections
On a War

Preface by Dorothy Fall

DOUBLEDAY & COMPANY, INC., GARDEN CITY, NEW YORK
1967

Map by Bernard B. and Dorothy Fall

To
Marine Gunnery Sergeant Byron G. Highland . . .
combat photographer,
partner in death.

Preface

ᗺᗺ

WHEN MY HUSBAND left this time for Viet-Nam there were those among us who felt we would never see him again. Even Bernard had put off his departure several times. First, it was the birth of the baby—his third daughter—in September, then there were lectures promised, his *Two Viet-Nams* to update and more articles to write. But finally, because he was committed and had accepted the Guggenheim Grant for this long awaited Sabbatical year, he set a departure date of December 8 and methodically began to assemble his gear.

It was unlike his usual preparations when he would be full of enthusiasm and anticipation for what he would find. I watched stoically wanting to urge him not to go but I could say nothing.

I stayed behind to prepare for an art exhibit in January and to give the baby more of a start in life before setting off for the other end of the world and a contemplated seven month stay in Hong Kong.

This was Bernard's sixth trip to his beloved Viet-Nam. He was first introduced to the area in 1953 when he decided to write his doctoral dissertation on the Viet-Minh, Ho Chi Minh's guerrillas who were then fighting the French. He was always proud to admit that he had gone on his own funds—the meager savings he had

9

accumulated during his student days. From his letters to me evolved *Street Without Joy*. The French censor had chided him for these letters. "Why don't you stick to love letters to your fiancée instead of these detailed reports and maps on French operations," he had said.

To obtain his information on the structure and degree of infiltration of the Viet-Minh, Bernard went deep into the provinces of Viet-Nam interviewing officials, tax collectors and village chiefs. The resulting analysis showed that the situation was much different from what the French command thought it was. The enemy held far more terrain than was known or acknowledged.

During these eight months he accompanied the French troops on operations, mostly in the North, and visited fortresses deep in Viet-Minh territory. His home base was Hanoi.

But it was following his next trip to Viet-Nam in the summer of 1957 that he began to feel the consequences of stating facts as one sees them, not as one would like them to be. Diem was in power and things looked fine from here, or so we were told. But Bernard noticed from Vietnamese newspaper reports that village chiefs were still being killed—three years after the Geneva cease-fire. From these facts and from trips into the areas he was able to map out what was now Viet Cong-held territory (that we were told did not exist). He returned to Washington with facts in hand and proof of corruption within the Diem regime. And he began to predict the events that would ensue.

Several job offers were rescinded but he held his ground. He was aware of memos circulating and of false accusations but he would not compromise.

During the subsequent ten years' worth of hundreds of articles and seven books we were to see one prediction after another come true. Meanwhile, my husband held onto his French passport because it would permit him to travel in areas forbidden to Americans. In 1962 he was granted a visa to visit North Viet-Nam and interviewed Ho Chi Minh and Pham Van Dong. He had decided, though, that he would become an American citizen after this trip for he had staked his roots here now.

In late 1963, just three weeks after the November 1 coup in which President Diem was overthrown and he and his brother,

Ngo Dinh Nhu, killed, Bernard landed in the hospital with a near fatal case of uremic poisoning. He had been in this state for a week; most people die after four or five days. His strong constitution and superb physical stamina would not permit it. An X-ray showed that he had a total blockage of both kidneys. The ureters were squeezed shut by something but the doctors did not know by what. Ten weeks, four operations and $8000 later it was discovered that Bernard was suffering from retroperitoneal fibrosis, a rare incurable disease which produces the growth of non-malignant fibrous tissue within the abdominal cavity.

President Kennedy was assassinated the day after Bernard entered the hospital and during my daily vigil I often envisioned Madame Nhu, whose own world had toppled, sitting before two dolls—one of President Kennedy and the other of Bernard Fall—eking out vengeance by sticking pins into them.

One ureter was freed of the fibrous tissue but the left side was too far gone and the kidney was subsequently removed.

My husband had always attributed his tremendous output to his "machine," never to his mental acumen. This in spite of the fact that he spoke three languages fluently and accentless and wrote brilliantly in each. He had the power of total recall and was capable of taking his facts and giving a penetrating analysis of a situation as well as a practical solution to one.

But now his "machine" was failing him. In March of 1965 the colon suddenly became strangled by the fibrosis, still alive within him. This was snipped away during an exploratory operation and there were no more symptoms. Nonetheless, Bernard felt that his days were numbered.

He left for Viet-Nam four months later, heedless of the protests of his doctors. Yes, he promised to behave himself. While I was receiving letters postmarked Saigon I read in the New York *Times* of his having been caught in an ambush while on patrol in the sticks.

He was fearless; he had to prove to himself that he was the old Bernard—hoofing it with the troops—in the mud and jungles of Viet-Nam. But also, he had to test his convictions and could rely only on information gathered first hand. This was the trip during which he was to change many of his opinions.

11

What ensued was a race against time. In the three years following his illness he produced his most penetrating articles and his greatest book, *Hell in a Very Small Place*. He worked like one possessed.

As he left, just six months ago, with his camouflage equipment and his sense of foreboding, he knew somehow that he would never return. Once in Viet-Nam, however, he was hypnotized and filled with his usual enthusiasm for life. He had to pursue each hunch. On February 19, just before he was to visit me in Hong Kong he decided to accompany the Marines on Operation Chinook —up in his old area, Street Without Joy. And there like the other men he wrote of so reverently he had his rendezvous with destiny.

Dorothy Fall

WASHINGTON, D.C.
JUNE 1967

Contents

჻

EDITOR'S NOTE

BERNARD B. FALL was killed by a booby trap on the Street Without Joy, in Northern South Viet-Nam, at 4:30 on the afternoon of February 21, 1967. He was forty years old.

At the moment of his death he was reporting the conclusion of a Marine Sweep. His last words were recorded on tape, a transcript of which appears in this book. *Last Reflections On a War* consists of Dr. Fall's tape recordings, unpublished pieces, and articles that have not been published in book form. It follows *Viet-Nam Witness* (1966), and augments it.

On November 21, 1966, Dr. Fall appeared on *Celebrity's Choice,* a WABC-FM interview program, conducted by Dick Hubert. The transcript of this program provides the only autobiographical account of Bernard Fall's life available. "Street Without Joy Revisited" was found among the author's papers returned from Saigon. It was perhaps the basis for a new study.

The pieces in the present book have been selected by Mrs. Bernard B. Fall.

Stewart Richardson

Celebrity's Choice:
November 21, 1966

Bernard B. Fall, Interviewed by Dick Hubert

ᏀᏔᎵᏋ

EACH WEEK a distinguished guest talks about his life and work and picks the most significant and memorable music in his life. Here to introduce tonight's guest and to play the music he finds important in life is our host, Dick Hubert.

HUBERT: Good evening. Our guest on *Celebrity's Choice* tonight is the distinguished expert on Viet-Nam—North and South—Bernard Fall, Professor of International Relations at Howard University in Washington and the music that he has brought along for tonight's program reflects an incredibly fascinating career that spans several continents, some of the most horrendous wars in modern times and an expertise on the most critical subject in America today—Viet-Nam.

Bernard Fall, I'd like to start out with your first piece of music which takes us all the way back to 1940 but before we get to it, I'd like you to tell us a little about where you were born and where you were brought up.

FALL: Well, my background, I guess, is about as mixed as my present life. I was born in Vienna, Austria, but actually never lived there, except having been born there—my father was working

Reprinted by permission of Dick Hubert Productions. Mr. Hubert is also Producer-Writer for ABC Television News.

there at the time. But, I am French—I was raised in France so I went to school there and when the Germans overran France my father was in the French Army and we saw the Germans marching in and this is where I got my first whiff of war at the age of twelve. I'll be forty, in fact, this week and this is where for the first time Beethoven came to my mind as something else except the good classic music. As you will see from the rest of my choices I am a very happy . . . lowbrow when it comes to music.

HUBERT: Well, tell us a little first about your upbringing there and about your family. What did your father do?

FALL: My father was a businessman in France. We had engineering materials and so forth as part of my father's business line and my mother was just the normal housewife. I have a sister, a younger sister and the rest of my family is in the book business in France—which is very handy when you happen to be an author as I am—you can always push your own books on your own family and I went to the normal *école primaire* the primary school in France and then to *lycée* and this is when the war broke out. You know, I was just an average young boy and to me war was . . . I'd seen war in the movies, of course, and war, somehow in European movies, always gets depicted as being either at night or in the middle of rain and I'll never forget . . . I was on vacation in Southern France when the war broke out and it was a perfectly sunny Riviera day. I was standing out in the open overlooking the Riviera. We lived on a hill—a beautiful house on the hill so I was waiting for the thunder and the rains to come down and nothing happened. In a way I was quite disappointed that war would start out on this perfectly banal, beautiful day.

HUBERT: Now, this particular day—was this in 1938?

FALL: 9—September 1939.

HUBERT: The official breakout.

FALL: Outbreak of war in Europe—Western Europe.

HUBERT: Now, what did your family do with this new situation? Did it change their plans? Did it change your life?

FALL: Well, my father was in the Army. Everybody was called up and there was talk that the Germans might be bombing Paris and so forth so my mother and family decided to stay in the South on the Riviera. Now, the joke was that the Italians declared

16

war on France as she lay dying, in June 1940, and we were literally on the front lines of the Italian advance. Yet, somehow, the Italians were never quite taken seriously. They were, in fact, wonderful people. They were not terribly interested in becoming the master race and I'll never forget . . . us going to school while Italian planes would fly overhead. No one ever really did take the war seriously. People would pick up their hunting rifles and go out, man the front lines against the Italians and so on and so forth. So, on our side, as the Austrians used to say about World War I— the situation was desperate but definitely not serious.

HUBERT: Now, where was your father during all this?

FALL: Well, he was being clobbered in Northern France by the Germans (chuckle). He was south and east of Dunkirk and he was part of this vast magnum of collapsing British and French forces retreating into Central France so we didn't know where he was. There was no V-mail or anything. He finally popped up after the war . . . after France was defeated in 1940—June—he popped up in some ill-fitting Army uniform and apparently he had made it. Well, obviously he had made it. So from there on in the Germans occupied my country and in 1942 I joined the underground.

HUBERT: Well, in 1940 when your first piece of music comes in in your life, you were the mainstay of the Fall family—father was away fighting the war.

FALL: That's right . . .

HUBERT: . . . and you were the senior male in the household.

FALL: . . . I was the male component in the family—right.

HUBERT: Well, tell us how this music comes in and how you remember it.

FALL: Well, . . . as France was defeated on June 25, 1940, the cease-fire was signed by Field Marshal Pétain and this era of German occupation started which was to end only four years later— you know, you sort of fiddled on the radio and at first French stations were off the air as they had been overrun by the Germans— some stations didn't function at all—others on a helter-skelter basis —others all you heard was German. And, all of a sudden there was this British station on the air and that British station on the air began with the very famous dot, dot, dot dash of course, of Beethoven's Fifth and also, of course, the dot, dot, dot, dash in

17

Morse Code means "V" and "V," of course, stood for Victory and anybody who in the dark days of 1940 was still willing to stand for Victory had not only our votes but certainly had our ears. And for four long years—the V—or, rather, beginning strains of Beethoven's Fifth became something that we all lived for and lived with. People risked their lives for it—just to listen to a British program or to the French program of the BBC. And, people were deported and executed in Germany for having just found their radio sets being on the BBC wavelength when the Gestapo walked in. This was enough to be arrested and deported—so, to me, Beethoven's Fifth is always connected with that.

[*Here the music of Beethoven's Fifth can be heard. . . .*]

HUBERT: Bernard Fall—the next piece of music in your life is a complete change of mood and a completely different time. It brings us up to 1944 and I'd like for you to bridge the gap in years and also in your life. You say you went into the underground—when, and how?

FALL: I joined the underground on a sunny afternoon of November 8, 1942. Now, you're wondering how you can tell anything as incredible so precisely. Well, what happened is that the American and British troops had landed in North Africa on November 8 and we, of course, were living in Southern France in Nice, on the shore of the Mediterranean. Algeria was across the Mediterranean—700 kilometers away—about 500 miles away and I had been part of a plain boy scout movement in France but at that time even the boy scouts were political—nobody liked the Germans. We'd been talking a lot about what we would do if we ever had a chance of getting to North Africa to join up.

I was coming home from school that afternoon and I met the boy scout troop leader who was a former French Air Force lieutenant colonel and I was then sixteen. And this was a man in about his late thirties and he said: "Listen, Bernard, you said you wanted to fight? Well, here's your chance. We've got a ship and we're taking off for North Africa tonight to join the Americans and the British and the Free French." Well, you can imagine making a decision like that on the spur of the moment. I literally walked down to the docks with my schoolbooks under my arm and from

18

the docks I called up my mother and—no, it was my father. I got my sister on the phone and said, "Well, Lisette, this is goodbye —I'm leaving for North Africa." You can imagine how my young sister took that one and she said: "Well, can we call you back?" I said, "No—we'll just have to leave."

Well, there was this French 8000 ton tanker sitting in port by the name of *Penerf* which is a Breton name and aboard the *Penerf* you saw these people coming from all over town as word had gotten around.

You see, here's what was happening. The Germans had not reached Nice yet. Nice was still in the Italian Zone of Occupation and the Italians had been very, very sloppy maintaining control so there was an even chance of being able to slip out of port. You see, the French Island of Corsica was further to the South and there was French boat travel from Nice to Corsica. So, if you got out of port you had a fair chance of being able to head for Corsica and then veer off away from Corsica into the open sea and ask for an American plane to escort you and if you were lucky you could get one. In fact, some ships succeeded in doing this.

Well, there we were—fifty of us—young ones, old ones, reserve officers, boy scouts—an incredible semblage of people and the tanker crew. The tanker Captain said: "Look fellows, I'm willing to try but if we get captured I'll say that you forced us to do it . . . there's no point getting everybody hanged." So, the Lieutenant Colonel Montier said "Yes, that's all right with us." Off we went; you know this whole thing sounds like a wild dream. We had actually hijacked a tanker. And again, like in a very bad dream—oh, about thirty miles and about three hours out there was an Italian torpedo boat. The Italians had never taken a prize on the high seas and we had never been captured so both sides played their scenario rather badly. When the Italians came aboard waving tommy guns and yelling *"pirata, pirata"* (pirates, pirates), and we sure enough found ourselves on the way back and to jail. And, you know, word finally got around this was a very serious thing—this was piracy on the high seas. We had actually captured a ship and, you know some of us had some ideas that we were going to get hanged for piracy because the only thing we had ever heard is that when you are a pirate you get hanged

19

from the yardarms. And, very fortunately, we were captured by the Italians and they either had a sense of humor or were heavily bribed—I think both occurred and we were released after a jail sentence . . . In my case, this was the funny thing—this had taken place on November 8, 1942—I turned sixteen on November 19 and I was released in the custody of my parents as a juvenile so I didn't get a criminal record as a pirate but it was a pretty close thing and from there on in I was wedded to the underground—this was it.

Well, things got very bad—my mother was deported as a hostage and she never came back and my father was tortured to death in 1943 by the Gestapo—we found his body in a ditch with twelve other people, two years later. Well, this was it. I hadn't known my father was in the underground. You didn't tell your own family what was going on. Of course, this is part of it in the system where everybody snoops on everybody else—the secret police watches everybody and the German secret police was rather good at it and it's quite incredible for Americans to believe that people could live like that—but we did.

So, I was then in Upper Savoy—from there on in I was on the Wanted list, I was in a real *Maquis*. Now, *Maquis* was really a combat outfit. There was no such thing as living at home like a solid citizen and then go out and shoot up a few Germans and then go back home and stay camouflaged. Oh, no, you actually fought all the way through. So, for us there was nothing except the endless tunnel. Either the Americans, British landed and the Free French and we would be saved or you'd just die—that's all there was to it—there was no giving up or being a prisoner—you landed in a concentration camp for extermination. And then the Americans landed.

HUBERT: And, strangely enough, with the landing of the Americans the mood of your music on tonight's program changes from the sad and yet hopeful strains of Beethoven to Glenn Miller. Now, explain this and your next piece of music.

FALL: You know, the whole liberation of France to me is going to be forever just one vast orchestration of Glenn Miller. As the American troops advanced, the first American AFN station was set up—the Armed Forces Network station on the Continent and Glenn

20

Miller was the rage of the day. Glenn Miller, as you know, was, in fact, in the armed forces at the time and he very unfortunately died in an airplane accident I think in the late fall, 1944. And his orchestra was there, live—it wasn't just something that you heard on a record—you actually could hear an actual transmission of Glenn Miller and it so much represented the Americans in the confident, rich, lovable characters. You know, this was not an Army of professionals—these were the American citizens—the guy on the street—the New York taxi driver—this was to us the first Americans whom we ever saw in our lives. And we were in the Alps— we were fighting our own war. The Americans weren't anywhere near us and we had some pretty grim German troops on the other side. But to hear every day, you know, the AFN and another piece of French real estate had been liberated and always Glenn Miller in between and as we finally linked up with the Americans, of course, then I was transferred to the French regular army, we all shoulder to shoulder marched into Germany. To me, the whole Western campaign—the whole end of World War II is always going to be Glenn Miller. I can't hear, can't even today listen to Glenn Miller without quite breaking up over it.

It sounds so terribly silly for a political science professor to be sentimental about "pop" music but this is really it. I'll never forget one particular day—we were in what we thought were pretty solid positions for in the winter of 1944 and then the Germans literally broke in out of the clear blue sky as it were and Glenn Miller was playing and it was "In the Mood."

By the time we came back—I mean probably three hours later and the radio had been left on: it was again, presumably after X-many station breaks—Glenn Miller was playing again—this is exactly why it became really engraved in me.

[*Here the* "In the Mood" *record of Glenn Miller is heard in its entirety.*]

HUBERT: Bernard Fall, I know that "In the Mood" not only recalls those days in World War II but strangely enough the same record came back into your life later on and I know we're going to have a jump in years but right now just let's hear that story about how you heard "In the Mood" again.

FALL: This was very weird. Finally, in 1962 I had obtained per-

21

mission to visit Communist North Viet-Nam which the Communists had taken over in 1954 after they had defeated the French at Dien Bien Phu and I sat in exactly the same hotel restaurant where I had sat in 1953 when the French were still fighting there and by sheer accident, I'm sure it was sheer accident, I had been given the same table I used to sit at and the whole—you must visualize now—North Vietnamese restaurant, this was probably the only one in the whole city that was fit to eat in for Westerners—isn't exactly a terribly pleasant place to begin with—the food's bad but that's not the only thing. It was absolutely sinister. There were maybe fifty tables and there were four persons in the whole restaurant: Me —a Chinese expert who in the fifteen days I was there never addressed a word to anybody including a Vietnamese waiter and a very nice Laotian Army Neutralist colonel and his very pregnant wife and you can imagine in a fifty-table restaurant—it was absolutely sinister.

And, as I came in there for the first meal in the evening there was this very screechy music—it wasn't Asian music—it was a Vietnamese version of Russian military marches, if you please. And, as I sat down, somewhere, somebody lifted off the needle on the P.A. system and on went a *very scratchy* 78 rpm version of Glenn Miller "In the Mood"—in Communist North Viet-Nam—out of courtesy to me (chuckle) and in a way I was quite touched.

HUBERT: Well, you know, you've gotten us into Viet-Nam and going to backtrack once again. Your next piece of music comes not in 1962 but in 1953. It's in Viet-Nam and I think many of our listeners would be interested in knowing how you became interested in this far away *then* French possession in the first place.

FALL: By sheer accident. I had come to the United States in late 1951 as a Fulbright research scholar to do my master's degree at Syracuse University in the State of New York and I had, in fact, done my theses and not on Viet-Nam . . . not at all on Viet-Nam but on the illegal rearmament of the German Weimar Republic —something perfectly esoteric and nobody's ever heard from it since. But, I had to finish—I had more time on my hands than I thought I would have and decided to do some work in a different field and I went to Johns Hopkins University School of Advanced International Studies in Washington and by sheer accident—they offered an

22

Asian concentration and for the first time there was a part of a course devoted to Indo-China and I took that. And I found the area rather interesting, as you said—well, the French no longer owned it as a colony but French troops were fighting there—this was in 1953 and this was actually getting to be a pretty nasty war except nobody knew anything about it. One of my good professors at the time— Amry Vandenbosch is still around—at the University of Kentucky— said, "You know, Bernard, you with your French background—you ought to get specialized in that area—you know, nobody knows much about it" . . . and I did. And, I went to Indo-China at my own expense in 1953 for my doctoral research for my Doctorate degree. And this is how by pure accident, one sunny day in Washington, D.C., of all places, in 1952 I got interested in Viet-Nam and it's been sort of a bad love affair ever since.

HUBERT: You know there are a lot of unusual aspects in your career and your music list tonight on *Celebrity's Choice* reflects that. Here we are in Viet-Nam with an Ella Fitzgerald song—"Cow Cow Boogie"—as a piece of music that is memorable in your life. Now— how and why?

FALL: As part of my research in Viet-Nam I wanted to find out what really went on—well, I did what most journalists I guess would do eventually—I went into combat and I flew with some of the Americans who were flying with the French at the time. They were from Civil Air Transport of General Chennault's—CATS as we called them C-A-T and I knew two of them, particularly. One of them was Steve Cusak—he was from Rochester, New York (like my wife) and another one whose name was Earl McGovern and who was better known . . . he was absolutely huge . . . Earl McGovern was gigantic! I don't know—he was 6'6" and weighed 350 pounds —something like this and he had a beard . . . no, he didn't have a beard but bushy eyebrows—he looked like having a beard. He was called "Earthquake McGoon" like the comic strip character of Al Capp's. In fact, the man was so big they had to build a special pilot's chair for him in the C-119 cargo transport plane. He just couldn't fit in a normal pilot's chair. And, I remember flying over Communist territory with Steve Cusak and you know, it's very dull—once you're up in the air it's a dull flight like all other flights and further- more, on a combat transport you don't have hostesses with coffee so

23

all you can do is just listen to music so you fiddle around on the buttons. You know, you switch to audio frequency and I'll never forget that that particular morning on one particular combat mission we were listening to an Anglican church service from Singapore. And, all of a sudden it was blanketed out by a stronger station which was, of all places, the U.S. station Manila and "Cow Cow Boogie" and we went . . . I was staying on audio frequency . . . we went into a shallow dive to dump our six-ton load of ammunition over a French encircled outpost—you can imagine—and all of a sudden there was Communist flak fire—we saw the traces passing by a wing. There we were flying—this was my first combat mission— I'm strictly ground-borne and with the Commie's flak firing at us, we had six tons of high explosives in back of us—we were listening to "Cow Cow Boogie."

Again, the perfectly incongruous scene—nothing fit. And, since nothing fit I think "Cow Cow Boogie" fitted perfectly well right with it and there's a sad tale to the story because Earthquake McGoon was shot down just about a year later. I have this actually in my new book *Hell in a Very Small Place*. He came in over Dien Bien Phu. Now, Dien Bien Phu the Communists finally revealed their very deadly capacity for antiaircraft fire which they are now showing to American planes in North Viet-Nam and Earthquake had six tons of ammunition aboard again . . . Howitzer ammunition and he was hit and his left engine was hit first and Steve Cusak was flying wingman in another aircraft. And, Steve heard as Earl said "I'm hit" and then he got hit again and this time it was his tail boom—the plane became unmaneuverable. And the last thing Earthquake said was, "Look's like this is it, son." We still don't know whether this was addressed to Steve in the other plane or to his own American co-pilot who was with him, whose name I do not recall. And the choice then was either let the plane go down straight down and maybe give the men a chance to jump or to ride the plane in and be sure he wouldn't crash into the French lines. You can imagine six tons of ammunition—it was all the French needed in Dien Bien Phu was to have a major ammunition explosion in it. And he rode the plane in and died with it.

[*Here the recording of Ella Fitzgerald's* "Cow Cow Boogie" *plays in its entirety* . . .]

24

CELEBRITY'S CHOICE: NOVEMBER 21, 1966

HUBERT: Bernard Fall, the next piece of music you have chosen takes us out of Viet-Nam for a while to an idyllic spot. You were telling me before the program that you have felt extremely fortunate in your life in that you've been able to do just about all the things in life that you wanted to do despite some serious illnesses.

FALL: That's right. I never knew how ill I was. It turned out I have a disease very few people know about. It's got a very long Latin name, of course, like all these things and it cost me my left kidney three years ago and four months, five operations and eight-thousand five hundred dollars later I came out of the hospital and I felt pretty despondent about the whole thing. But—I had a very good surgeon and since advertising for the medical profession is unethical I can't advertise the name over the phone—but I was lying there pretty despondent, you know, having lost my left kidney, and he finally walked in and said: "Look, you idiot," he said, "you only got one brain and one heart—if they stop, you're dead! So, all right, you only got one kidney—if the kidney stops, obviously you're in trouble." So he said, "Quit talking about it and start living" . . . and, I did. But, so, it's never stopped me from anything. I'm just now going back to Viet-Nam for another year's stay in Viet-Nam and chances of dying in Viet-Nam are much better from any other cause but the trouble I have. But, before that—you're right. I was very lucky in a way because ever since a child since I was a small boy I dreamed of being able to do research and jungles like many kids do—you know, that's where you get so many comic strips dealing with the subject being very popular. I was very lucky I could do it. I always meant to write and I do, and I always liked school and I teach. So . . .

HUBERT: And you always liked to travel and your next piece of music takes us to a land that was always exciting and a little mysterious for you. Not Viet-Nam, but Tahiti.

FALL: Tahiti. . . .

HUBERT: And you brought a record along for tonight's program and it's a very special one. Tell us about it and why it recalls such fond memories for you.

FALL: Well, I think when I was nine years old I first read Nordhoff and Hall's, *Mutiny on the Bounty,* and you can't read that book without really getting enamored with the whole idea of fair maidens

25

in the midst of swaying palms on an island in the middle of the Pacific. It just is that vivid. And ever since—so, all right, I had seen the jungles of Indo-China (chuckle) and I think of the desert of the Soviet Union and so on but somehow—I had even been in Hawaii but Hawaii wasn't it. Hawaii was Miami East . . . or, Miami Far West. It was just a big American City with a little bit more palms than Southern Florida but not very much more. A little bit greener than Southern California but then again not very much more. Yet I am always assured that the outer islands are unlike it but the outer islands are full of plantations which isn't again the real thing, either. And furthermore, there aren't any Hawaiians on Hawaii— about 30,000 Hawaiians out of 600,000 people. Between the immigration of the Asians and alcohol and syphilis they were taken care of, unfortunately.

HUBERT: But Tahiti is another story.

FALL: Tahiti is an entirely different story. At least it was. I'll tell you why the past tense begins to apply. So, when we were in Cambodia I was professor at the Royal Institute of Administration, in Cambodia in 1961–1962. I decided that there were several ways of getting back to the United States. The easy way is via Japan— the normal way is by way of Hawaii and the real way out way is via the South Pacific, Australia, the Fiji Islands and Tahiti and . . . well, there was a slight problem with my wife who is a good, nice American girl and who knew darn well that I was going to Tahiti to watch those beautiful fair maidens of my youthful dreams. And she put before me a rather cold-blooded choice. She said "All right— you can go to Tahiti, if you take the kids and I" (my wife)—she would go via Japan which she wanted to see because of its art treasures. And the sheer thought of getting stuck in Tahiti with two little girls sorta'—I knew it would cramp my style completely . . . I may as well take my wife along as a baby sitter. So, we all opted to go to Tahiti together.

Now, you won't believe this—this was before the French decided to put their atom bomb development center into the Pacific. It was really true! It was a beautiful island with thoroughly friendly people and we actually had a real palm thatch hut on the beach not far from where Gauguin used to paint, there on the lagoon. And, in front of the lagoon was this huge barrier reef and on the barrier reef was the

26

hulk of a French destroyer which had been thrown on it in 1914, I believe, by a typhoon. I mean, it is just unbelievable again—the sort of thing that was unbelievable . . . eh . . . a little bit more of everything would be totally camp but it just worked out right.

It was wonderful and there was the music. It's entirely different from Hawaiian music. It's stronger in spirit, if you will, and also the dances. You know, once you've seen Tahitian girls dance—forget about Hawaii—you'll never go back again and, unfortunately, this was our trouble. We had to go through Hawaii to get back to the States after having been in Tahiti. And, Hawaii is very nice, really, I guess but Tahiti had spoiled us completely.

HUBERT: We're going back to the year 1962 for Bernard Fall and this is "Manea."

[*Here the record plays in its entirety . . .* "Manea"]

HUBERT: Our program is rapidly coming to an end, Bernard Fall, and there's one more piece of music I do want to get in even briefly because it takes us back to your primary interest—Viet-Nam. And, strangely enough it's an American "pop" song and again we have the case of very strange music coming in—in very unusual places. Explain this one.

FALL: Well, I returned to Viet-Nam in 1965 and this was now the Viet-Nam of the Americans. It was an American Army but it was a different army from the one I had seen in 1944. These were not the citizens—these were the professionals. This was a very young army—really. It was young enlistees, young draftees, nineteen and twenty years old and this was also the first war which is drowned out by transistor radios. Everybody is going around with a five-buck transistor radio in his pocket. In fact, the Australian troops were seasoned veterans, most of them—they refused finally to go out and join combat operations with the Americans and Vietnamese because among the Americans and Vietnamese you would always find somebody who would have a transistor radio going on in the middle of an operation or—you know, if you carry one in your pocket and if you crawl on your belly, as luck would have it, you can push it on and all of a sudden you're going to reveal yourself with a nice blaring pop song. So, in Viet-Nam the whole country is literally overshadowed not by Glenn Miller but by American pop and one that stuck in my mind is precisely the one which I brought along

27

here which I think is sung by a group and in a way, you know, it's a very . . . sort of a sad . . . wars are never, never pleasant things. Anybody who thinks that war is pleasant even with the benefit of twenty years hindsight—you know, the old veteran stuff. You know, "War is great stuff." Well, it's great for the survivors —not great for the people who are killed in it. Nor for the Vietnamese peasants who get napalmed or the troops who get ambushed but in a way, this is a very funny war because it's understated on the ground. It's not a serious war. You know, this is a war when you describe a very, very, very sad story of woe, people getting killed—the answer is going to be, "sorry about that." Sort of a war with Batman language built in. For example, the enemy is "Charlie," "Victor Charlie." The radio language for VC—Viet Cong . . . but . . . as . . . that isn't all. For example, killing is "zapping" or "waxing" or zapping includes shooting down airplanes, for example or a tank gets "zapped." An object, too, can get killed. And, for example, a helicopter, helicopters get broken down into "slicks" which are unarmed transport helicopters. "Frogs" which have machine guns and "hogs" which have M79 grenade launchers and, for example, when you say "Charlie zapped a slick" you are actually saying that the Viet Cong shot down a troop transport helicopter. That's why I call it Batman language. And the music is true Batman music. It goes along with this sort of thing.

[*Here is played a "pop" recording of* "What a Day for a Daydream" . . . (*guitars, mostly*)]

HUBERT: True Batman music, in a way. The music of Viet-Nam as "In the Mood" typified World War II for Bernard Fall—"What a Day for a Daydream" typifies Viet-Nam.

Bernard Fall, our time is at an end. This has been a fascinating hour for me. Before we go, though, I always ask our guests what comes next. I know for you it's a new book and another trip to Viet-Nam. Do you feel apprehensive about going back again?

FALL: Not in a personal way. In other words, it's not a matter of fear of getting shot at. I've been wounded twice—in World War II —and shot at so often and fell into an ambush together with Charlie Mohr of the New York *Times* last time I was in Viet-Nam so it's not that. It's just simply and purely for the first time I'm really apprehensive about what I'm going to find. You know, Viet-Nam to

28

all accounts is really taking a terrible beating for a small country or for a country that size. We've never really fought that intensive a war over that small a piece of real estate, if you want to use hard-boiled language. So, in a way for the first time I'm just wondering what's going to be left of "my old Viet-Nam" and it's always very sad when you come back to a place and you sort of wonder what they have done with it—whether it's the last time you saw Paris or the last time you saw Tahiti—Tahiti before and after the French atom bomb or Viet-Nam before and after the American blitz.

HUBERT: Well, I hope that when you do come back from Viet-Nam which will be what, in about a year?

FALL: mm, hmmm.

HUBERT: that you will come back to *Celebrity's Choice* so that we can talk about what you found there, the people, the life, and even the music.

Bernard Fall, thank you so much for being my guest tonight and good luck.

FALL: Thank you very much . . .

PART I

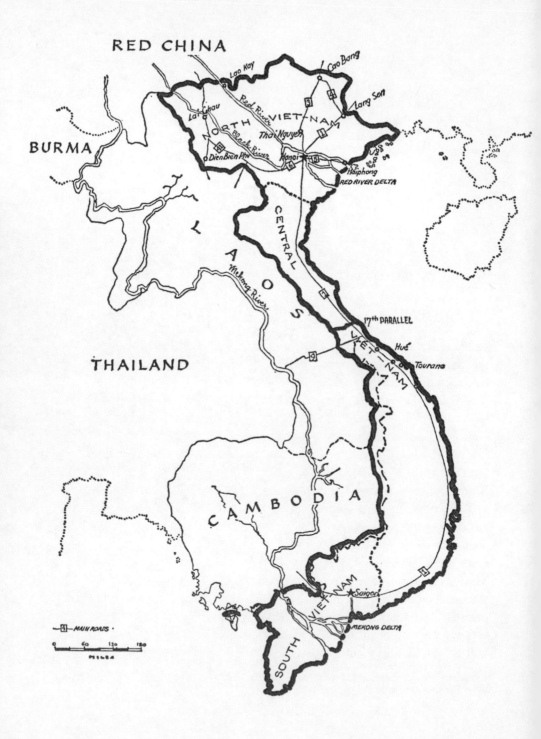

RED CHINA

BURMA

THAILAND

Lao Kay

Cao Bang

Red River

Lai Chau

3

4

Lang Son

VIET-NAM

NORTH

Thai Nguyen

Black River

Dien Bien Phu

Hanoi

15

Haiphong

RED RIVER DELTA

CENTRAL

L A O S

Mekong River

17th PARALLEL

VIET-NAM

9

Hué

Tourane

CAMBODIA

SOUTH

VIET-NAM

Saigon

MEKONG DELTA

4 MAIN ROADS

0   60   120   180

MILES

2000 Years of War
in Viet-Nam

⟨✴⟩

THERE ONCE was a country called Viet-Nam, at the eastern rim of the Southeast Asian mainland where it abruptly terminates in a balcony jutting out into the South China Sea. Significantly, German geographers called the area *Hinterindien* ("Beyond-India") and left it at that; but as early as 1812, Malte Conrad Bruun, a Danish-born geographer working in Paris, recognized the essential characteristic which made it different from the rest of Southeast Asia—the intimate mixture of Indian and Chinese civilizations. It was Malte-Brun (as he was known) who gave the area the name "Indochina."

To be sure, the part of Indochina that is now called Viet-Nam (it has carried various versions of that name—Dai-Viet, Annam, Nam-Viet—for more than a thousand years) has not disappeared from the maps as a geographic location. It is still there, the size of New Mexico, stretching out like a very elongated "S" for more than a thousand miles from just north of the equator to the twenty-fourth parallel. The Vietnamese like to think of their country as dragon-shaped, dragons being considered luck-bringing animals.

It is Viet-Nam as a cultural and historic entity which is threatened with extinction. While its lovely land has been battered into a moon-scape by the massive engines of modern war, its cultural identity has been assaulted by a combination of Communism in the North and superficial Americanization in the South.

Viet-Nam's location has made it not only a melting pot of cultures but a battleground for foreign armies and foreign ideologies. The history of the South has been shaped by the kind influence of the Buddha; that of the North, where China has always prevailed, by the far sterner philosophies of Confucius and Lao-tse. And as far back as history and mythology can recall, the Vietnamese have fought among themselves, though maintaining a surprising amount of cultural unity. Many remains of a long and glorious past, which had with-stood the inroads of dozens of invasions and which archaeologists had lovingly preserved, have now disappeared without a trace.

Like much of surrounding Southeast Asia, Viet-Nam was cut off from the rest of the world by the huge Himalayan glaciers of the ice age. The earliest traces of civilization are the so-called "choppers" —sharpened stones which were used as tools—dating back to 12,-000 B.C. The first specifically Vietnamese culture emerged around 5000 B.C. in the caves and grottoes near Hoa-Binh, in what is now North Viet-Nam. "Hoabinhian" man belonged to the Australoid group moving from Central Asia southeastward into Indonesia and Australia; he may have been as dark-skinned as the present-day Melanesians of New Caledonia and the Solomon Islands. By 2000 B.C. a second wave of Australoids, armed with double-edged axes, entered the country on their way south. They are known as Bacso-nians, after the Bac-Son area north of Hanoi where their remains have been mostly found. They slowly spread throughout Southeast Asia, from Malaya to the Philippines, and became the first "Viet-namese" to settle the country permanently.

The third wave from Central Asia brought many of Southeast Asia's present inhabitants, in the form of the first Malays, who set-tled Java, Malaya, and the coastal area of Viet-Nam from Saigon to what is now the imperial city of Hué. The newcomers brought with them cattle, some metals, rudimentary irrigation, and upright stones, or megaliths, which have a striking resemblance to similar monu-ments found in places as distant as Europe and Easter Island. In Viet-Nam they also left magnificent burial chambers at Sa-Huynh (near Quang-Ngai, where American troops fought bitter battles last year with the Viet Cong), and near the rubber plantations of Xuan-Loc and Bien-Hoa, just northeast of Saigon.

But around 1000 B.C. a new flood of people began to emerge from Central Asia: the Han Chinese. Endowed with a strong social organization, a sophisticated writing system, an advanced knowledge of agriculture, and, even then, an incredible propensity to multiply, the Han rapidly overran the small kingdoms that covered China south of the Yangtze. Like the moraine off a glacier, this new layer of humanity began pushing down the narrow Indochinese funnel into Southeast Asia. Until recently archaeologists felt that much of Viet-Nam's Bronze Age culture, particularly the beautiful finds at Dong-Son, was "imported" from the Han civilization about 500 B.C. But one of the most brilliant of the new generation of French researchers, Bernard Philippe Groslier, suggests that part of the Dongsonian culture may have been indigenous to Viet-Nam. Archaeological diggings by North Vietnamese at Thieu-Dong, a few miles from Dong-Son, in 1960–61, seem to indicate as much. They uncovered a Bronze Age culture of fifty-five graves and more than five hundred objects predating Dong-Son. The correctness of their findings will have to be verified by outside researchers, since the theory of an "autonomous" Vietnamese Bronze Age culture owing nothing to the Chinese suits Vietnamese nationalism on *both* sides of the seventeenth parallel. With Dong-Son, Viet-Nam entered the civilized world as we know it. Beautiful bronze statuary and huge drums of clearly Dongsonian origin began to show up throughout Southeast Asia and as far away as the Indonesian archipelago and the western Pacific. By the third century B.C. the Han invaders had driven the small kingdoms of South China into tight beachheads on the China Sea; they were also threatening Dong-Son. But the Dongsonians did not give up easily. Pushing southward, they entrenched themselves in snug little deltas surrounded by almost impenetrable jungle, and became the forerunners of the great Hinduized Champa kingdom.

One of the kingdoms of the Yangtze region defeated by the Han in the third century was that of the Vietnamese. (The Chinese ideogram for them was *Yuëh,* pronounced "Viet" by the Vietnamese.) As the Han advanced, the Vietnamese retreated southward. By

257 B.C. we begin to encounter the first formal diplomatic correspondence between the pursuer and the pursued. But a country as huge as China was hard to keep together, especially since the advance element of settlers (as was often the case in Western colonization efforts) was made up of convicts, adventurers, and other rough-and-ready types. Occasionally they would strike out on their own or would even join the opposition. That was the case with a Chinese front-line general by the name of Chao-T'o (Trieu Da, in Vietnamese) who conquered the Vietnamese in 207 B.C. and proceeded to install himself as king of the country—which by then comprised a small part of what is now North Viet-Nam.

The Empress of China immediately proclaimed a complete blockade of Viet-Nam, forbidding in particular the export of such "strategic" items as iron plowshares and of female draft animals. The principal effect was to stiffen Vietnamese resistance. When Trieu Da changed his title from king to emperor, matters seemed to be rapidly coming to a head. But in the end the essential wisdom of the rulers prevailed. Han Wen-ti, the emperor who succeeded Empress Lu in 179 B.C., sent an ambassador to Trieu Da with a diplomatic note whose text—fortunately preserved for posterity—would do no dishonor to any future negotiator of the Vietnamese problem:

> Respectfully to the King of Nam-Viet. I am most distressed in my heart and afflicted in my thoughts . . . I have learned that you have recently sent troops to the border to pilfer and ravage. Not only did the Trang-Sa [area] suffer, but [your] Southern Command suffered even more. Under such conditions how could even your Kingdom derive a single advantage from this? Surely, a great many officers and soldiers will be killed, many excellent generals and officials will be wounded; wives will be deprived of their husbands, children of their parents, parents of their offspring. To gain one and lose ten—I do not consent to act like this. . . .
>
> You are ruling in full independence; yet you have changed your title to that of Emperor. When two Emperors exist at the same time and no ambassadorial chariot establishes connections between them, struggle will ensue. But to struggle unyieldingly is not a deed for men endowed with humanity. Let me then share with you, and forget, our earlier differences . . .

The old Vietnamese king promptly replied that all that had happened was just a terrible "misunderstanding" and that he had made

36

himself emperor, as the French translation says, *"quelque peu pour se divertir"*—as a lark. Trieu Da reaffirmed his vassalage to the Chinese emperor, changed his title back to king, and sent a tribute of white jade, bird plumage, and rhinoceros horns. This arrangement settled Sino-Vietnamese relations for more than half a century, with the only penetration of Chinese culture being a peaceful one.

Meanwhile another phenomenon, which to this day is the key to all Vietnamese attitudes, came to the surface—a violent internal struggle between those who felt that good relations with China, even at the price of vassalage, was important, and those who felt that Viet-Nam would soon become nothing but a Chinese province if it tolerated the Sinicization of its every cultural trait, from its language to the manner in which rice was irrigated. Unfortunately that controversy developed at the height of one of China's expansionist phases, when it was trying to achieve both a common border with India and a broad bastion on the Pacific: in 111 B.C., after a brief campaign, the Chinese overran the young Vietnamese state. Three years later they occupied Korea. The Chinese occupation of Viet-Nam was to last, with a few brief interruptions due to rebellions, for 1050 years, until A.D. 939.

At the same time, in what is today South Viet-Nam, a more peaceful penetration from India and points farther west was taking place. Bulging out into the South China Sea, South Viet-Nam has always been a welcome stopover for sailors on the China trade routes, and it was not surprising that many of its early colonizers came by sea. In the South, mythology and history abound with tales of Indian princes and Buddhist monks alighting from big sailing ships and bringing to the primitive populations of the lower Mekong the enlightenment of their advanced civilizations in addition to the liberal teachings of the Buddha.

Strangely enough, there are no contemporary Indian texts available to us about the kingdoms they established in Southeast Asia. But the Chinese, ubiquitous traders, travelers, and diplomats that they were, have again left us detailed descriptions of the opulent cities which then dotted what they called the kingdom of Fu-Nan —its Indian name being unknown—located in the South Vietnamese Mekong Delta and southern Cambodia. Historians viewed some of the Chinese texts with disbelief until French aerial surveys of the 1930's and 1940's revealed the patterns of hundreds of elaborate canals and of vast cities grouped around them like so many Venices. It may have been at this time that the first Europeans reached Viet-Nam. Whether or not Romans actually visited the port city of Oc-Eo has not been clearly established, but the fact remains that a Roman coin dating to Antoninus Pius (A.D. 152), and Sassanid brooches have been found there, along with thirty other clearly Roman objects. There is little doubt, in any event, that by the third century A.D. Oc-Eo had become a crossroads of civilizations. Here Chinese ships deposited their merchandise and passengers to be picked up by Indian ships bound westward; and here they picked up cargo and travelers seeking to find their way to the huge and mysterious Chinese empire. Chinese records also show that in the middle of the third century A.D. the first Indian missionaries, seeking to spread the gospel of Buddhism eastward, stopped over in Fu-Nan before going on to Canton. The rulers of Fu-Nan soon recognized the power of the great nation to the north, and like the Vietnamese, paid a nominal tribute to China.

But to the east of Fu-Nan and south of the kingdom of Viet-Nam, a new power was emerging—Champa. The Chams, who were mentioned by the Chinese for the first time in A.D. 192, were the Norsemen of the South China Sea. Their raiding ships preyed upon the slow, unsuspecting Chinese trading junks—emerging from veritable "fjords" whose names sound familiar even today: Danang, Qui-Nhon, Nha-Trang, Cam-Ranh, Phan-Rang. Fu-Nan, peaceable and unprepared for war, became an easy target for the raiders. By the end of the sixth century, Fu-Nan had disappeared altogether, and the beautiful cities around Oc-Eo, sacked and destroyed repeatedly, began to sink into the mud of the Mekong. Where they once were, there are now a few "strategic hamlets" in the midst of abandoned rice fields seared by napalm and crop-killing chemicals. But for almost a thousand years after its disappearance, Christian chroniclers would spin tales about the marvels and riches of Transgangetic India or the Golden Chersonese. What they were looking for were the golden cities of South Viet-Nam.

Now it was Champa's turn to become a regional trade center. Cities like Khautara (Nha-Trang), Panduranga (Phan-Rang), and

Indrapura were known to Arabic seafarers from Baghdad and India, and were in regular touch with Java and China. After numerous wars in which they gave as good as they got, the Chams also decided that it was the better part of wisdom to pay a symbolic tribute to China and to exchange periodical embassies with her. Toward the eighth century a truly magnificent culture blossomed out along what is now the shore of northeastern South Viet-Nam. Champa, however, was afflicted with the same drawback as seafaring powers such as Portugal and Holland: it had to rely on trade even for its food and was constantly vulnerable on its land side.

Such was the fate of Champa in the face of the progressive inroads of the Viets. Internal troubles in China had resulted in a gradual weakening of its power, and Viet-Nam had liberated itself from the Chinese yoke. Like their other neighbors, however, the Vietnamese had learned a useful lesson: a small state cannot long exist on the Chinese periphery in a condition of permanent hostility. The result had been an offer of tribute and a renewal of a relationship of loose suzerainty. Aside from a brief period of Chinese occupation in the 1400's, that would be the relationship between the two until the late nineteenth century, when the French took over.

With the Chinese mollified, the Vietnamese rulers turned their sights southward. There the Chams had let fertile agricultural land lie fallow in their preoccupation with trading, raiding, and building temples, while the already teeming Vietnamese had been constricted to their lowland deltas in the Red River region. What began now was a nasty episode of colonialism with overtones of genocide. The Vietnamese began to destroy the Cham state piecemeal, city by city and province by province. By the end of the fifteenth century Champa had not only disappeared from the map but almost all its population had disappeared as well. Today a few ruins and about fifty thousand Indonesian-looking *montagnard* people, who now follow the Moslem religion of their blood brothers in Malaya and Indonesia, are all that survives of that once proud kingdom.

Even the physical remains of the Chams are disappearing under the pounding of war. Last fall a New York *Times* correspondent visited a small open-air museum near Danang which the French had built to house Cham relics. He found it littered with "bat droppings, American beer cans, and rusty C-rations tins . . ." During the Buddhist uprising in May, 1966, snipers had used the museum as a sanctuary; while little damage had been done to the building itself, the heads of three of the museum's statues had disappeared.

The Vietnamese had embarked upon their own version of the Chinese Long March, and even had a war cry: *"Nam Tiên!"* ("Let's March South!"). Yet, as Groslier noted with a tinge of regret, "that vigorous movement was only the triumph of demography—not of a civilization." The Vietnamese carried south with them a thoroughly Sinicized civilization, and it suited them so well, intellectually, administratively, and artistically, that they showed little incentive to change it.

There was one trait that the Vietnamese had not borrowed from the Chinese—their enduring patriotism. It was to be put to a severe test many times in their turbulent history, but probably never to a greater one than when, a tiny nation of perhaps a million people, they stood up to the mighty Mongol empire.

Peking had fallen to the Mongols in 1215. By 1257 the first Mongol invasion—contemporary figures speak of 200,000 men— flooded the Red River valley. The Vietnamese, as they would so often do later, abandoned their cities and headed for the hills, leaving their capital to be burned by the invaders. But the Mongols, still unused to the tropics and tropical diseases, were defeated by the environment; after a fruitless pursuit of the Vietnamese, they withdrew. A few years later, Kublai Khan made a second attempt at crushing Viet-Nam, not because he needed the backwater kingdom on the Gulf of Tonkin, but because it blocked the overland route to Champa, which the great Khan wanted as a naval base for further operations in Southeast Asia. Marco Polo left us a description of the campaign against what he calls "Ziamba," which took place about 1268 after a landing by sea and left the Vietnamese in the center of a Mongol pincer.

In 1284 the third Mongol invasion of Viet-Nam began. At first there was an understandable feeling of hopelessness as once again the Mongols ravaged the lowlands; more acclimated now, they were less likely to be dislodged by climate alone. That was the moment

40

when a great military leader and thinker stepped forward: Marshal Tran Hung Dao. He withdrew to the mountains, wrote his *Essential Summary of Military Arts,* and began to train his troops in what we now call guerrilla warfare. His principles could just as well have been written by Mao Tse-tung or Dao's present-day successor in Hanoi, General Vo Nguyen Giap, the victor of Dien Bien Phu: "The enemy must fight his battles far from his home base for a long time . . . We must further weaken him by drawing him into protracted campaigns. Once his initial dash is broken, it will be easier to destroy him."

And that is exactly what happened. In 1287, after the Vietnamese had whittled down the Mongols through protracted guerrilla warfare, the latter decided to withdraw. Tran Hung Dao planted thousands of iron-spiked stakes in the Bach-Dang River north of Haiphong through which the Mongol fleet had to pass. The ships arrived at high tide, when the stakes were submerged. A small Vietnamese naval force cleverly decoyed the enemy into a fight which looked like an easy victory until the Mongol ships found themselves stranded or gored on the stakes by the momentum of the outflowing tides. That was the moment Marshal Dao's infantry chose to attack and defeat the invaders.

But once more wisdom prevailed: the following year Viet-Nam voluntarily offered to pay tribute to the Mongols in Peking. A last Chinese invasion under the Ming emperors, in 1407, was eventually defeated by the same mixture of guerrilla and attrition warfare, and a new dynasty of Vietnamese kings, beginning with Lê Loi in 1418, reigned until the end of the eighteenth century.

With no dangerous enemies left, the Vietnamese settled down to what seems to be their favorite national pastime: bitter quarrels among themselves in general, and between Northerners and Southerners in particular. In the North the Lê kings had fallen under the spell of powerful feudal lords; in the South the Nguyen feudal family had for all practical purposes taken control. By 1613 the "two Viet-Nams" had not only broken apart but the South had constructed at Dong-Hoi its own version of the Great Chinese Wall. In fact there were two walls, one six miles long and the other twelve, both of them eighteen feet high. Dong-Hoi is only a few miles north of today's division at the seventeenth parallel.

But this was the great epoch of European trade and colonial expansion, and the arrival of the Westerners further complicated the split. Thanks to the more modern arms which became available, it also made the conflicts between North and South more deadly. To be sure, the contact with Europe from Marco Polo's time on had never been broken, but trade had proved unrewarding. The Dutch, who had opened a trading station in North Viet-Nam as early as 1637, lost two fleets of warships when they helped the Lês fight the Nguyens in several disastrous campaigns; they finally closed up shop in 1700. The British tried in 1683 and quit in 1697. The French opened a trading post in 1680 and closed it in 1682. With all of India and China and the Spice Islands for the picking, the European merchants turned their eyes and capital elsewhere.

Not so the Catholic missionaries. To them, the Vietnamese, with their mélange of Confucianism, Taoism, ancestor worship, and remnants of Hinduistic beliefs, were ripe prospects for conversion. On January 18, 1615, the first Italian and Portuguese Jesuit missionaries landed in what is now Danang, and their initial successes led the pope to send a permanent mission to Viet-Nam, headed by a French Jesuit, Alexandre de Rhodes. Monsignor de Rhodes remained there for twenty-two years, and by the time he was banished in 1649, tens of thousands of Vietnamese had embraced Catholicism. But Rhodes had done more than that: he had transliterated Vietnamese from the Chinese characters to the Latin alphabet, with the adjunction of a few diacritical marks to account for the multitonal character of the Vietnamese language. A door had been forced open which would never close again.

In the meantime the Nguyen had taken over the Long March southward, moving into the Mekong Delta. But they, in turn, were to be faced with the rise of a "Third Viet-Nam" at their backs— just as a hundred and eighty years later the Viet Cong was to divide Viet-Nam into three areas. In 1771 three brothers from Tay-Son village in the South rose against the Nguyen with demands for social reforms and reunification. They found a ready echo among the landless peasants oppressed by their feudal lords, and among the merchant class, distressed at the loss of internal as well as foreign trade because of the country's division. Soon, all the Nguyen rulers save one young prince, Nguyen Anh, had been murdered, and by June, 1776, the Tay-Son were masters of most of South Viet-Nam.

Two years later the Tay-Son had defeated the tottering Lês and their supporters in the North. Only Nguyen Anh, holed up in the Mekong swamps or sometimes fleeing to neighboring Cambodia and Siam, still held out against all hope. In his despair the young prince approached the French bishop in the Mekong area, Pigneau de Béhaine, and persuaded him to go to France to secure help from the French king, Louis XVI. France, a short while earlier, had won a war over Britain (and with it, the independence of the American States) and had footholds in India; perhaps she would be willing to help a young Asian ruler as well.

In 1784 Monsignor Pigneau embarked for France, taking with him Nguyen Anh's son, four-year-old Prince Canh, who became the darling of Versailles. But in spite of a treaty of assistance signed in 1787, France, bankrupt from wars and cracking under the stresses of oncoming revolution, could do very little. The governor of French India, Count Conway, sent four warships to Viet-Nam in August, 1788, which returned with a pessimistic report on the chances of Nguyen Anh's success. Undeterred, Monsignor Pigneau and the young Prince Canh sailed from France with a single privately bought warship and three hundred French volunteers attracted by the promise of land. They landed in Viet-Nam in mid July, 1789, the week the Parisians stormed the Bastille.

Incredible as it may seem, the tide was eventually turned by this minute infusion of modern military know-how, coupled with the fact that the Tay-Son were now more preoccupied with another Chinese invasion in the North and had neglected to deliver on promised reforms. But the overthrow of the Tay-Son was a long and arduous process. Not until July, 1799, did Qui-Nhon, the key Tay-Son fortress in the South, fall, after a brutal siege which Monsignor Pigneau personally directed. He had only a few months to enjoy his victory. He died in October and was followed to the grave a year later by his pupil, Prince Canh. Nguyen Anh proceeded to exterminate the Tay-Son leaders, and by 1802 had crushed the movement from north to south. A few years later he made himself emperor under the name of Gia-Long. For the first time in almost two centuries Viet-Nam was a single country, from the China Gates in the north to the Ca-Mau Peninsula at its southernmost tip.

The influence of the small group of Frenchmen who had come with Monsignor Pigneau waned as rapidly as their small numbers were depleted by disease or homesickness. But two of them had an influence which to this very day has not been wiped off the Vietnamese landscape: Théodore Lebrun and Olivier de Puymanel. They were both military engineers, and their star-shaped forts soon dotted the landscape—for Gia-Long had ordered the construction of a citadel in every provincial capital and at other strategic points. Above all, Gia-Long wanted a modern port city in Cochinchina, and from 1789 to 1792, Lebrun and de Puymanel laid out a modern city in the south, with broad rectilineal boulevards facing a protected river harbor where there once was a fishing village called Saigon. When Gia-Long died, in 1820, Viet-Nam not only was a consolidated state but was secure and prosperous; it had even incorporated what was left of Cambodia. It is to Gia-Long that Vietnamese hark back when they dream of their country's greatness.

Gia-Long's successors, however, did not match their ancestor in realism and intelligence. Rather than face up to the realities of growing European intervention as Siam and Japan were reluctantly doing, they attempted a retreat into isolationism and began to expel Western merchants and to persecute Christian missionaries and converts. Figures vary, but the best-documented sources show that about 130,000 Catholics, including hundreds of priests and several important church dignitaries, were murdered between 1827 and 1856. The largest single persecution of Christians since Nero, it goes far to explain the present-day distrust between Catholics and Buddhists in South Viet-Nam.

It was the persecution of the Catholics which brought about the first documented intervention of American military force in Viet-Nam. The old U.S.S. *Constitution,* under the command of Captain John ("Mad Jack") Percival, was showing the flag in Asian waters when he was informed that the Vietnamese were about to put to death the French bishop Dominique Lefèbvre in Hué. Percival put into the nearest Vietnamese port, Danang, on May 10, 1845; he marched a Marine detachment ashore, captured several high Vietnamese officials (who no doubt did not even know

that America existed), and held them hostage until, four days later,
Hué assured him that the bishop would not be harmed. When
Washington later found out what had happened, it was properly ap-
palled, and in 1849 sent its consul at Singapore to the court at
Hué to apologize. It is doubtful that a single one of the Marines
who waded ashore at Danang in 1965 had an inkling that his appearance was a return engagement.

The French who landed in Danang in 1856—ostensibly to save
the Catholics from persecution—and then secured Saigon and the
surrounding Mekong Delta in the following decade, knew that there
had been Frenchmen there before them. But this time they came
to stay as a colonial power, convinced that they were bringing enlightenment as well as progress and the benefits of colonial commerce. Often the errors made at the beginning when two civilizations
collide—whether it be that of the French and Vietnamese in the
1860's or that of the Americans and the Vietnamese a hundred
years later—fatefully condition the whole development of the relationship. That was to be the case now. Since the late fifteenth
century, Viet-Nam had elected its local governments and this had
proved an effective shield against the imperial government's high-
handedness. "The Emperor's writ stops at the bamboo hedge [of the
village]" is an old Vietnamese saying. The arriving French colonials
began to tamper with those hallowed institutions, thus breaking one
of the most important links in Vietnamese society. The French,
unfortunately for themselves, understood this too little and, above
all, too late; but it took the incredible blindness of the late Ngo
Dinh Diem to abolish local elected government altogether. When
he did so, in 1956, the Viet Cong had the issue it was looking for.
Appointed village chiefs were killed by the thousands, and the first
round of the second Indochina war went to the opposition by default.

The French colonial government probably did no better or worse
than most colonial governments. A university was established in
Hanoi as early as 1904; vast irrigation systems eliminated the disastrous floods or droughts which had beset Viet-Nam's agriculture
and transformed the country into one of the world's food baskets;
and epidemics were completely wiped out by a network of Pasteur

45

Institutes. But the French failed to provide the Vietnamese with a real say in the political development of their country, allowed too few of them to obtain an advanced education and too few of them to rise high in the administrative hierarchy of their own country. French-type cities gave the country a veneer of Westernization beneath which a small but vigorous intellectual class grew increasingly impatient with the colonial framework.

One result was the growth of the secret societies that had always been part of the Sino-Vietnamese civilization. This is a phenomenon largely unknown to us: in the West, only Communism is specifically geared to operate as a clandestine political party. It was a combination of Marxist ideology and the secret societies of Viet-Nam that produced the *one* effective political organization the country has ever had—the Indochina Communist Party, later known as the Vietnamese Workers' Party under its creator, Ho Chi Minh.

For those who refused that alternative but were reluctant to work with the French, there were only two choices: exile or an escape into meditation and religion. It was France's best expert on Vietnamese society, Professor Paul Mus, who once spoke of *"le goût du merveilleux"*—the "hang" for the supernatural—of the Vietnamese people. In the 1920's and 1930's this gave rise to new religions such as the Cao-Dai, a mixture of spiritism and a type of ecumenical Buddhism in which Christ, the French poet (and atheist) Victor Hugo, and Winston Churchill, have a fitting place.

During the Second World War both the French and Vietnamese settled down to living with their Japanese masters. The latter turned out to be even less willing to understand the inhabitants than the whites were; but they brought to the Vietnamese a chance to shake off the French yoke. The Japanese collapse, however, left a total void, and the only group which was not only willing but also capable of taking power in Viet-Nam was the Viet-Minh, which included Communist as well as non-Communist nationalists under the leadership of Ho Chi Minh. His Democratic Republic of Viet-Nam, proclaimed on September 2, 1945, returned Viet-Nam, however briefly, to the ranks of independent nations; but the return of the French and the divisions among the Vietnamese Nationalists made a conflict almost unavoidable.

46

Last-minute efforts in 1946 to head off the oncoming Indochina War failed as French and Viet-Minh moderates were swept aside by the extremists in both camps. As the war ground on, a new division of Viet-Nam began to take shape: the French, and the Vietnamese regime under their control, held all the cities and towns; the Viet-Minh held the villages and the jungle. The French lashed out in ineffectual "search-and-destroy" operations, but the Viet-Minh, following Marshal Tran Hung Dao's doctrine, refused to be drawn into a major battle. Finally, the French offered them 17,-000 troops in the valley of Dien Bien Phu as "bait," just as the Mongols had attempted to corner Dao in the plain of Bach-Dang. In a grueling fifty-six-day fight the Viet-Minh won. It was a victory of Communism, to be sure, but it was also a victory of which every Vietnamese would henceforth be proud, just as Americans, regardless of where their personal sympathies lie, are proud of Gettysburg.

But unlike Gettysburg, which insured the eventual reunification of the United States, Dien Bien Phu sealed the division of Viet-Nam into a northern Communist and a southern non-Communist state; their cultures would soon diverge under the competing influences of Russian and Chinese training in the North and American training in the South. In both zones the French cultural overlay flaked off under the impact of new techniques and, in the South, of a far more massive influx of foreigners than the country had ever seen and one which it simply could not absorb. In the North common poverty at least insures that the living standards of the urban areas are not markedly different from those of the countryside. In South Viet-Nam the cities have become the home of incredible traffic jams—an American wag has baptized Saigon "Hondaville"—and the social decay that attends war. Meanwhile the countryside literally dies under the blows of the largest military machine ever unleashed on an area of this size. And in that blistered countryside lives the "Third Viet-Nam"—the Viet Cong and its northern allies, who hide in deep underground burrows, as if returning to the Stone Age cultures of Hoa-Binh and Bac-Son.

It was in 1931, after yet another abortive rebellion against the French, that a young Vietnamese author and poet, Pham Quynh, told the French colonial minister, Paul Reynaud (who would be France's premier in the dark days of June, 1940): "We are a people who are looking for a country and have not yet found it." Thirty-six years later that search still goes on, more desperately than ever.

"A Grain of Rice Is Worth
a Drop of Blood"

THE LATE FRENCH STATESMAN Georges Clemenceau is credited with the *mot:* "A drop of oil is worth a drop of blood." Today in Southeast Asia and the Far East, Clemenceau's quip might well be changed to read: "A grain of rice is worth a drop of blood." And perhaps Red China and North Viet-Nam are willing to pay the price.

Almost two-thirds of the world's population, or about two billion people, live in the Far East, in a wide arc that stretches from Pakistan in the west to China and Japan in the north and Indonesia in the south. This is the area of the world where rice is, in the literal sense of the word, the staff of life; it represents more than 60 per cent of the total grain production, with wheat a poor second at 20 per cent and corn an unimportant third at less than 10 per cent.

In what used to be called "normal" times, a poor crop in China and India meant the death through outright starvation of perhaps seven million people; and even today, with American, Canadian or French wheat surpluses available, a middling crop in Asia can wipe out economic progress for that year as the hungry countries deplete their hard-currency reserves to feed their teeming populaces. Red China, though grimly bent on industrialization at almost any

Reprinted by permission and first published in the New York *Times*.

price, had to buy close to six million tons of "capitalist" wheat for hard cash to prevent what no doubt would have been a hunger rebellion; and riots broke out in Calcutta in October, 1963, because of a small rise in the price of rice.

Even worldwide philanthropy cannot close the world's "rice gap" in the face of Asia's population explosion. As a sober-worded report by a Ford Foundation team of experts pointed out in 1959: "If India's food production increases no faster than present rates, *the gap between supplies and target will be 28 million tons by 1965–66. . . . No conceivable program of imports or rationing can meet a crisis of this magnitude.*" (Emphasis in the original text.) Indeed, Indian grain production dropped from 81 million tons in 1960 to less than 77 million in 1963 and is hardly likely to reach the bare minimum of 100 million tons planned for the end of the current economic plan. Rice alone dropped from 34 million tons in 1961 to 31 million in 1963. Figures for Red China indicate a disaster of similar magnitude in the making, in spite of massive imports from abroad and forced dietary switches from rice to corn or potatoes.

This is what makes mainland Southeast Asia—the peninsula embracing Burma, Thailand, Malaya, Cambodia, Laos and the southern segment of Viet-Nam—so terribly important in the present struggle; excepting Malaya and Laos, these countries constitute the only food-surplus area in Asia and the only fertile part of the continent that could be called "underpopulated." Thailand alone, for example, normally is the world's fourth-largest grain exporter, after the United States, Canada, and France; and if it were exploited as intensively as parts of China and all of Japan, it could probably export three times as much. The same holds true for the other exporting countries of Southeast Asia.

The "have" nations of Asia—those that raise more grain than they consume—are these:

	Exportable Surplus, 1963	
Burma	1.8	million tons
Thailand	1.6	″ ″
Cambodia	0.35	″ ″
South Viet-Nam	0.3	″ ″
East Pakistan	0.2	″ ″
Taiwan	0.11	″ ″
AREA TOTAL:	4.36 million tons	

50

It must be emphasized that the above figures are not truly representative of the export capacity of the "have" countries, for 1963 was in many places a year of typhoons and floods; and, in the case of South Viet-Nam, one of heavy insecurity. In normal peacetime (1939), South Viet-Nam exported more than 1.5 million tons of rice, after having covered North Viet-Nam's perennial deficit of about one-quarter million tons, and even throughout the years of Japanese occupation it exported more than one million tons annually. Prewar Burma exported more than three million tons and Cambodia more than half a million.

Around this small "nucleus of prosperity" looms a whole hungry continent whose over-all grain production has barely kept pace with its population increase and which in many cases keeps from starving by accepting large-scale handouts (such as America's "Food-for-Peace" program) or by massive and unpopular dietary switches.

The "have-not" nations—those that raise less grain than they need—are:

	Import Requirements, 1963		
China (mainland)	6.0	million	tons
India	4.0	"	"
Indonesia	1.5	"	"
Ceylon	0.55	"	"
North Viet-Nam	0.5	"	"
Malaysia	0.3	"	"
Ryukyu Islands	0.06	"	"
Laos	0.05	"	"
Philippines	0.03	"	"
Nepal	0.01	"	"
AREA TOTAL:	13.00 million tons		

As this table shows, the "have-not" nations of Asia far outweigh in their demands what the "have" nations can spare.

Programs of intensification of agriculture are under way in most such countries. In Red China and North Viet-Nam, however, political mythology usually gets the best of sound agriculture; in Indonesia military *konfrontasi* ("confrontation") with Malaysia takes precedence over much-overdue agricultural inprovements; in India the runaway birth rate throws the whole rural economy into what, at best, can be described as the Red Queen plight: It must do all the running it can just to stay in one place, and if it wants to get anywhere, it must run twice as fast.

51

This would, of course, be less of a problem if the Southeast Asian rice economies were not so woefully inefficient. Almost none of them has reached pre-1939 acreage yields and almost none of them uses the easily available fertilizing, irrigation, and seed-selection methods which Japan has been using with success for decades and which give the Japanese farmer an acreage yield triple that of the Southeast Asian farmer.

The reasons for this are manifold. Guerrilla-torn areas do not lend themselves to agricultural experimentation. In many cases, the substitution of inefficient "squatters" for large European-run rice plantations also contributes to the lower productivity. And, unfortunately, many of the young, independent regimes accord a lower priority to rice growing than to eye-catching stadiums, triumphal arches, tourist hotels, and gigantic steel mills. Foreign-aid programs, in most cases, had little choice but to go along with the desires of the new rulers. Thus, only minimal amounts of aid went into this key field. Yet experts have calculated that even a short-term crash program in the culture of rice could radically transform Asia's food picture.

But rice planting is more than an economic activity: It is a way of life, a whole *Weltanschauung* in itself. First of all, it is probably the most backbreaking normal human activity. Each hectare (2.6 acres) of rice field requires *ten thousand* tons of water which—except for the few areas where irrigation systems are available—must be pumped or scooped by various primitive means: water wheels worked by hand or with bicycle pedals; wicker baskets, or mere pails, carried thousands of times uphill in those areas of Asia where rice is grown on terraces along the slopes of steep mountains. In almost all areas of monsoon Asia, two rice crops a year are produced to feed a continent whose relatively small fertile areas are fantastically overcrowded. In a few areas, such as Thaibinh province in North Viet-Nam, three rice crops a year have been grown.

In the Far East rice is grown in small seedbeds for up to two months and then replanted, stalk by stalk, into deeply irrigated fields which have previously been plowed with the help of water buffaloes. To imagine the incredibly backbreaking quality of rice planting one must imagine what it would mean to plant a wheat field stalk by stalk in 95-degree heat while standing in muddy water up to one's knees for 10 hours at a time. It takes all the human manpower the family (or even the whole village) can muster to do the job in the short span of time when replanting must be done. If too much rain produces floods, the seedlings cannot be planted in time; if there is a drought before the seedlings have taken hold, the crop will die. Like all peasants throughout the world, the rice farmer lives in deep symbiosis with nature, and the exacting nature of rice farming ties him closely to his neighbors.

The big irrigation dikes must be maintained collectively and are the responsibility of whole villages or even districts; no one can be allowed to shirk his duty in maintaining them. I recall a deeply moving sight during the French-Indochinese War, in 1953, when a sudden flood in the Red River Delta washed out a major irrigation dam. The whole population of the area—perhaps tens of thousands of people—was seen swarming over the dike, working busily at reinforcing it. On one side of the dike there were French sentries protecting the working farmers; on the other side one could see the flat helmets and olive-green uniforms of "Viet-Nam People's Army" patrols. Neither side fired on the other; there was a war on, but the protection of the rice crop took precedence over it.

The "collectiveness" of rice farming also extends to its other aspects, and becomes embedded in the mores and religions of Southeast Asia. Josué de Castro, the great Brazilian economist and former chairman of the executive council of the United Nations Food and Agriculture Organization (F.A.O.), points out in his magistral study "The Geography of Hunger" how Confucianism and ancestor worship are in fact necessary adjuncts to the economics of rice farming:

"The doctrines of Confucius would not have penetrated and taken such deep root in the soul of the Chinese people if his precepts of love for one's family and worship of one's ancestors had not coincided with the people's economic interests. . . . The need for hands to grow food, thus fending off the chronic hunger, and the need for hands to help in the terrible hours of famine, have built a whole

53

complex social structure favorable to a high birth rate. [The Chinese] must have an ample excess of sons, so that after they have been cut down by disease, plague, famine, and war, there will still be some left to work the soil and worship the name of his ancestors."

That the life cycle is built around rice also holds true in the Buddhist countries of Asia, where water festivals, the plowing of "holy furrows" by the sovereign and harvest ceremonies are all-important in the life of the rural population. And this rural population represents about 90 per cent of all the people of the area. It is not often heard from, yet it is the rural population which, in the long run, is the object of the various "hot" and "cold" wars fought today throughout southern Asia.

In mainland China, as later in Communist-held areas of Viet-Nam, the changeover from the traditional pattern to the new mold was at first slow and gradual. The Communists began with an immensely popular land-rent and usury-reduction program (which, incidentally, was adopted in the non-Communist areas later); followed at a later stage by a breaking up of the big estates, whether owned by indigenous Chinese or Vietnamese owners, or by European corporations. Thereupon followed a period in which landless farmers received outright small parcels of rice land, often after the legal owners had been given short shrift before a "People's Court."

But that small parcel of land often came without the proper agricultural tools or the absolutely indispensable draft animals, and a process began which Lenin himself openly explained to his critic Kautsky almost 50 years ago:

"The proletarians tell the peasant: 'We shall help you to realize your desires in the direction of ideal capitalism. . . . At the same time we shall demonstrate to you the impossibility of such a system and the necessity to pass on to the collective culture of land.'"

In Communist China and Viet-Nam, this process was followed almost to the letter. The scarcity of tools and buffaloes led to the creation of "production cooperatives" and "work-exchange teams." They, in turn, led to the merging of adjoining plots into larger and more economical plots. It was when the Asian Communist regimes

began to make the latter process compulsory that the peasantry discovered it had been mousetrapped into collectivization. But then, it
was too late to rebel successfully.

It will remain a matter of debate among scholars and politicians
alike whether the Chinese Communists took over the Chinese mainland so successfully because they played their role of "agrarian
reformers" to the hilt, but the fact is that the Chinese Nationalists
had certainly failed to keep the allegiance of China's 500 million
farmers.

The war being fought in South Viet-Nam today, which largely
equals the French Indochina War in terms of manpower and treasure
committed and in lives lost, also has strong agrarian undertones. In
South Viet-Nam, large-scale absentee land ownership existed as it
never had in the North, even under the French. Vietnamese and
French rice estates of 20,000 acres and more were not unknown in
the rich Mekong Delta, with the result that up to 1955 about 2 per
cent of the landowners held title to 45 per cent of the rice land. And
since many landowners held senior government posts, land reform
(at first enacted by Emperor Bao-Dai in 1952 and later promised
by every subsequent government, including the present one under
General Khanh) was agonizingly slow.

The official land-reform programs involved resurveying all the
land about to be expropriated; long negotiations with the landlords
as to the price they were going to be paid; the complicated taking-
out of loans by the peasants; and the proper establishing of priorities
for the families of refugees, war victims, veterans, etc. But the Communist land reform in the areas held by the guerrillas since 1946
was often brutal and simple: outright confiscation from the landlords. The Communists did not tell the peasants who received this
land that it would some day be taken away again for collectivization; but they did tell them that it might be lost under Saigon's
land-reform program. This fear was a ready-made issue for the
Viet Cong.

Denis Warner, an old Asia hand, said of Diem's land reform in
his recent book, The Last Confucian: "The much-vaunted rural
help program did not exist. Land reform was a flop." Peasants

throughout history have rebelled for less than that, and much of the huge civilian effort which is now being made in the counterinsurgency field in South Viet-Nam involves convincing the farmer that his own government in Saigon and its American ally are willing to make up to him for past errors. Victory or defeat in Viet-Nam may well hang on whether he will be convinced in time.

It is officially conceded today that perhaps five million or more rural Vietnamese are under the effective control of the "Southern Liberation Front"—some estimates in fact run as high as seven million—and that they will have to be won back, at least in part, if the military counterinsurgency program is to succeed. This may well become the key test of the success or failure of General Maxwell D. Taylor's new ambassadorship to Saigon.

But even in so pro-Western a country as Thailand, rice is not only an economic factor but an important political factor as well— as it must be when it represents (as it also does in Burma and Cambodia) more than half of the country's export income. When American grain donations to India under Public Law 480 allegedly cut into Thai exports, a wave of public indignation swept the country's controlled press. Its gist was a barely veiled threat that further such American "interference" in Thailand's trade might well result in a political realignment of the country toward neutralism. American explanations that exports under P.L. 480 covered only quantities which India could not have afforded to import commercially (and thus did not cut into Thai exports) fell on deaf ears. Clearly, rice, in that case, was a more serious matter than political alliances (a view which such grain exporters as Canada and France fully share).

Needless to say, the Asian Communists have their own troubles with rice and the rice peasants. The incredible mistakes of Chinese land reform are a matter of record and the utter failure of the commune system, from which the Russians refused to rescue Mao, even contributed to widening the split between the two major Communist powers.

North Viet-Nam imitated Red China's mistakes up to a point and with the same dire results. After an initial stage of land reapportionment to individual small farmers, those farmers were grouped into "cooperatives." Holdouts or so-called "rich farmers" were tried and executed before specially created land-reform courts. On November 4, 1956, while the attention of the world was focused on Suez and Budapest, the peasants of Ho Chi Minh's own home province of Nghean rebelled against collectivization and had to be put down with gunfire. North Viet-Nam had to hold back for a time on the pace of its land-reform program, and commune-type farms today are rare in North Viet-Nam; the few that exist are run by People's Army soldiers and provide food for the armed forces. Yet land reform already has left its imprint on the North Vietnamese country-side: When I flew to Hanoi from Laos in 1962, the collective farms were easily recognizable by the larger expanse of their rice fields. Those still held privately had preserved their pocket-handker-chief pattern within their maze of small dikes. According to official North Vietnamese figures, 94 per cent of all rice land has already been collectivized.

North Viet-Nam, in spite of relentless efforts to supplement its de-ficient rice production through supplementary crops on nonirrigable land, such as sweet potatoes, corn and yam roots, still falls short of making up for the prewar imports from South Viet-Nam, cut off since the Geneva cease-fire of 1954. As in the case of Red China, the first detailed population census made in North Viet-Nam in 1960 was a serious blow to the hopes of the North Vietnamese planners; for it showed that North Viet-Nam had close to a million more people than believed and that its population increased 3 per cent a year, or half a million new mouths. Merely to break even (that is, give the 18 million North Vietnamese their meager 22-pound-per-month individual rice ration) means that North Viet-Nam *must* put every year at least another 80,000 acres of new rice land to the plow. It has never reached that figure.

This is precisely what makes underpopulated, rice-rich, easy-going South Viet-Nam—hardly anyone bothers to plant two crops *there*—such a tempting target for North Viet-Nam. And this is what makes all of Southeast Asia such a desirable prize for Red China.

Were all of the present rice exports of Southeast Asia directed to feed China and North Viet-Nam alone rather than going to India, Indonesia and even West Africa, both Asian Communist states would be freed of the major problem which hobbles all their industrial, military, and political ambitions—food. The Western nations, which have it within their power to alleviate those shortages, are of divided minds as to what the full political impact of self-sufficiency in rice would be on Hanoi and Peking.

Would "full-belly" Communists be easier to deal with than the lean Red revolutionaries in China and North Viet-Nam?

Or would an even further tightening of the present Western blockade bring about the "imminent" Communist Asian collapses which some inveterate Western optimists have been regularly predicting for the past decade?

Or would an easing of the rice problem in Communist Asia merely provide Hanoi and Peking with the necessary wherewithal for further aggressive moves deeper into Southeast Asia?

All this, and much more, rides on the humble Asian rice peasant as he patiently tends his water-covered fields lying like bright mirrors under the hot tropical sun. In 1964 indeed, a grain of rice is worth a drop of blood in the Far East.

Man Behind a War:
Ho Chi Minh

⚬⚬⚬

Saigon

"YOU KNOW, it's damned difficult to go out and tell people to hate a guy who looks like a half-starved Santa Claus," was the way one American member of the Saigon psychological-warfare services explained one of his problems to a journalist recently. And he said it with feeling. And an American officer well-versed in American history and faced with the hundredth affirmation that Ho Chi Minh was the George Washington of Viet-Nam, regardless of what the politics of the Vietnamese were, quipped:

"All right, so he *is* the George Washington of Viet-Nam. But do *we* have to get stuck with *all* the Benedict Arnolds?"

And that, basically, is one of the troubles in making the whole Vietnamese war credible to the public: Hitler, Mussolini, and Tojo —particularly against a background of *Panzerdivisionen,* Black Shirts, and Imperial Navy battleships—not only looked loathsome, but *were* loathsome; in addition to commanding the kind of military force which obviously could (and almost did) destroy their opponents. Stalin also provided us with a convenient hate-figure which could be easily caricaturized with a blood-dripping knife protruding from under the hooked mustache; and Mao Tse-tung does not do badly what with 700 million Chinese playing Yellow Peril as if hired by Central Casting.

But with Ho Chi Minh, we enter the era of what could be called the "Hate Gap." It is as difficult for the United States to believably depict a frail seventy-seven-year-old gentleman with a whispy beard and rubber sandals, ruling a country the size of Florida with an army the size of the Swiss militia and a 100-plane airforce, as a "threat to the freedom of Southeast Asia" and to America's position in the world; as it is for a 200-pound lady to find sympathy when she jumps shriekingly on a chair because a mouse crossed the floor in front of her. To be sure, North Viet-Nam is a Communist state and Ho is a Communist, and North Viet-Nam is involved in the Viet Cong insurgency in the South. It is equally a fact that, while Ho was (and is) president of the country, a land reform was rammed through which, even according to North Vietnamese sources, caused "many unlawful executions." But, unfortunately for the Hate Gap, it was Ho who stopped the land-reform excesses and fired the party hacks directly responsible for it.

Contrary to other world leaders on both sides of whatever tattered curtains there are still left, Ho constantly underplays himself rather than the reverse. Where other leaders want to be known as the genial inspirers of their country's arts, sciences, and literature (not to mention politics), Ho has thus far abstained from expressing his views on art in general or pictures of himself in particular; does not pretend that assiduous lecture of his writings will aid North Vietnamese scientists in overcoming their technological handicaps, and has thus far confined his literary efforts to one brief French-language theater play, *Le Dragon de Dragon* (1923 vintage, and a flop to such a point that no Hanoi theater has thus far given it a try), and to brief political pamphlets and speeches, only a few of which will long be remembered even by the literati of the CIA who, like the Roman haruspices, love to dissect that sort of thing in order to discover the portents of Hanoi's future moves. A small volume of poems written while Ho was in a Chinese nationalist prison in 1942–43, has some merit because the haunting verse at least reflect the personal feelings of Ho at a time when, for once, he was totally at the mercy of others.

60

There are not yet any mountains, towns, or even factories named after him—at least officially. The only terrain feature named after him, was named by the French Army in Indochina and inherited by its American successors: it is the famous "Ho Chi Minh Trail," the seemingly endless network of jungle paths, supply depots, and rest camps on the way from North Viet-Nam to the South and located in Laos, the most inhospitable confines of the Cambodian frontier, and the deepest jungles of South Viet-Nam.

To the unconditional enthusiasts, all this reflects a passion for real humility, in the same sense that Stalin and the Communist Chinese leaders wore, and wear, unadorned military uniforms. Yet the latter were—at least until the dust settles around the Red Guards—as slavishly adulated as leaders ever were anywhere in the world. He also wears a suntan version of the Stalin-Mao uniform jacket. But as a Japanese Socialist legislator noted, when he visited him in November 1966, Ho's uniform was badly frayed at the collar, as if, in a poor country at war, he could not afford to have a new one. And that precisely is the point of difference between Ho and the other uniform-wearing types: he may not be as humble as his warmest admirers think, but he really is a simple man with simple tastes and *really* prefers to wear a comfortable old cotton suntan jacket and sandals rather than a stiff sharkskin uniform and formal leather shoes. Anybody with sense, living in Viet-Nam and in an unairconditioned French governor's palace—now North Viet-Nam's White House— would do likewise, providing he is not stiff-necked about protocol, and Ho decidedly is not. But he knows what he likes. *Time,* which makes it its business to be well-informed about small things, informed its readers breathlessly that, in 1955, Ho liked to smoke Philip Morris cigarettes while offering local brands to his visitors (being a non-smoker, I was not able to verify that distinction) but that in recent years, like many other smokers, he has switched to the filter-tipped Salems.

Yet, the seeming precision of the known details about Ho's life conveniently hides the large unknown areas of his life, gaps of four or five years in which he *may* have been married, *may* have been in Boston, Mass., *may* have been with Mao in China; or *may* have studied at the Lenin School in Moscow. The worst part of it is that even the Communist press has never been quite able to make up its mind about Ho. His birth dates are mangled as to day, month, and year, and the London *Daily Worker* in 1932 published an eloquent obituary of "Comrade Nguyen Ai Quoc," Ho's pseudonym of the time, which led many sources to speak later of a "second Ho Chi Minh" who is at least as mysterious as the presumed second assassin of President Kennedy. (In actual fact, however, the ever-vigilant French *Sûreté*—the French counterpart of the FBI—got a good close-up photograph of one of Ho's ears in the early 1920's when he called on a senior French police official in Paris, and I am assured that more recent pictures perfectly match that early one.) The same holds true for Ho's personal life. Even Mao Tse-tung is acknowledged to have a normal family life—in fact he married a very pretty actress who may yet develop into a political power of her own—and so did, up to a point, Stalin. In the case of Ho, his most ardent panegyrists state, he gave his whole life to the Cause: to this day no one has been able to pin down the story that, while in China in the 1930's, he had a wife and a daughter whom he loved a great deal and who died during the war against Japan. One of his closest associates, Tran Huy Lieu, an old revolutionary and now the director of the Historical Research Institute in Hanoi, formally denied this story, but he at least acknowledged that Ho had had an older brother and an older sister, both of whom never engaged in politics (though they were arrested for a time by the French police because of their brother's activities), stayed on the family farm, and died uneventfully a few years apart in the 1950's.

Actually, Ho was born on May 19, 1890 at Kim-Lien, about 14 miles from the now much-bombed city of Vinh in Central Viet-Nam, 140 miles north of the 17th parallel which divides the country in two parts since the 1954 cease-fire. Vinh is the capital of the province of Nghé An, an area of jungle-covered mountains and narrow, heavily-populated plains and had in the past produced more than its fair share of strong-willed men who resisted outside invaders against all comers, be they Chinese invaders, unworthy Vietnamese rulers, or the French colonials. Ho's father, Nguyên Sinh Huy, was among them. Though emanating from a poor family, he had, through sheer hard work and tenacity, passed the Vietnamese equivalent of a doctorate of philosophy (pre-French Viet-Nam, like China, had a sophisticated, though limited, school system) and had become a minor mandarin in the imperial administration. An ardent patriot, he had witnessed the arrival of the French in the deep south of Viet-Nam with great misgivings, and when a new young Vietnamese emperor, Nam-Nghi, ascended to the throne in 1884 and led his own government officials into open guerrilla war against the French, Ho's father joined in enthusiastically. The bemused French were at first unable to cope with a revolt led by a country's whole elite and aptly dubbed by them *la Révolte des Lettrés* (the Intellectuals' Rebellion) until they finally succeeded in crushing it in 1888 when they captured the young monarch with his last men in Nghé An, precisely.

Ho's father, heartbroken, vowed not to serve the colonial power or the native administration under its control and returned to Kim-Lien where he still owned a house and a plot of land—a normal procedure for Vietnamese officials in disgrace and one of the reasons why they will, to this day, own a farm and plot of land in their native town, regardless of how much other wealth they possess. Ho thus was born into a family in which the presence of the French was bitterly resented and in which patriotism was an article of faith to be practiced at all times. The defeat and deportation of Nam-Nghi— the French deported him to their safest overseas territory, Algeria— merely drove the anti-French resistance underground. Like their cultural brothers, the Chinese, the Vietnamese love conspirations and secret societies, and Ho's father was a member of such an anti-French resistance movement, and when a son was born to him in 1890, he gave him the name of Nguyên (which was the family name) That Thanh (Who Will Be Victorious). By the time young Thanh was old enough to attend the village school, he carried messages for the anti-French underground, and when he transferred to the French *lycée* at Vinh, he soon came to the attention of the principal for his fiery political tirades and was dismissed from the school, probably in 1905. "Poor grades," said the teachers. "Politics," say the North Vietnamese historians.

Ho's father, determined to give his son the best of all possible educations, succeeded in getting him enrolled in the most prestigious high school (in fact, it was close to a modern prep school) in Viet-Nam, the *Lycée Quôc-Hoc* in the imperial capital of Hué. *Quôc-Hoc* was an interesting experiment: created by a mandarin by the name of Ngo Dinh Kha (one of whose sons was to be murdered in 1963 as President Ngo Dinh Diem of South Viet-Nam), it was to blend all that was best in French education with a solid anchoring in Vietnamese culture which the French *lycées* in Viet-Nam of course did not offer. As such (it exists to this day) *Quôc-Hoc* was to become the hotbed of Vietnamese resistance to all outside influences. Fierce nationalists such as Diem, equally fierce Communists such as North Viet-Nam's General Giap and Prime Minister Pham Van Dong; are among its graduates. And in 1966, its students, espousing the cause of Buddhism this time, nearly toppled the South Vietnamese regime of General Ky and with it, almost shook the whole American effort in Viet-Nam to its very foundations. At *Quôc-Hoc,* Thanh (or Ho, by his later name) now received whatever nationalistic underpinning his inbred fervor needed—but *Quôc-Hoc,* like the rest of Viet-Nam, was after all under French control. He left the school around 1910 without a diploma, thus ending his formal education save for attendance at such Communist party schools as the University of the Toilers of the Orient and the Lenin School in Moscow. He has no claim to the title "Dr." which some Asians (notably almost all Indian writers) constantly bestow upon him.

But even without his degree, Ho now had more education than all but a small élite of his Vietnamese contemporaries. Notably, he spoke and wrote superb French, and does so to this day; in addition to equally good Mandarin and Cantonese, fluent Russian, good English, and passable German.

We find him now teaching school in the sleepy south-central Vietnamese fishing town of Rhan-Thiet, at the *Lycée Dac-Thanh,* which had a nationalistic curriculum patterned on that of *Quôc-Hoc.* But as everywhere else, teachers were paid starvation salaries and Ho, then as now more of a "doer" than a contemplative thinker and theoretician, soon tired of academe. In 1911 he was in Saigon and attended some trade school, probably in the field of cooking and baking since he later was to be employed in that field and since, for a Vietnamese, such a specialty was a sure way to more lucrative employment in a European household. (It has by now probably been forgotten that a minor "flap" ensued between Jackie Kennedy and the household of former French Ambassador Hervé Alphand when it was bruited about that the Alphands' Vietnamese cook was

64

being lured into White House employment.) In early 1912, Ho thus landed a messboy's job on the French liner *Latouche-Tréville*. Unwilling to besmirch his good family name by the lowly job he now held, Ho adopted a new name, the first of many: Ba (Three); probably because he was the third child of his family.

By opting for a French ship on the European-Atlantic run, Ho had also made a key political decision: he had opted for the West against the East, and, eventually, for Moscow against Peking. For there were, at that time, many Vietnamese (particularly among the conservative nationalists) who made the contrary decision of continuing to look toward China for guidance, or even toward the rising Japanese state. Such nationalist leaders as Phan Boi Chau, witnessing the rise of Dr. Sun Yat-sen's Kuomintang, in fact emigrated to China and created the *Dông Du* [Eastern Voyage] movement which many young Vietnamese followed for over twenty years. A royal prince, Cuong-Dê, led another small group of nationalists to Japan, some of whom returned to their home country when the Japanese invaded it. But Cuong-Dê himself was to die there, a bitter man, in the 1950's. North Viet-Nam's main party theoretician (and, in fact, also its leading exponent of the Peking faction) clearly understood this option for what it was in a small book on Ho published in Hanoi in 1966.

"What attracts [Ho] in those [Western] countries is their ideology of freedom, of the sovereignty of the people, of democracy, of science and technology . . . Why did he not follow the promoters of the Eastern Voyage movement to Japan and China? He thought that to fight the French colonialists with the help of the Japanese militarists, would be to 'hunt the tiger only to be eaten by the wolves.' And to become an adept of Liang Kai-tsiao [a Chinese writer] would be to opt for a reformist path rather than a revolutionary one."

In all likelihood, Ho's decision was not at all based on ideology then, but its ultimate consequences for him and the movement and state he leads were the same and they would be of even greater importance to those who were to fight him—the French first and the United States later.

Life aboard ship was a sobering experience to the young Vietnamese. At that time, a good crossing to West Africa or North

America took fifteen days or more for a smaller vessel, ample time to become acquainted with the foibles of the white master race in the deck cabins and those of the white crews below deck: "A handful of well-fed bourgeois lives in luxury," says Truong Chinh, "while the immense majority, the workers; is confined to misery." There is no question but that Ho was deeply impressed by what he saw, and particularly the inherent contradictions of a society in which he was addressed, like a child, by the familiar *tu* when he was in Viet-Nam, but as *Monsieur* as soon as he landed in France; where an African could be killed almost with impunity merely for looking at a white woman in the American South, but where the same African could buy a white prostitute in Marseilles; where white nations could pretend to rule the non-white four-fifths of the world for the sake of "civilizing" them—with the help of soldiers and sailors who were as illiterate and superstitious as those about to be civilized.

A few months before World War I broke out, Ho had had enough of seafaring for a while. He settled down in London and, now speaking not only French but English, learned during his time at sea, found employment at the posh Carlton Hotel, where the incomparable Escoffier was holding forth as probably the greatest chef of his time, to the point that Frenchmen would go to London— a feat probably not repeated since—in order to eat well. Escoffier liked the slim and quiet Asian boy and soon promoted him to the pastry division, a choice spot. Again Ho had ample opportunity to see the constant side-by-side existence of crass riches and seamiest poverty as, in order to supplement his meagre cash income—for, it must not be forgotten, he worked in the West to be able to send remittances back home to his family in Kim-Lien—he shoveled snow in London schools early in the morning before going to his job at the Carlton. But it is said that the latter has left him, to this day, with a gourmet's taste for fine eating, and (like some American presidents) an occasional desire to take his turn at the cooking stove in his Hanoi residence.

What exactly happened next is again lost in party mythology and hagiography. His close associate and prime minister, Pham Van Dong, says in a small pamphlet published in 1961 that Ho again returned to sea during the early part of the First World War; which would be clearly consistent with the then prevailing situation: war-time food restrictions made pastry cooks a drug on the market, but high shipping losses due to the Kaiser's U-boats put a premium (as well as premium wages) on men who were willing to go to sea. But Truong Chinh's 1966 version of the facts asserts that Ho, on learning that France was shipping almost a hundred thousand Indochinese (mostly Vietnamese) to France to either replace French manpower in the war plants or, like the British Indians on the Somme or the French Senegalese at Verdun; to serve in the trenches; immediately went to France in order to spread his na-tionalist views among them. For Ho, in London, had for the first time since he was an adult, made contact with a formal political group, the Chinese-dominated "Overseas Workers Association." That association, though ostensibly concerned with improving the working conditions of foreign workers most of the time excluded from the local labor unions (a grim practice often still alive in Britain with regard to the West Indians and in the U.S. with regard to Negro labor—and not necessarily in the deep South), had also begun to address itself to the problem of political organization of its members once they returned to their respective homelands. As the later histories of nationalist movements in British colonies clearly show, those overseas workers associations, by virtue of the fact that they were dealing with a compact urban audience generally pro-tected by the laws of free assembly which willy-nilly applied to them in Britain and France (but not in British India or French Indochina), became an important adjunct to the eventual libera-tion of their homelands.

In the case of Ho, both Dong's and Chinh's accounts are in fact not mutually exclusive. There is strong circumstantial evidence that Ho *did* return to sea on the deadly Trans-Atlantic wartime runs, visiting Boston, New York, and other East and Gulf Coast ports, because he later wrote vivid accounts of what Dong calls "the barbarities and ugliness of American capitalism, the Ku Klux Klan mobs, the lynchings of Negroes." A pamphlet written by Ho in Moscow in 1924 and entitled *La Race Noire,* seems to be in part based on what he heard and saw in the United States during his trips in 1914–16. But there is no question but that he moved to France in early 1917 and that his motives were political, this time.

And indeed this was a good time to do so. In Viet-Nam, another young emperor, Duy-Tan, had led a rebellion against the depleted French colonial troops in 1916 and had been, like Nam-Nghi, crushed in the nick of time and deported to Reunion Island in the Indian Ocean. And in France, a mutiny had broken out in the war-weary French Army in 1917 and been put down with cold ferocity by the French commander-in-chief, General Philippe Pétain (in 1914 the regimental commander of Lieutenant Charles de Gaulle)—and with the help of loyal Vietnamese military police units.

[Duy-Tan himself deserves a biographer of his own. He stayed for 25 years on Reunion Island, became an electrical engineer there, ran its radio station with the outside world and, in World War II, was one of the leaders of the anti-Vichy Free French underground there. He joined the French Army under his personal name of Vinh-San, became a Free French major but still was an ardent advocate of Vietnamese independence. Faced with Ho's rising Viet-Minh movement in 1945, de Gaulle decided to return the prestigious Duy-Tan to Viet-Nam as France's best middle-of-the-road bet against Ho's left-wing hotheads. Duy-Tan agreed, but on condition that he first could return to Reunion to pick up his family there. His plane crashed near Bangui, in Central Africa, and he still is buried there under a marker reading "Vinh-San, Major, French Army. *Mort pour la France.*" Had he lived, Viet-Nam might be a neutralist-leaning monarchy, like Morocco or Cambodia, with Duy-Tan as monarch and Ho Chi Minh as premier.]

But something else had happened in 1917. A Communist revolution had broken out in Russia under Lenin. The Tsarist Empire opted out of the war and proclaimed a heady new faith whose tenets included immediate national independence for all colonial territories (a promise the new regime promptly reneged in 1924, when one of the colonials from the Georgian Republic by the name of Joseph Dzhugashvili—better known as Stalin—took over in Moscow) not only at home, but throughout the world. To Ho, this was a blinding flash of recognition: here was *his* program, but clearly presented and part of a seemingly coherent philosophy, and a political party with worldwide aspirations not only willing to work with him, but to accept him as a welcome equal among equals! In France, that party still was the French Socialist Party. Ho joined in the acrimonious debates which pitted the old-line Socialists wedded to the idea of gradualism in everything, against the adherents of the new faith, and in the process met almost every French politician who was to be of any importance through the 1950's. To this day, whenever he meets Frenchmen, he immediately asks questions about *mes amis*. But, as is the case in the life of every old man, there are fewer and fewer of them: Léon Blum is dead, Vaillant-Couturier is dead, Edouard Herriot is dead, Albert Sarrant is dead . . .

But, while politics made for heady moments, the little Vietnamese refugee in Paris also had to earn a living, and Chinese calligraphy, laboriously learned in the village school at Kim-Lien twenty years earlier, suddenly proved useful. Ho used his knowledge of careful brush strokes to establish himself as a photo retoucher at 9, Impasse Compoint, a small dead-end street in Paris' then somewhat run-down 17th *arrondissement*. The Socialist Party's newspaper *La vie ouvrière* of 1918 even carried small classified advertisements testifying to Ho's adventure into Free enterprise:

"You who wish a living remembrance of your relatives, have your photos retouched at Nguyen Ai Quoc's. Handsome portraits and handsome frames for 45 francs."

Apparently, the business did not exactly flourish, as probably fewer and fewer of the war-weary French wished to have "living remembrances" of their relatives and Ho, with the war at an end, began to travel throughout France to visit the barracks and housing developments where the Indochinese war plant workers, now idle, and the about-to-discharged troops were awaiting repatriation. What with essential food imports and supplies pre-empting shipping badly depleted by the German U-boats, repatriation convoys had low priority and the almost hundred thousand Indochinese (most of whom were Vietnamese) proved a magnificatly fertile terrain for political indoctrination. They had seen the whites (and not only the French: Britishers and even Americans, as well) at their worst: dying and being afraid of it; black-marketeering and whoring through four war years; rebelling against their commanders; discriminating against them (and, above all, against the Negroes) on racial grounds. They had also seen, as Mao Tse-tung was to express it only a short while later, how much power was really growing out of the barrel of guns. And Ho, as well as other Vietnamese exile leaders, now came around to put all this dispersed knowledge into a well-rounded political context of both nationalism and socialism. In a way, the Indochina War against the French, and, hence, that against the United States; started right there in the repatriation camps of 1918–19, and with the Vietnamese serving with the French forces then: In 1919, a Vietnamese sailor, Ton Duc Thang, serving aboard the French battle cruiser *Waldeck-Rousseau* in the Black Sea, engineered a mutiny together with a Communist petty officer by the name of André Marty, for the purpose of turning the ship over to the newborn Soviet Russian government! He paid for this abortive mutiny with a nineteen-year hard labor sentence in the infamous Poulo Condore prison island off South Viet-Nam's coast. But today, Ton, aged 84, is Ho's Vice-President in North Viet-Nam.

The next formative shock for Ho was the great 1919 Versailles Peace Conference, held in the glittering mirrored ball rooms of Louis XIV's palace. Versailles, held out the hope of not merely being another big-power palaver where the map of the world would be carved up by a few superpowers, but—as America's President Woodrow Wilson had hoped—was to be the cradle of a just peace for all and bring the right of self-determination to nations yet unborn. Precisely, the aspiring leaders of such nations, or pseudo-nations; from the Balkans and the Caucasus, Eastern Europe and South Asia; hovered in the wings in the hope of finding a powerful champion for their causes—and sometimes found them. Britain was interested in promoting weak vassal states in the Moslem parts of the Russian Empire and in dismembering Turkey; France was interested in Eastern European satellites of her own, in addition to parts of the Middle East; the United States backed the Irish and Czechoslovakia, and the Italians wanted footholds in the Eastern Mediterranean. But this was still a white man's world: *nobody* backed independence for any African or East Asian country—a lesson which the Gandhis and the Nehrus, the Haile-Selassies, and Ho Chi Minhs, weren't about to forget. Ho and some of his friends had laboriously drawn up a very modest eight-point program which covered one side of a sheet and had had it printed over Ho's signature. The finished product did not look very impressive, and the French printer, faced with an unfamiliar-sounding name, even had managed to misspell Ho's name to a Donald-Duck-sounding "Nguyen Ai QuAc." But there was no time (and probably no money) to have the program reprinted and Ho and his modest *Cahier de révendications* [Petition of Claims] were off to Versailles via suburban railroad.

But before beginning this undertaking, Ho had to get the proper clothing from a second-hand store: pinstriped suit, pinchwaisted overcoat, derby hat, and, adding a note of nonchalance, a light tan muffler hanging over the left shoulder. As it was, Ho and his friends wasted their time and money. Versailles nowhere records that a petition for "Annamite" (as the term then was) independence had been officially taken under consideration and Ho's petition, with its demands for more basic freedoms, better education, and appointment of a Vietnamese delegation to advise the French government on its Viet-Nam policy; never even got a hearing. Time and again, the thin Asian in his shabby elegance was shunted from impassible usher to busy-looking secretary until he finally gave up in despair. And with Versailles died Ho's hopes of a "liberal" solution for his country, and he was also able to observe now what the other unsuccessful petitioners were muttering among themselves—the Irish in the lead: armed revolution was the answer, the road to power via the terrorist's bomb and the guerrilla's gun barrel. One big country, absent from Versailles, was right at that very moment proving that very point—the Soviets in Russia—and their example was wildly debated by every Socialist Party in the world. What if their slowly evolutionary road to Socialism was the wrong one? What if capitalism *really* was in its death throes throughout the world as a result of the Great War? Defeated Germany was seething, Soviet cavalry under the mustachioed Marshal Budyönni was in the process of overrunning the newly-created Polish state [he was stopped in the nick of time before Warsaw by a French-advised Polish army. One of the Polish-speaking French advisers was a Captain Charles de Gaulle]. There were anarchists throwing bombs in the United States, Red flags were flying in Milan, Italy, huge strikes racked Britain. In every major Socialist Party, congresses were

71

convened to reevaluate the situation, as the more radical elements pressed for World Revolution now.

In France, the clash came on Christmas Day, 1920, in the quiet Loire Valley town of Tours, at the 18th National Congress of the Socialist Party. He participated, according to the record, as "Comrade Indochinese Delegate." A period picture shows us a sallow-faced young man with deep-set black shining eyes, surrounded by well-fed, jowly, French faces turned toward him as he spoke. With incredible single-mindedness, Ho pleaded for adherence to the Third International for one single reason: the colonial question. Nothing else mattered. Relentlessly, and to the obvious discomfort of the mainland French delegates, Ho ticked off one French crime in Indochina after another:

> . . . In its selfish interest [France] conquered our country with bayonets. Since then we have not only been oppressed and exploited shamelessly, but also tortured and poisoned pitilessly. Plainly speaking, we have been poisoned with opium, alcohol, etc. I cannot, in some minutes, reveal all the atrocities that the predatory capitalists have inflicted on Indochina. . . .

And he ended his appeal with a passionate plea that the "Socialist Party must act practically to support the oppressed natives." There was an uncomfortable silence. Then Jean Longuet, no one less than the grandson of Karl Marx and thus enjoying considerable prestige in the Party, observed somewhat lamely:

"I have spoken in favor of the natives."

But to Ho, words were no longer enough. On December 30, as the congress ended, Ho once more spoke up, and this time he was not pleading for understanding. It was *he* who had understood:

> . . . I understand very well one single thing: The Third International concerns itself a great deal with the colonial question. Its delegates promise to help the oppressed colonial peoples to regain their liberty and independence. The adherents of the Second International have not said a word about the fate of the colonial areas.

And thus, Ho Chi Minh, on December 30, 1920, opted for Communism as a way out for Viet-Nam, on totally nationalistic grounds, and at the same time became a founding member of the French Communist Party. The option of course changed his whole life: from an isolated individual in a hostile community he now

72

became a much sought-after Party functionary in a worldwide movement new enjoying the financial backing of a struggling but nonetheless powerful state: the Soviet Union. Funds suddenly became available for more lecture trips inside France; Ho started the Intercolonial Union in 1921 as a "front" to attract members from other colonial territories to the Party. The Union's paper, *Le Paria,* reflected Ho's own inimitable, direct, style, hammering away at concrete problems; never bothering with doctrine. As one peruses Ho's writings forty years later, one can only be amazed at how *little* they offer: most of them are polemic tirades about some obscure French official in some remote province who beat up his houseboy, raped the kitchenmaid's daughter, and closed the village school. It would be difficult to pin down the "essential Ho" in a small booklet of his quotations, as was done by the Chinese Cultural Revolution in that best-seller of the millennium, *Quotations from Chairman Mao Tse-tung;* for Ho, throughout his whole life, did not seek to convert the world to anything—except to accepting the existence of an independent Viet-Nam, united from North to South. In fact, that singlemindedness about a country nobody had ever heard of, when so many other important issues were at hand in the advanced Western countries, often irritated the senior Comintern leaders who, like Jean Longuet, felt that they had done all that had to be done once they had passed a few resolutions condemning colonialism in general. But the published records of the Fourth and Fifth Comintern Congresses, held in Moscow in November–December, 1922 and in June–July, 1924 (Ho also attended the Peasant International [Krestintern] meetings in Moscow in 1923), are full of repeated statements by "Comrade Nguyen Ai Quoc" about the question of colonial revolutions. In fact, in remarkable statements preceding by forty years the Lin-Piao statement that "the countryside of the world will encircle the cities," Ho made an impassioned plea at the Fifth Comintern Congress that the best way to defeat the industrialized powers was *not* by labor agitation in the industrial centers of the West, but by the instigation of a ceaseless series of debilitating colonial wars of national liberation.

It was Ho who turned out to be right, of course.

In view of his recognized competence in this field (or, perhaps, to get rid of this single-minded pest), the Comintern appointed Ho to its Southeast Asia Bureau, and he was also appointed as the Colonial Representation on the ten-man executive committee of the Krestintern. At the same time his hatred of French colonial practices came to an all-time pitch as he began to sign articles with a new pseudonym: Nguyen *O Phap* ["Nguyen Who Hates the French"]. That was finally a bit too much for the French Communist leadership, and Jacques Doriot, its own overseas affairs specialist (who died in 1944 as a lieutenant in the German *Waffen-SS*), told him to tone down his statements. It is perhaps this worsening of relations with the French CP—Ho was never to become close to it again, feeling quite correctly that, when it came to France's colonies, the CP's attitudes were far too "French"—and the relative lack of support for his views among the highly-Westernized intellectuals who then ran Communism in Moscow; which may have decided Ho to return to the Far East to put into practice what he had been preaching. China was, in late 1924, in the throes of revolution. In Canton, South China, the anti-warlord elements of the Chinese Republic had regrouped and of their generals, Chiang Kai-shek, was in the process of reconstituting a modern, disciplined army under the guidance of an important Russian mission, headed, on the civilian side by Michael Borodin, and on the military side, by General "Galin" (in reality, General Vassily Bluecher, later on executed by Stalin). Ho's job, officially, was to serve as Borodin's secretary-interpreter. In actual fact, it consisted in reorganizing the important Vietnamese exile community in South China, principally in Canton and Hong Kong.

Adopting a new pseudonym (the actual list of all his names is almost endless), Song Man Tcho, Ho now was in his favorite element: talking directly with his own countrymen, organizing them to liberate the Fatherland. He soon had established an efficiently-operating "Revolutionary Youth Associations" whose members, after training in Canton, began to reinfiltrate Viet-Nam and soon began to organize strikes in schools, plantations, and mines. Heavy-handed French repression only broadened its impact and provided new recruits for Ho in Canton. Among them was the son of a high-ranking mandarin of the Vietnamese imperial court. Ho immediately recognized his true value as a brilliant mind and devoted friend and sent him to the Nationalist Chinese military academy at

Whampoa, superintended by Chiang Kai-shek with the help of Russian and German military advisers and one of the best military schools in Asia. The young mandarin did well and, in his free hours, also studied Marxism. Soon he became Ho's most trusted lieutenant. Today, the mandarin, Pham Van Dong, is Prime Minister of North Viet-Nam.

For other recruits, Ho had different methods. Some of the young Vietnamese revolutionaries emerging out of Viet-Nam could not be interested in the new faith preached by Moscow. Their return to Viet-Nam, after military training in Canton, would have endangered the Communist underground structure which Ho was slowly putting into place; and their names often found themselves conveniently "leaked" to the French *Sûreté*. But, in Viet-Nam, this was not a onesided phenomenon. With the fractionalism which seems to be the constant bane of South Viet-Nam to this day, the Vietnamese somehow managed to have *three* bitterly-quarreling Communist parties between 1925 and 1930 which were not above selling each other out to the French, in addition to selling out their Trotskyist and nationalist competitors; and the two latter, knowing where the information leading to their arrest had come from, in turn revealed what they knew of the Communists. It is this mutual decapitation of leadership which permitted the French for so long to ignore the legitimate aspirations for self-government of the Vietnamese and which, to this day, accounts for the instability of institutions in South Viet-Nam, where the bitter lessons of the 1930's were never learned.

But Ho, in the meantime, had other problems. In 1927, Chiang and his Russian advisers broke over the role the rising Chinese Communist Party was to play in the Republic—the break ending in a wholesale massacre of the CCP, brilliantly described in André Malraux's novel *Man's Fate*. Ho escaped being engulfed in the catastrophe at the last moment by fleeing westward across Yünnan to placidly Buddhist Thailand. The Vietnamese community there gave him shelter and Ho began to preach his faith among its villages, traveling in the handy disguise of a saffron-robed, shaven-headed Buddhist monk. But the contemplative life even of false bonzehood could not suit Ho for long: in 1928, he mysteriously showed up in Brussels at a Communist-sponsored Congress against

Imperialism, traveled on to Switzerland and even fascist Italy, worked in a Berlin racked by the financial crash of 1929 and the rise of Nazism, probably touched base in France, and then, just as suddenly, re-disappeared in the Far East via the Trans-Siberian railroad to Vladivostok, whence he took a British ship to Hong Kong (being an unwelcome—or, conversely, a most wanted—guest in Nationalist China), where he took up residence in the first days of 1930. Communism had fallen on evil days in the Far East of 1927–30. In Indonesia, a premature Communist rebellion, launched against the advice of the Comintern, had brought about the complete destruction for a full twenty years of the Communist apparatus. In Malaya, an intercepted Comintern agent, Joseph Ducroux, "spilled his guts" to British intelligence about the whole Communist structure in the Far East; the Chinese-dominated "South Seas Communist Party" had for all purposes collapsed with the crushing of the CCP in 1927; and the Vietnamese Communists not only were as divided as ever, but had gotten tangled up in an anti-French nationalist uprising in 1930—which they at first wanted to sit out in view of its obvious hopelessness—and were being swept in droves into French prisons.

With all this going on, Ho received a message from the Executive Committee of the Third International to clear up the Party mess in his own country: "The most important and most urgent talk for all Indochinese Communists consists in founding a revolutionary party of the proletariat, i.e., a mass Communist Party. It should be a unified party and the *only* Indochinese Communist Party."

It would have been sure death to hold such an important meeting inside Viet-Nam, and warily, one by one, the key leaders filtered outside to Hong Kong, where Communism was not particularly welcome either, but where at least the Vietnamese Communists were less well known. There is an element of high comedy in the fact that the original reunification meeting of all Communist factions took place at the Hong Kong stadium in the middle of the bleacher section, while a wildly disputed soccer game was in progress and thus conveniently blanketed whatever equally wild disputes the Vietnamese party factionalists were thrashing out. Like a floating crap game, the meetings were continued all over town between January 6 and February 3, 1930. But on the later date, Ho was able to report that a unified ICP was now in existence, just as the Comintern had demanded, although it took until October, 1930, to include Cambodian and Laotian sections, to make it truly "Indochinese." But that organizational success bore little immediate fruit. Soon, the most important party stalwarts in Viet-Nam—Pham Van Dong, the future General Giap, the Party's first secretary general, Tran Phu (who was to die in prison)—found themselves arrested by the French and sentenced to long jail sentences. Ho himself, now camouflaged as Chinese businessman Tong Van So, had taken over the southern section of the Far East Bureau of the Comintern, and thus was on Ducroux's list of operatives when he was arrested in Singapore. On June 5, 1931, the police caught up with him and he was given a six-month prison sentence. That seemed mild enough, except that Ho, as a French subject which he technically was, had been sentenced to death *in absentia* by a French tribunal at Vinh, the capital of his native province, for subversive activities and rebellion against the French Republic; and now the French were demanding his extradition from Hong Kong.

But in the genteel world of Anglo-Saxon law, legality once more prevailed. Ho's court-appointed lawyer, Frank Loseby, argued that Ho was a political refugee and thus not subject to extradition. The case went on appeal all the way to the Privy Council (the British equivalent of a Supreme Court), where Ho's side was brilliantly argued by Sir Stafford Cripps, and Ho indeed was found not to be subject to extradition. Still, he was a marked man. He could not stay in Hong Kong (he was in any case under a British mandate of expulsion after his conviction), but neither could he go to Indochina nor, for that matter, neighboring China, without great risks. With the help-beyond-the-call-of-duty of Frank Loseby, Ho eventually managed to slip out of Hong Kong into the nearby but isolated province of Fukien. Here, as in the case of his relations with the French *Sûreté* in the 1920's, assertions were variously made that he obtained his liberty and getaway papers by making a deal with the British Intelligence Service. Obviously, neither Ho nor the I.S. were above making such deals (and in 1943–44, he *did* make a deal with the American Office of Strategic Services to help it find downed U.S. pilots and provide it with intelligence in exchange for guns), but there simply is no evidence to prove the assertion, and Loseby's personal help—he was to remain a fervent admirer of Ho until his death in the 1950's—was far more likely under the circumstances.

Fukien, to this stormy petrel of Asian Communism, must have been like the bonze's robes in Thailand, an eminently safe but highly boring means of staying alive. Little wonder that one year later he again was in the only place in Asia then where a substantial Vietnamese community could be found, the International Concession in Shanghai, whose neighboring French Concession also contained Vietnamese colonial troops. A young American correspondent met him there fleetingly, after having become the first foreigner to observe Mao Tse-tung's guerrillas first hand: Edgar Snow. But above all, Ho was desperately seeking contact with the Comintern apparatus, now prudently lying low. Earning his life as a teacher in a Vietnamese school, he began to make contact with local Vietnamese and Chinese Communists, but his big break came when his one-time Communist chief from France, Vaillant-Couturier, visited Shanghai and put him in touch with the Chinese apparatus. There is more than one curious aspect to Ho's self-admitted temporary isolation. To be sure, what with the total destruction of the Southeast Asian Comintern apparatus due to the Ducroux affair and the collapse of the Indochina Communist Party after the abortive 1930 uprisings, it was understandable that what was left of the Chinese Communist Party outside of Mao's forces which were about to embark on their historic 10,000-mile "Long March," was not about to advertise its presence all over Shanghai. But there may have been another aspect as well: Ho, under death sentence by one colonial power and just released from the prisons of another for reasons which a good Communist might find difficult to swallow, now lived in Shanghai under the thinnest of disguises. To an apparatus as badly burned as the Communist structure in Asia was in the early '30's, to isolate Ho Chi Minh as a potential *agent provocateur* until more was known about what exactly he said and did while in British custody, was just normal prudence. The same was done during World War II in the European resistance movements against the Nazis when an arrested resister found himself released by the Gestapo under suspicious circumstances (in fact, considering the reputation of that organization for summarily executing or deporting people on the flimsiest of suspicions, *any* release was suspect). Hence, it is not surprising that it took the authority of as senior a Communist as Vaillant-Couturier to "introduce" Ho to the Chinese and also Vietnamese Communists among whom he in fact lived. One of the latter was Nguyen Leng Bang, who was later to become one of Ho's closest associates as his envoy to Peking and Moscow. Finally, early in 1934, the Communist apparatus succeeded in smuggling Ho back to Moscow, where he already had been preceded by a fairly large group of Vietnamese trainees studying in many fields, from aircraft engineering, such as Lê Hong Phong (later secretary general of the Party, and executed by the French), plain *agitprop* (agitation and propaganda) at one of the political schools. Ho naturally went to the latter.

Ho first attended the Institute for National and Political Questions in Moscow, and then the famous "graduate school" for senior Communist leaders, the Lenin School. But Moscow, in 1935–38, also provided an education of a far different sort: the Stalin purges. It would be interesting to know (and this writer is sorry he didn't ask when he had the opportunity of doing so) what Ho's feelings were as he saw some of his best former friends accused, convicted, and executed for crimes which they patently did not commit—and, in some cases, could not have committed—had they wanted to. What is even more remarkable is that Ho, as a well-known member of the Comintern group, was not purged right along with them, for hundreds of thousands of people of lesser distinction than he became victims of Stalin's mania. There may have been some good reasons, however. First of all, Ho had been absent from the U.S.S.R. when the major break came between Stalin and the "internationalist" wing of the Party structure; Ho, as a "doer" rather than a theoretician, had never participated in the fundamental debates between Stalinists and their opposition; and lastly, he probably then was unconditionally loyal to Stalin, and Stalin knew it. This became particularly clear when the threat of Nazism began to loom large on the horizon and the Communist parties decided in 1936 to apply a policy of "popular fronts" with the Western democracies.

Known as the "Dimitrov Line," that new policy was a particularly bitter pill for the colonial Communist movements such as the Indochina Communist Party, for it meant foregoing the advocacy of outright independence in favor of a policy of cooperation with the French colonial regime. For a man who had, all his life, advocated nothing else, the application of the Dimitrov Line was a real watershed. Ho, who had returned to Kunming, South China, in 1937, gritted his teeth and rammed the line down the throat of his reluctant followers in its most minute vagaries. His report on the success of this policy, addressed in 1939 to the Comintern, shows this quite clearly:

1. The Party cannot, at this moment, formulate demands of too high an impact (national independence, parliament) without incurring the risk of falling into a Japanese trap.

At present it behooves us to ask only for democratic rights, freedom of organization, of assembly, of the press, of expression; and a general amnesty for all political crimes, as well as legalization of the Party.

2. To attain that aim, we must develop a democratic front, including not only Indochinese but also progressive Frenchmen; as well as the working class and the national bourgeoisie.

3. With regard to the bourgeoisie, the Party must show a great deal of cleverness and flexibility. . . .

4. As far as the Trotskyists are concerned: no alliances, no concessions. They must be at any costs unmasked as the front men of the Fascists. . . .

7. In order to accomplish its tasks well, the Party must struggle energetically against sectarianism and narrowness of views, study Leninism-Marxism, raise the level of political consciousness of the cadres, and establish close relations with the French Communist Party.

8. The Central Committee shall control the Party's press to avoid all errors of tactics or strategy.

This was probably Ho's nadir. Ho had to forswear publicly all he had stood for, had to cooperate with the people he hated most; and had to sell out his Trotskyist allies of yesterday, with whose help the Communists had in the past decade succeeded in beating French-sponsored candidates in the legislative elections of Cochinchina [the latter, as a French colony rather than a protectorate, enjoyed a measure of legislative representation]. And the worst was not yet over. Not authorized by the Comintern to expose himself through a premature return to Viet-Nam, Ho was assigned as a low-level communications operator in the Chinese Communist 8th Route Army, then fighting the Japanese, and as secretary of his unit's Chinese Communist Party cell—his fourth party membership, counting the French, the Indochinese, and his direct Comintern affiliation. In the meantime, the "Dimitrov Line" had been a total failure: Stalin and the Western democracies did not come to an agreement on a common front against the Axis powers (Germany, Italy, and Japan); Stalin did a turnabout and made friends with Hitler; and the colonial Communist Parties, which had operated very much in the open for three years and thus were vulnerable to police supervision; were immediately destroyed when France and Britain found themselves at war with Germany. Much of what was left of the ICP inside Viet-Nam wandered into French prison camps, and some of its leaders went to the guillotine. As in the case of the Chinese Communists in 1927, Moscow had blundered miserably again a decade later in sacrificing local parties to its own interests—a mistake which it was to continue to make with desperate regularity later on as well.

The physical divorce from Russia which the latter's invasion in 1944 by Nazi Germany entailed for the Asian Communists, proved to be a real boon—for their own local requirements could for once take precedence over Moscow's views. In the case of Ho, this meant resumption of the anti-French *and* anti-Japanese line, in favor of an outright struggle for national independence. And in 1941, the only outside power relevant to that cause was China—not that of Mao (then a small guerrilla holding in the northwestern part of the country) but that of Chiang Kai-shek which then controlled all the border approaches to Viet-Nam. In late 1940, Ho became the political commissar of a Red Chinese training mission under General Yeh Chien-ying, sent to train Nationalist guerrillas, including a nucleus of Vietnamese exiles, in the South, at Liuchow, Kwang-Si Province. In February 1941, after an absence of exactly *thirty* years, Ho set foot on Vietnamese soil in Cao-Bang Province, where he lived in a grotto at Pac-Bo throughout the whole spring of that year, thinking, writing orders, planning the future. The "Museum of the Revolution" in Hanoi today carefully preserves the battered rattan suitcase and the other few belongings which were his during that period. On May 10, 1941, the badly-depleted Central Committee of the ICP met at Pac-Bo to discuss the new line it was to adopt. He was ready with his plan: the French would be defeated by the Japanese (Japan already had put pressure on

Vichy France for bases in Indochina), the Japanese in turn would be defeated by the Allies—and in the resulting vacuum, the Vietnamese Communists, as the only really well-organized party in the country, would have a chance of gaining power *if* there was mass support. But there could not be mass support for an overtly Communist-dominated movement, and there certainly would not be any Chinese Nationalist support for it. And Ho proposed to his associates a new "front" organization; a new "Dimitrov Line" of his own. After nine days of discussions, the new movement was agreed upon. Called the League for Revolution and Independence, contracted in Vietnamese to *Viet-Minh,* the Front was born on May 19, 1941, Ho's fifty-first birthday. It was probably then also, when Chinese support became urgent and such support, if requested by the known Comintern agent Nguyen Ai Quoc, would have met with opposition in Chung King; that the name "Ho Chi Minh" first was used by him.

But Ho's troubles were not yet over. Apparently unwilling to accept Chinese demands to include a majority of pro-Chinese "Quislings" into the Viet-Minh leadership, Ho was arrested by a Chinese warlord on August 28, 1942 on the interesting, if somewhat, conflicting accusation of being both (a) a Communist, and (b) a French [sic] spy. Chinese prisons, regardless of political coloring, have never been known for their loving care of their inmates, and Ho not only lived in stocks, but was shifted from jail to jail in heavy shackles and on foot. It was a time of bitter trial, and Ho found solace in writing poems which reflect both his fortitude as well as his deepfelt commitment to Vietnamese culture, such as his quatrain on "Crushed Rice."

> The rice grain suffers under the blows of the pestle;
> But admire its whiteness once the ordeal is over!
> Thus it is with men in the world we live in;
> To be a man, one must suffer the blows of misfortune.

When he was finally released on September 16, 1943, Ho was a sick man and had learned a hard lesson about dealing with Chinese warlords. He now agreed to work with them on their terms (at least on the surface) while casting about for allies. They came in the form of the Americans from the Office of Strategic Services, the predecessor agency of the CIA. The relationship was no one-way street: Ho needed weapons, training and, above all, *some* counterweight to the warlords; and the OSS needed intelligence from Viet-Nam and some means of rescuing American pilots shot down during air raids over Indochina. Ho's guerrillas could provide both, and did.

All Americans who knew him then agree that he was an "awfully sweet old guy" who, far from selling the Communist line, was interested in one single thing only: national independence for Viet-Nam. His hatred of the French seemed unquenchable. When a French liaison officer disguised as an American, arrived in his camp with an OSS detachment, Ho quickly exposed him and had him deported back to China under threat of a worse fate if this were to occur again. How much of this was show and how much of it was real is hard to fathom: in other areas of Viet-Nam, stay-behind French detachments operated harmoniously with the Viet-Minh. Perhaps Ho, sensing the anti-colonial feelings of his American guests, put on a "show" for them just as this very often occurs in Saigon today where great demonstrations of anti-French feelings in front of Americans are immediately followed by private apologies to whatever Frenchman is handy—very often by the same government official who had just resoundingly proposed the abolition of French schools, the closing of all French businesses, and the use of the vernacular in a highly technical field in which Vietnamese terms simply are not available. In any case, American material aid to Ho was of a minor nature and probably had not been the subject of a high policy decision, and Ho soon discovered that the Americans, for all their personal friendliness, were not going to be of much use in backing him against two of their major allies, the Chinese or the French.

There was nothing left for him but to rely on speed, organization, and his own native cunning. As Japan was collapsing in the first days of August, 1945, Ho convened a "National Congress" at Tan-Trao, north of Hanoi, which decided to take control of Viet-Nam before the arrival of the Allies, so as to confront them with the *fait accompli* of "people's power," as the ICP's secretary general, Truong Chinh ["Long March"] then put it. Similar tactics had worked beautifully in Poland and, almost, in Greece at the very same moment. They also worked like clockwork in Hanoi and

83

Saigon. With the French administrators in Japanese jails, government had fallen into the ineffective hands of Japanese-backed conservatives under the figurehead leadership of Emperor Bao-Dai. Two days after VJ-Day, Ho's forces staged an uprising in Hanoi which went over to the Viet-Minh in an explosion of joy. On August 25, 400 miles further south, the abandoned emperor handed over the Great Seal to representatives of Ho's provisional regime, while 1000 miles south of Hanoi, in Saigon, Tran Van Giau, one of Ho's most ruthless southern associates, took over that city. On September 2, 1945, Ho proclaimed the independence of the "Democratic Republic of Viet-Nam (DRVN)" from the balcony of the French municipal theater in Hanoi to a delirious crowd of a half-million. By the time the British landed in Saigon and the Chinese Nationalists pilfered their merry way into Hanoi, Ho's new republic was a going concern and had all the weapons of the 50,000-man 38th Imperial Area Army (plus the French military stocks which the Japanese had held) in its hands. This was probably the swiftest and most bloodless Communist takeover on record, but it was not to remain so as Ho's followers began to settle accounts all over the country.

But Ho again, ever the realist, realized that Chinese support had gone as far as it could. From now on, if further relied upon, it would swallow Viet-Nam as it had done several times in the past. Yet the alternatives were pitifully few: Russia was far away, preoccupied with Eastern Europe and the huge devastation at home; the Chinese Communists were in deep trouble and not likely to win their own guerrilla war in the near future; the Americans seemed to have lost all interest in the tiny Southeast Asian appendix to China, which was America's main future area of Asian interest. That left the hated colonial power, France, with whom one would have to come to acceptable terms. It must have been a bitter decision to make, and the nationalist extremists with whom the Chinese had sprinkled Ho's regime, did not take it lying down. A later deserter from Ho's cabinet has left us with a vivid report on the dramatic cabinet meeting of early March, 1946, in which it was decided to allow 15,000 French troops to return to North Viet-Nam.

The right wing argued that, come what may, China was at least a "blood brother" and that it could be counted upon to "protect"

Viet-Nam against further Western encroachments. The left argued that the French had a left-wing government—wasn't Maurice Thorez, the French Communist Party leader, vice-premier of de Gaulle?—which would surely give independence to Viet-Nam eventually, and would provide it in the meantime with badly needed assistance. Ho had witnessed the sterile debate in silence. But then he suddenly sprang up, looked both disputing groups in the eye, and explained:

"You fools! Don't you realize what it means if the Chinese stay? Don't you remember our history? The last time the Chinese came, they stayed one thousand years!

"The French are foreigners. They are weak. Colonialism is dying out. Nothing will be able to withstand world pressure for independence. They may stay for a while, but they will have to go because the white man is finished in Asia. But if the Chinese stay now, they will never leave.

"As for me, I prefer to smell French sh—— for five years, rather than Chinese sh—— for the rest of my life."

On March 6, 1946, Ho and the French signed an accord, permitting French troops to return for five years, with France recognizing the DRVN as a "Free State within the French Union." On May 31, Ho and his entourage left by French warship for a state visit in France to negotiate the final independence treaties with the former colonial power. What followed next is too complicated a story of French blunders to be told here. Involved in their own perennial government crises (Ho had to wait until July 6 'till the French could form a government to negotiate with him!), the French left colonial matters to the "specialists," i.e., the ultra-conservatives of the Ministry of Colonies. Ho, for his part, naïvely overestimated the power of his old Socialist and Communist friends in Paris, or even their willingness to grant independence to his country. Settled down in a minor hotel near the Place de l'Etoile, graced for the occasion by a red carpet as befits the protocol for a chief of state, Ho had time not only to ponder his own fate, but to become acquainted with another nationalist awaiting a change in *his* country's fate at the hands of another colonial power: David Ben-Gurion, the future president of Israel.

At that time, Ho was deeply moved at hearing Ben-Gurion's account of what had happened to the Jews during the Second World War, and British intransigence bode ill for Israel's future, while Viet-Nam's case seemed on its way to an early settlement. He spontaneously offered Ben-Gurion Hanoi as the location for an Israeli government-in-exile; an offer which the Jewish leader did not turn down: after all no one else had thus far made as generous a proposal. But Ho's own affairs were suddenly taking a downward turn. All the fine promises made by the French liberals in the spring were now slowly being whittled down to nothing by the "specialists" from the rue Oudinot, where the Colonial Ministry was located. In fact, as Ben-Gurion was to note wrily, Ho's descending fortunes could be measured by the progressive shrinking of the protocolary red carpet. On Ho's arrival, it had extended from the sidewalk to his room. As the summer wore on, it was limited to the lobby, then to the staircase, and finally, simply to the corridor in front of Ho's suite. Finally, on September 14, 1946, the break came. The French proved unyielding on the unification of Viet-Nam and at home not only the right wing but now the left wing as well was clamoring for results. In a dramatic night session, Ho and the French Overseas Minister, Marius Moutet, signed a *modus vivendi*—an "agreement to disagree"—after Ho had vainly pleaded with him to relent somewhat on the terms. Moutet, "boxed in" by his own "hawks," explained that he was unable to do so, and Ho signed, muttering audibly: "I'm signing my death warrant."

He also knew that the failure to agree meant eventual war with France. Dead tired, he walked into Ben-Gurion's room and said: "There is nothing left but to fight," a lesson that Ben-Gurion was not to forget a few months later. As Ho walked back to his room, the remaining red carpet in front of his door had disappeared altogether. On December 19, 1946, at 8 P.M., nearly all the French electrical plants throughout Viet-Nam, carefully sabotaged in advance, blew up. The lights went out all over the country as Viet-Minh shock troops began to attack French garrisons from south of Saigon to the Chinese border. The war for the reunification, with minor cast changes in the South, is still going on to this day.

For Ho, at 56, this meant a brutal change of roles. Until now he had been the underground agent, the Comintern *apparatchik,* writing reports and holding together networks of agents. At best, he had been a guerrilla leader, although the specifically military tasks had soon been delegated to young General Giap. Now he was *in* Viet-Nam, a country he knew very little (in fact, far less than France, Russia, or China) and which was totally isolated from any major source of Communist power. Even the Greek rebels, though exposed, had access to Yugoslavia, Albania, and Bulgaria. He had access to nobody until December, 1949, when Red Chinese troops finally reached the Vietnamese border. Yet he fought on, and against a French *communist-backed* government, for nothing else but purely Vietnamese *national* objectives, and that fact is terribly important to this very day. He was not interested in proving that capitalism was on the way to the scrap heap of history; that "liberation war" (the word, of course, was used but, thank God, had not yet been discovered by the Pentagon) was the wave of the future; or that the French (and the U.S., which began backing them in 1950) were "paper tigers." He fought because he felt that Viet-Nam must be one single state because it was unviable as a divided one and because the French were trampling upon Vietnamese national dignity.

This came to the fore quite clearly during the first of at least four unsuccessful peace attempts with France, made in May, 1947, when the war was only a few months old. The French, though seemingly winning militarily, sent a highly competent negotiator to meet Ho at the *Pont des Rapides* [Rapids Bridge] north of Hanoi, just inside Viet-Minh lines. He was Professor Paul Mus, one of France's most renowned Viet-Nam specialists and a consistent advocate of Vietnamese independence, then serving as a paratroop captain in Indochina. The French Army had given Mus a set of negotiating points with a certain amount of leeway, but on one point the Army was adamant: Ho had to surrender to the French all the foreign specialists who were serving with his forces. There were indeed then with the Viet-Minh a bevy of Japanese officers afraid of Allied war crimes courts and even a sprinkling of Germans from the Nazi missions in China, as well as some Foreign Legionnaires of various nationalities. These foreigners, in the absence of any outside aid, were of tremendous importance to Ho, for they were the only men capable of training his forces in the use of the Japanese, French, and American weapons (the latter bought from the Chinese or smuggled in via boat or airplane from the Philippines) with which they were equipped. The French Army correctly had identified this training problem as the one chink in his armor: if he yielded on that point, he was quasi-powerless to resume the struggle. In addition, by surrendering people who had sought asylum with him, he would dishonor himself in front of his own people and "lose face."

Mus, who had been raised in Viet-Nam and knew Vietnamese mores well, heatedly argued that this point would surely abort the peace talks, if nothing else would; but the French High Command remained adamant: Ho would surrender his specialists, or the war would go on until victory.

As Mus presented Ho with the French proposals in a small thatch hut erected near the bridge, he saw an incongruous sight in one corner. There was a shiny French champagne cooler filled with cracked ice, cradling a bottle of what was obviously a bottle of French champagne. The sheer logistics of getting both ice and champagne (not to speak of the cooler and proper glasses) in that kind of setting must have been staggering. To Mus it was clear that this meant that Ho *expected* to sign the agreement and that the champagne had been brought to celebrate the welcome event. He rapidly went over the various points: return to the status quo of December, exchange of all prisoners, resumption of political talks— all these he could accept without difficulty. But then he came to the "Leonine clause," the surrender of the specialists.

Unblinkingly, Ho looked at Mus and said slowly:

"Monsieur le professeur, you know us very well. If I were to accept this, I would be a coward. The French Union is an assemblage of free men, and there could be no place in it for cowards."

Said it, shook hands with Mus gravely, and walked back into the jungle for seven more years of war. A war that Ho Chi Minh won.

Since then, Ho and the regime which he heads have changed little. Like in the past, when French Intelligence provided selected journalists periodically with the interesting, if untrue, "inside information" that Ho was either dead, or about to die of tuberculosis, or a helpless puppet in the hands of (a) General Giap, (b) one or another party leader, and (c) Stalin, Malenkov, or Mao; we have now "Hanoiologists" who claim that Ho is (a) "senile, of course,"

(b) a tool in the hands of Giap or some party leaders, and (c) Peking's stooge.

The hard fact is that Ho, at 76, is just as old as de Gaulle, and ten years younger than either Adenauer or Churchill were when they led their country in some difficult situations—and admittedly better than some of their younger successors. On the basis of his past experience with the French and the Chinese, or, for that matter, Stalinist Russia, he is likely to distrust any arrangement from which he cannot pull back if events turn against him. As Ho looks at the world, his trust (in Stalin, in China, in the French in 1946, and in the Geneva participants of 1954) has always been betrayed. And when it became clear that the reunification elections which were to take place in 1956 were not going to be held, the callous non-support by *both* Red China and Russia must have been an eye-opener to him as to how much trust he could place in his closest allies once their own most essential interests were not involved in an issue which, nevertheless, involved an essential Vietnamese interest.

He and his closest associates have a hard-headed faith, thus far not contradicted by events, that the Vietnamese people (and particularly the North Vietnamese above the 17th Parallel) will take an immense amount of punishment if the issue is simple and clear, i.e., that it is they who are aggressed and that they are holding out for reunification of their country, and even if it were to take twenty years and involved the destruction of Hanoi and Haiphong—events which Ho, in a nationwide speech on July 17, 1966, predicted would happen. In contrast to a city-bound culture as we have in the West, Ho, for all his cosmopolitanism, is essentially a product of the Vietnamese village. In 1946–47, he almost immediately abandoned to the French every city in the country: Saigon and Hanoi, as well as "vital" Haiphong; fully realizing that what was really vital in that kind of war, were not the cities, the bridges, and whatever puny industries he had then or has now, but the allegiance of his people.

When I saw him last in Hanoi in 1962, the Viet-Nam war still was a localized conflict between a huge South Vietnamese regular army and ten thousand American advisers facing a small guerrilla force. But Ho had few illusions.

"It took us eight years of bitter fighting to defeat you French, and you knew the country and had some old friendships here. Now the South Vietnamese regime is well-armed and helped by the Americans. The Americans are much stronger than the French, though they know us less well. It may perhaps take ten years to do it, but our heroic compatriots in the South will defeat them in the end."

That was before the bombing began over the North, and before the Russians got involved with sophisticated antiaircraft weapons and Mig-21's. But it was also before a half-million Americans were sent to Southeast Asia. But Ho continued:

"I think the Americans greatly underestimate the determination of the Vietnamese people. The Vietnamese people have always shown great determination when faced with a foreign invader."

Perhaps Ho will, in the next few months, show himself ready to settle once more for the half-country he has consistently been forced to settle for ever since the French rolled up the red carpet on him in Paris in 1946. Or perhaps he will settle down to ten years of war, just as he settled down to seven years of it when Professor Mus faced him with unacceptable demands.

But in that case, we only have five more years to go.

The Other Side
of the 17th Parallel

☙✺❧

THE BOMBS that have fallen around Hanoi and Haiphong have shifted the focus of the whole Viet-Nam war away from the guerrilla-infested swamps and jungle of the south to the little and backward Asian country (the size of Georgia, with a population of 19.8 million people) that apparently is willing to take on the United States single-handed.

Not too much is really known in the West about North Viet-Nam. Western visitors to the land beyond the 17th Parallel are few, stay in many cases only for several days, and often are not equipped with sufficient background to be able to learn much from their sojourn there. Travel in the countryside was not easy or comfortable even when the North was peaceful in the early 1960's. In many places bridges and roads destroyed during the French Indochina War had not yet been fully reconstructed. Now, with communications under constant American pounding, travel has become well-nigh impossible, as well as dangerous.

Most Western visitors to North Viet-Nam have come back with uniform impressions—of "bleak austerity," towns thronged with bicycles, a countryside "littered with broken bridges and pulverized roads," to cite the words of a recent British visitor, James Cameron.

Reprinted by permission and first published in the New York *Times*.

91

All such views simply depict the result of twenty years of guerrilla Communism, of a decade of forced-march "Socialist construction," and of eighteen months of war with the mightiest power on earth, the United States.

How North Viet-Nam got the way it is and what makes it tick is a longer story which too often fails to come into focus. Yet it is necessary to know as much as possible about this small state, for it will, of necessity, play a key role in whatever settlement of the Viet-Nam crisis will eventually be achieved.

Born as the "Democratic Republic of Viet-Nam" (D.R.V.N.) on Sept. 2, 1945, under the presidency of Ho Chi Minh—and recognized as a "free state, with its own government, parliament, army and finances," by the French in 1946—the Hanoi regime has lived ever since on a roller-coaster of near-disasters and seemingly hopeless wars. Plunged into an eight-year war through the machinations of a Saigon-based French colonial bureaucracy which simply outmaneuvered its own weak home governments, the D.R.V.N. defeated the French despite the desperate odds. At the ensuing ceasefire conference at Geneva in 1954, she won almost one-half of the country and over 60 per cent of its population, as well as a doubtful promise to win the rest two years later in an election which never took place.

When Ho's troops entered French-evacuated Hanoi in October, 1954, the city itself was a representative sample of the shambles in which the rest of North Viet-Nam—the war never had reached the present-day intensity in the South—was left; the evacuating French and non-Communist Vietnamese troops and officials had taken along with them everything movable, from essential records and statistics to the radium from X-ray rooms of the city's hospitals, and much that could not be taken along had been rendered unusable. In the countryside, a spring's bitter fighting had prevented much of the necessary planting and the broad cleats of French tank treads had done the rest.

The massed flight of 860,000 refugees, over a half-million of whom were Catholics, from the southern part of the Red River Delta, left several provinces a virtual desert. In the areas which for years had been under Communist control, French fighter bombers, though far smaller in number than today's American air fleet in Viet-Nam, had methodically wrecked everything of value; and in a fit of anti-Western rage the Ho regime in the jungle had early in the war ordered the razing of every Western-type concrete structure in the guerrilla zone.

Both sides had wrecked each other's communications with a will: no bridges existed, no roads which were not either mined by Ho's troops or cratered by French bombs, no telegraph wire that had not been cut down, no powerlines which were capable of carrying electricity outside the urban areas. This was North Viet-Nam in late 1954. Many departing Frenchmen were betting on the country's early collapse from the sheer exhaustion of its Pyrrhic victory—or its immediate absorption by its mighty Red Chinese neighbor.

It was the Soviet Union that helped North Viet-Nam withstand this first shock. A quick "triangular" transaction in which Russia delivered cement and other goods to Burma in exchange for Burma's delivering 150,000 tons of rice to Haiphong saved North Viet-Nam. The institutions of the new regime got hold of the country's essential control mechanism and clamped their authority on the restive, war-weary population. North Viet-Nam had passed its first survival test.

The new institutions that emerged from the jungle hills were those of a "people's democracy"—which the country already had become before the Indochina War broke out—with some modifications. Ho remained the country's President, but his faithful associate, Pham Van Dong, a high-ranking mandarin who was also a graduate of Nationalist China's prestigious Whampoa Military Academy, became his Prime Minister. The old Indochina Communist Party, ostensibly abolished in 1945, had been reconstituted in 1951 as the *Viet-Nam Dang Lao-Dong* (Vietnamese Workers' party) and it represented the real center of power in the country.

As in every other Communist country, agriculture was the major stumbling block of North Viet-Nam, and, even without the present war, would still be a major difficulty. Taken as a whole, Viet-Nam has agricultural surpluses in the South under normal circumstances (but the South will *import* 400,000 tons of rice from abroad this year) and, prior to World War II, the North regularly incurred a

93

250,000-ton yearly deficit made up by Saigon. This held true until the split-up of Viet-Nam in 1954.

Traditionally, North Viet-Nam's peasantry cultivated its own small plots, and while there was a great deal of usury, about 98 per cent of the farmers owned their own land (by contrast, in South Viet-Nam, 6 per cent of the landowners until very recently held 45 per cent of the land under cultivation). Hence, while the South is in real need of land reform, any kind of reapportionment in the North was merely a matter of ideological faithfulness to Marxist dogma. This, in fact, was well illustrated in a Russian study in *Voprosy Ekonomiki* in September, 1957, which pointed out that—prior to the land-reform law enacted in 1953 and applied with great ruthlessness in 1955–56—a North Vietnamese "landlord" owned on the average 0.65 hectares (i.e., less than two acres) of riceland. After land reform, so-called "rich farmers" were allowed to keep 0.21 hectares and agricultural laborers received 0.15 hectares. According to later reports, a total of 702,000 hectares (one hectare equals 2.47 acres) was distributed to 1.5 million landless peasant families; i.e., every family got about one acre—or not enough to live on.

In fact, the lack of *real* landowners (those who indeed could be classed as such had of course fled southward in 1954–55) compelled Hanoi to put on trial as "reactionary landlords" men and women who not only were by no stretch of the imagination rich landowners but in many cases had a good record of anti-French fighting. In the hands of pro-Peking leaders such as the party secretary, Truong Chinh, every village felt compelled to produce it own "quota" of such reactionaries. Perhaps 50,000 were executed. By the time Ho Chi Minh, on the warning of People's Army elements, stepped in in August, 1956, to reverse the course, it was too late.

The faithful commander of the People's Army, General Giap, sharply criticized the overzealous land-reformers that year before the 10th Congress of the Lao-Dong party's central committee: "We have made too many deviations [from the correct line] and have executed too many honest people . . . seeing enemies everywhere, we resorted to terror, which became far too widespread. . . . While carrying out our land-reform program we failed to respect the principles of freedom of faith and worship in many areas."

The pullback came too late to avoid a short-lived peasant revolt in Ho's own home province of Nghe-An on the very day—Nov. 4, 1956—the Russians overran Budapest and the British and French landed in Suez. It took a good part of the North Vietnamese 325th Division to crush it. But both Ho Chi Minh and the prestigious Giap could show their people that the fault lay with the pro-Peking faction of the Party, and not upon the North Vietnamese regime as a whole—a view which many Vietnamese, both in the North and South, often take when something anomalously harsh occurs in the North. "It's not Ho Chi Minh, or Giap, or [Premier] Pham Van Dong," they will say, "it's those pro-Chinese fellows in the party." There is some reason to believe that the Hanoi government likes to keep that impression very much alive inside the country as well as abroad.

There was no real way back. By 1965, over 90 per cent of the small-plot farmers had been regrouped into "cooperatives" and this time with little apparent brutality. The reason was simple: most of them had found out that it was impossible to make a family's living on an acre plot of land and provide a surplus with which to feed the cities and growing industries. Attempts at supplementing the deficient rice crop through so-called "secondary" crops in land unsuited for rice—and on which yam roots, cassava or corn were planted—did not succeed too well because of Vietnamese resistance to the change of diet.

The moment of truth in the field of agriculture came when the very accurate 1960 population census told the planners in Hanoi what they had feared all along: a disastrously high 3.6 per cent yearly birth rate makes a shambles of all attempts at raising per capita food consumption, short of a crash program designed to increase both acreages and yields. Merely to break even with the yearly net increase of about a half-million mouths to feed would have meant to put another quarter-million new acres under cultivation yearly—and a 1962 program intended to do so failed completely, by all accounts. Hanoi says that bad weather and floods in two consecutive years had much to do with it.

In 1965, the North Vietnamese leaders took the almost unheard-of step for a Communist country of admitting a Western development expert inside their borders for a hard look at their agricultural situation. René Dumont, a French development economist with a towering reputation for his surveys of Madagascar, Cuba, and West Africa (and with a reputation for brutal frankness, which is unknown in most national or international aid bureaucracies), handed Pham Van Dong a detailed report which flatly contradicted earlier optimistic estimates or reports of accomplishment and addressed this warning to his hosts: "Things must be looked straight in the face and it must be recognized that the Five Year Plans were, at least in the agricultural field, far too ambitious." And Dumont did not hesitate to lay part of the blame on the botched land reform, which "may well have traumatized a number of unjustly hurt families, including those of members of the [anti-French] resistance."

What all this means to the average North Vietnamese, now also burdened by constant air raids, can be easily guessed. To be sure, food production has gone up since 1954—from 1.9 million tons of rice to perhaps 2.8 million—but in 1954 the North still imported rice from the South and since then its population has increased by as much as 40 per cent. And, unlike Red China, North Viet-Nam has little that it can export which would provide it with the foreign exchange necessary to purchase food abroad. Contrary to the great myth of North Viet-Nam's "extensive trade with the Free World," the latest official U.S. figures available show that in 1963 North Viet-Nam imported $919,000 worth of wheat flour (the North Vietnamese have, in the cities at least, continued to be bread eaters) and $438,000 of corn, while *exporting* $1.03-million worth of rice, most of it to British-owned Hong Kong. North Viet-Nam may not be starving—but its people have been on tight rations for twelve years.

In the industrial field North Viet-Nam has a clear advantage over the South. All the country's useful minerals and metals seem to be north of the 17th Parallel (just as all the surplus food and coffee and rubber are in the South), and the French left behind a small legacy of cement plants, shipyards, textile plants, and semi-industrial workshops, along with vast exploitable mines yielding coal, iron ore, and uranium phosphate. The Sino-Soviet bloc's economic-aid program—which, in round figures, breaks down into $750-million from Red China, $400-million from Russia and $100-million from the smaller Asian and European states—has over the past decade provided North Viet-Nam with an industrial infrastructure which under no circumstances would make her what some optimists have called "a second Japan." But it could, given normal conditions, transform her into a Southeast Asian industrial equivalent of Belgium.

A Soviet-built machine-tool plant in Hanoi turns out, on the basis of my personal observation in 1962, creditable medium-size turret lathes. An electro-chemical complex north of Hanoi produces a variety of items from paper to antibiotics. A steel combine in the mountain midlands (the first in Southeast Asia) turns out a pitifully small amount of steel—about 200,000 tons a year (American production: 100 million tons)—but enough to cover the country's basic needs. Uranium phosphate, produced near the Chinese border along with tin in a modernized French-built concentration plant, was exported to China as early as 1952 and is in all likelihood a part of Communist China's source of fissionable materials.

Two of the great weaknesses of the North Vietnamese industrial structure are the lack of qualified engineers and the difficulty in obtaining sufficient electrical power. While one is always likely to find, at any North Vietnamese industrial site, a few "comrade experts"—the Chinese will scuttle as far away as possible from the Western observer; the Eastern Europeans will be glad for the diversion from the routine provided by the foreign visitor—there are simply not enough of them to go around. And as is often the case with American advice in South Viet-Nam, such expert advice is sometimes not received too gladly, no matter how sound it may be. The result often is that the advice is at times called for only after the mishap has occurred.

"It often looks as if a midshipman had been given the command of a cruiser as his first post," one Western observer said of the management of North Viet-Nam industry. "And it often works out just that way."

The Soviet Union has made the solution of North Viet-Nam's industrial power problem her own task, and has set up a long-range program to build a whole series of large power plants throughout the country. One of them—in fact, the only one of the series which has been fully completed thus far—at Uong-Bi, near Haiphong, was disabled by U.S. air strikes last year and this spring. It is not known how much the destruction of the plant affected North Viet-Nam's ability to send reinforcements or munitions to the South, but Soviet propaganda made much of the destruction of a Russian-built civilian plant.

The impact of American bombing already has completely changed the complexion of the North Vietnamese economy. Targets set for the Five Year Plan ending in 1965 were, of course, not reached and no new plan has been announced. Instead, "temporary" short-term targets are set for a given economic sector. In actual fact, this amounts simply to a maximum effort at keeping the country going under the increasing tempo of U.S. air raids. There is mounting evidence (from a variety of Western sources) that official American assertions to the effect that thus far only a limited segment of North Vietnamese communications targets has been hit simply no longer correspond to the facts. North Vietnamese cities such as Vinh, Thanh-Hoa and Nam-Dinh have been extensively damaged, and the absence of published aerial photographs of those cities is often taken abroad as proof that this fact is being hidden from the Free World public.

The effects of the war on North Viet-Nam's territory have been to thwart these economic aims: the balancing of its agricultural economy and the creation of a moderate-sized industrial base which would produce most of the light machinery required by the small country, and provide a moderate amount of light machines (drills and turret lathes), canned tropical fruits, coal, and cement for export. The gradual destruction of the Hanoi-Haiphong "sanctuaries" and of perhaps another dozen or so industrial sites would not, contrary to what has been said, throw North Viet-Nam "back to the Stone Age," but would largely deprive it of everything that it has built with tremendous toil and at the price of enormous sacrifices by its population since 1954. And in the view of as staid an observer as *The Times* of London, North Viet-Nam "wants unity and independence far more than it cares for [its] factories."

The same view is echoed by Charles Fourniau, a French professor who recently returned to Europe after teaching in Hanoi for three years and who spoke to North Vietnamese officials about the possibility—they considered it a certitude—of the total destruction of their cities and industries by American air operations. Their views were that if all those objectives were destroyed, "the Americans would bring us back to the situation in which we were after [the defeat of the French in 1954 at] Dien Bien Phu, but that alone would not insure our defeat." Reconstruction, they continued, would be fairly rapid because then they would have the technicians which they lacked after the French Indochina War and "we do not doubt of the massive aid we would receive from the whole Socialist camp." These are brave words when one is a Georgia-sized country and faced with the mightiest country in the world, but it must be remembered that this is exactly what happened to North Korea, and it was indeed reconstructed by its partners.

Politically, North Viet-Nam is what it proclaims itself—a "dictatorship of the proletariat" led by middle-class revolutionaries. The liberal-sounding constitution which the Hanoi regime had proclaimed in November, 1946, was replaced in 1960 by a new document full of virulent denunciations of the West and of praise for the "farsighted leadership . . . of President Ho," who holds almost unlimited powers under it. This is further emphasized by Ho's choice for Vice President. He is Ton Duc Thang, a faithful companion in his 80's (Ho Chi Minh is 76) who, as a sailor in the French Navy in 1919 aboard the battle cruiser *Waldeck-Rousseau,* almost succeeded in turning the ship over to Communist mutineers while it was operating in the Black Sea against Soviet revolutionaries. Ton, who is also the president of the Viet-Nam Fatherland Front, created in Hanoi in 1955 to further the cause of Vietnamese reunification, is hardly likely to become a competitor for power.

Premier Pham Van Dong, just turned 60, is a possible but unlikely successor. An able administrator and a warm person from close up, Pham Van Dong apparently has not succeeded in becoming popular in his own right but enjoys Ho's full confidence. They are (as this writer knows from personal experience) on a "thou" basis and work closely together. General Giap, as the victor of Dien Bien Phu and the commander of the People's Army, now 54 years old, has all the prerequisites of future power save one—in the Communist scheme of things, regular army officers hardly ever attain political power.

But, as in all Communist states, the realities of power in North Viet-Nam lie with the Communist party of the country. Forged in clandestine operations ever since its creation in the bleachers of Hong Kong's soccer stadium in 1930 while a game was in progress, the party lost its whole first layer of leadership on France's colonial guillotines until in 1940 Truong Chinh—a *nom de guerre* which means "Long March"—took over as party secretary. He paid for the botched land reform of 1956 with his job, and he must bear the onus of being known as pro-Chinese in a country where the Chinese are intensely disliked. Now returned to grace (perhaps under Chinese pressure) as chairman of the legislative standing body, he and Nguyen Chi Thanh (a youth leader who rose to become the People's Army's chief political commissar with the rank of lieutenant general until "kicked upstairs" as head of the ailing Ministry of State Farms) are the main exponents of the "Peking hawks" in Hanoi. In recent weeks, Saigon and Washington rumor mills aver that Nguyen Chi Thanh is now in South Viet-Nam, leading the Viet Cong insurgency.

Other leading candidates for future prominence in North Viet-Nam are the party's secretary, who, by the rules of Communist power, should be the second-most-powerful man in the country, Le Duan; and Le Duc Tho, the chairman of the party's organization bureau, a member of its central committee and, particularly, of the party's Committee for the Supervision of the South.

There are—by the same curious process which in South Viet-Nam gives power to generals such at Air Vice Marshal Nguyen Cao Ky, who are in fact North Vietnamese—many former Southern guerrilla leaders in power in Hanoi: Nguyen Duy Trinh, one-time Foreign Minister, who in 1946–54 led the famous "Zone 5" bastion south of Danang; Pham Van Bach, then president of the Viet-Minh executive committee for South Viet-Nam and now president of North Viet-Nam's Supreme Control Organ; Pham Ngoc Thach, an M.D. who had been a Southern guerrilla leader and is now North Viet-Nam's Minister of Health, to name a few.

The party had its share of problems in the past, when it was criticized by the Cominform as being far too bourgeois-dominated.

The 1956 peasant uprising increased the party's distrust of the peasantry even further and a membership drive in 1957 was specifically directed at recruiting factory workers and intellectuals into the fold, after the earlier purges had diminished the party's strength from 700,000 to 420,000.

According to a recent report, from Hanoi, the party has admitted about 300,000 new members since 1960, of whom one-half are described as "poor contract farmers," 27 per cent as "middle-class farmers," and 16 per cent as "workers." It can be assumed that the remainder are intellectuals and perhaps from the urban middle class—what is left of it.

But as in all Communist states, conformity is achieved by a variety of devices, ranging from the schools to "block committees" headed by some nosy housewife who will report a sudden unaccounted-for increase of wealth in a neighboring household, to the surely ubiquitous, if discreet, police apparatus. Yet, perhaps because the North Vietnamese won their own "war of liberation" almost alone or because of a last irrepressible remnant of French-influenced defiance of established authority, they are, as a people, more relaxed in their contacts with Westerners than any other Asian Communist country and than most Eastern Europeans.

In my case, at least, unescorted spur-of-the-moment forays into parks, pagodas, or shops would usually end in talks with uninhibited local citizens who would unabashedly admire my Western finery and camera and end up asking whether there *really* were lots of cars in New York. This does not mean that the D.R.V.N. operates unlike other police states. A few years ago it cracked down on Hanoi's intellectuals with the same kind of brutality with which it had brought its peasantry to heel. All that can be said of the system is that, on the face of it, it may not *appear* more oppressive to its people than what most Afro-Asian countries offer their citizens at this particular stage of their development.

It would be futile to define the atmosphere, the freedom or lack of freedom, which prevails in North Viet-Nam in terms of, say, the East European satellites or of a parliamentary democracy such as India. In comparison to Red China, it certainly is freer in terms of individual existence, and more flexible in terms of ideology. The word "communes" still is not used in Hanoi polite society and life still is much family-centered; or at least was until the air raids brought about mass evacuations of children and university students. The very fact that Hanoi must deal with its own Peking hawks at the same time that it maneuvers to get sophisticated Soviet weapons via Chinese transit roads must create a degree of internal controversy rarely seen in a Communist state. This controversy must have been further heightened by the recent intensification of American bombing.

It was Ambassador Averell Harriman, the State Department's perennial troubleshooter, who once said of the North Vietnamese, "Their hearts are in Moscow, but their stomachs in Peking." This may become even truer if the port of Haiphong is blocked by American bombs or sea mines.

But what finally does keep the country glued together under the tremendous pressures of the moment is the People's Army—the P.A.V.N. Battle-hardened, and well-trained, it is probably, man for man, one of the finest infantry forces in the world today, numbering a half-million first line ("Main Force") troops and over one million trained reserves, not to speak of women and youths now being drilled in special brigades and antiaircraft units. How good the P.A.V.N.—or "Pavins"—really are is being attested to in South Viet-Nam by their American opponents. When they feel they must, the Pavins will hold their ground until they are pulverized. Or they will silently slip away to fight another day—and probably at the same place.

In North Viet-Nam the P.A.V.N. has readily absorbed the sophisticated Soviet equipment it has received, manning scores of missile sites and radar installations and flying advanced MIG-21 jet fighters. Veteran American pilots who flew combat missions in Europe and Korea attest that the "flak umbrellas" over North Viet-Nam are as deadly (if not more so) as those in the other wars. Official figures seem to bear them out: during the more than three years of the Korean conflict, 816 Allied planes were lost to enemy ground fire, while 241 combat aircraft were lost over North Viet-Nam in one single year of air operations and about 70 over South Viet-Nam.

Figures on lost helicopters (the Korean figure includes *all* craft) are kept secret.

But beyond the sheer fanaticism of the P.A.V.N. regular and the quality of his equipment, there are the uncontested qualities of his military commanders. In almost continuous combat since December, 1944, when General Giap led a first 34-man platoon from Nationalist China into still-French-occupied North Viet-Nam, the senior division and staff commanders have gained experience in the blood-drenched campaigns against the French, culminating in the smashing victory at Dien Bien Phu. They are unpurged, loyal to their chief, Giap, and their leader, Ho Chi Minh; and have thus far (with the exception of such pro-Chinese elements as Nguyen Chi Thanh, who had been the army's chief political commissar) stayed out of the ideological quarrels that have rent the Red Chinese Army. Contrary to their Chinese counterparts, they have not been stripped of all rank insignia, told to exchange places with their own private soldiers, or been accused of indulging in excessive professionalism at the expense of their ideological indoctrination.

It will take a great deal more (and no doubt something other than bombing) to convince such men that their tactics may be wrong; that the war they are engaged in has become hopeless; and that they are facing an enemy whose relentlessness is superior to their own. A simple look south of the 17th Parallel, with its musical-chair game of unit commanders and governments, would not change their views, regardless of the presence of awesome American power.

They are not only aware of, but convinced of, the primordial importance of the political environment in which a war is fought. And they have in the past—contrary to both Saigon and Washington—admitted their mistakes, regrouped, tried a new tack, and succeeded. They lost severe battles in the 1950's, too, but redeemed themselves at Dien Bien Phu. And while they realize that an American Dien Bien Phu will not take place in the *military* sense, they still can see how it can occur through other means.

"The victory at Dien Bien Phu has shown," said General Giap at anniversary ceremonies for the battle, "that under present circumstances even a small and weak people, once it has adopted a correct line . . . will necessarily win final victory."

103

What all this will mean over the long run in the war to which the United States has committed itself is difficult to analyze clearly. But given what is known of the North Vietnamese leadership, it seems obvious that the further escalation of the bombing of North Viet-Nam has made it almost impossible for the Hanoi regime to abandon the South Vietnamese Liberation Front now, as Stalin and Tito abandoned the Greek Communist guerrillas in 1948–49. From a peripheral skirmish—as were the Communist-led guerrilla wars in Iranian Azerbaijan in 1946, in Malaya, in Greece, or in the Philippines—the Viet-Nam war now has graduated into a sacred cause.

As the war has escalated into the North, internal propaganda has switched more and more from a theme of "warm fraternal support" for the Southern insurgents to the concept of a *single war;* of which North Viet-Nam is, in the recent words of North Viet-Nam's tough Labor Federation leader and Attorney General, Hoang Quoc Viet, a "wide rear area," while "the South has become a wide front line, a place where we and the enemy are fighting each other directly."

By an incredible irony, then, escalation of the war into the North may have further contributed to a "unification" of the Communist war effort as well as a larger commitment by Hanoi to a settlement which it considers honorable for both itself and the Viet Cong.

North Viet-Nam Between
Peking and Moscow

ᑐᔕᑐ

THE MARCHING SONG which you have just heard is a very popular North Vietnamese People's Army song—that of the "artillery haulers of Dien Bien Phu." Those were the thousands of unarmed coolies who, in the face of heavy aerial bombardment by French Air Force B-26's and Navy "Privateers," dragged over a hundred American-built artillery pieces to the battlefield of Dien Bien Phu early in 1954.

Like their American Air Force and Navy successors in 1965, those French bombers sought to destroy the supply routes leading from the battlefields in Viet-Nam to nearby Communist sanctuaries. The North Vietnamese coolies took an incredible pounding, but the rhythm of Communist supplies rose from about 300 tons a month in 1953 to over 4000 tons a month in 1954—most of it carried on the back of the "artillery haulers."

In 1954, it was this mixture of North Vietnamese guerrilla tactics, Red Chinese logistics, and Russian equipment; which finally produced a Communist victory, first on the battlefield inside Viet-Nam and then, at Geneva in July, 1954; at the conference table. And the possibility of a return to a similarly potent combination has been haunting the political planners in Washington

Unpublished lecture.—*Ed.*

ever since. In fact, the gist of the hearings recently held in Washington by the House Foreign Relations Committee on the incidences of the Sino-Soviet split dealt in fact mainly with the influence the split (or its lack) might have on the Western posture in Southeast Asia. The consensus of the specialists called before the Committee —and they ranged from college professors to retired military figures—was that a Sino-Soviet split *did* exist, and that it *does* have an influence on what is going on in Viet-Nam today. But the experts by and large also agreed that such a split could be healed very suddenly, should Russia feel that the very survival of the Communist bloc was threatened through the destruction of one of its members while the Soviet Union simply stood idly by.

This threshold may well be reached very rapidly, now that American airpower apparently is being used methodically and deliberately to destroy North Vietnamese objectives, much in the same way as it was used twelve years ago in North Korea. And thus Hanoi finds itself on the horns of a dilemma which, like Washington, it must resolve in the next few weeks to come: accept the Chinese theory of "liberation wars" and keep on fighting in the hope that its own physical destruction is nothing but a "surface phenomenon" which an eventual victory over South Viet-Nam will more than make up for. Or accept the more prudent Russian attitude and settle once more for some minor concessions; or, worse, for nothing else but a return to the *status quo,* as in Korea.

There is, however, a difference between the Sino-Korean situation of 1953 and the Vietnamese situation in 1965: in the case of Viet-Nam, the Communist regime would have been deprived of the fruits of its victory *twice,* and *both* times by Russian design. In 1954, the Communist Viet-Minh forces could have either pushed the French into the sea within a short period of additional fighting (or caused, as in the 1960's, the South Vietnamese government to collapse); or obtained a far better division of the Vietnamese territory in their favor, by obtaining a boundary on the 14th parallel or by retaining large terrain pockets in the South. The Soviet Union, for her own designs—allegedly, in exchange of French promises not to push for a European Defense Community embodying a German Army—pressed hard on North Viet-Nam to accept a territory which was far smaller than what it had gained on the battlefield, and which, in fact, is smaller by about 4000 square miles than South Viet-Nam is.

The same risk now looms large again over the horizon in Hanoi—and, understandably, the North Vietnamese leaders might well view such new Russian pressures with dismay. Yet, without the relative protection offered by Soviet air defense missiles and modern fighters (neither of which Peking can offer in meaningful quantities, if at all), a further military confrontation between Hanoi and the United States may well bring about a return of North Viet-Nam to little more than what it was when the war with France ended: a country dotted with gutted villages—and now possibly occupied by a Red Chinese Army. It was former Under Secretary of State Averell Harriman who once summed up Hanoi's dilemma by saying that its leaders had "their hearts in Moscow but their stomachs in Peking." One may well wonder how long this would continue if the relationship with Moscow remains one of unrequited love.

How all this came about makes perhaps for one of the more curious tales of the rise of Communism throughout the world.

The Vietnamese Communist movement, contrary to that of China or Korea, was born in Western Europe, among the 80,000 Vietnamese war production workers and soldiers whom France had brought to her shores during World War I. The traditional French Socialists saw in the colonial citizens of France a convenient platform to broaden their support and were the first French party to make a determined effort to gain a following in the colonies— probably the only colonial power to do so; for even the British Labor Party never did much more than to attract a few colonial intellectuals while they were in Britain but did not seek to set up Labor Party branches, say, in Nigeria.

One of the Vietnamese thus attracted was a slim, wispy young man then known as Nguyen That Thanh. Born in 1890 as the son of a small-town Vietnamese mandarin he soon left the fold of his family to seek freedom abroad, first working as a mess boy aboard French ships and later as a cook's apprentice at the Carlton Hotel in London. There, in 1914, he came into a contact with a Chinese-led "Overseas Workers" association, which seems to have been his first contamination with Western-style politics. Turning to France

107

in 1917, we find him doing odd jobs in Paris, but already making contacts with the French Socialists, including Charles Longuet, Karl Marx's grandson, and Marcel Cachin.

When peace came in 1918, young Thanh began to travel from one French war plant to another and from one military camp to another, contacting Vietnamese workers and soldiers as he went. Agitation was rife as ships were slow in becoming available for the repatriation of the men to Asia. In France, also, the Socialists (as elsewhere) were faced with the fact of the new Soviet Revolution, and the increasing split between the Socialist and Communist factions of their parties. In France the split came during Christmas week 1920, at the Loire town of Tours. History has left us with a photograph of that remarkable meeting, showing a mass of sweltering, overfed, mustachioed French faces turned toward a smooth-shaven emaciated Asian face lit by intense black eyes, who had spoken up at the meeting as a delegate of the French overseas Socialist groups. It also has left us with the young man's words:

"I don't understand a thing about strategy, tactics, and all the other big words you use, but I understand very well one single thing: The 3d International concerns itself a great deal with the colonial question. Its delegates promise to help the oppressed colonial peoples to regain their liberty and independence. The adherents of the 2d International have not said a word about the fate of the colonial areas."

On the 30th of December, he voted for the creation of the *French* Communist Party and became one of its founding members. Today, that young man is North Vietnamese President Ho Chi Minh. That single-minded adherence to the "national liberation" criterion threads itself through all of Ho Chi Minh's acts.

As a French delegate for the colonial areas, Ho also intervened at the 5th Comintern Congress in Moscow in June–July, 1924, and the record again leaves us with the following:

"I want to know if the Congress is going to make a special appeal to the colonial peoples.
Chairman Kolarow: The Colonial Question is on the agenda. . . . . . .
Comrade Nguyen Ai Quoc: The appeal should be directed at the colonial peoples. . . . . .

And later on, at the Congress, Ho Chi Minh was to present a scathing indictment of the French and British Communists who, according to him, were less anticolonialist than certain bourgeois groups such as the League of Human Rights.

To this day, Ho Chi Minh has remained less a theoretician of Vietnamese Communism than an operator of national-liberation methods for the purpose of achieving Vietnamese national objectives—although this is not, of course, true of the more recent generation of Vietnamese Communist leaders. This explains why he supported Stalin (whom he once called as the only true exponent of the anticolonial liberation idea for the colored peoples) in the 1930's against his former friends of the Comintern whose tactics he probably disliked because of their gradualism and because they were more interested in fighting fascism in Europe than colonialism the world over.

Sent with the Soviet delegate to Chiang Kai-shek, Borodin, to Canton, in December 1924, Ho Chi Minh (he was still under other aliases) finally had an opportunity of organizing specifically Vietnamese groups for anti-French operations in his nearby homeland. He took over a non-Communist refugee organization and transformed it into the "VN Revolutionary Youth Movement" in 1925. VN refugees were trained in Chinese Nationalist military academies such as Chiang's own Whampoa, and infiltrated back to VN to organize struggle groups against the French. One such graduate was Ho's later associate and Prime Minister of North Viet-Nam, the aristocratic Pham Van Dong.

It is perhaps ironical that at this stage, the Chinese influences on the Vietnamese Communists were more of the Nationalist than the Communist variety. And the total sell-out by Russia of the Chinese Communists in 1927, which nearly destroyed the nascent CCP, further weakened Chinese Communist influence on the Vietnamese Communists—and perhaps also weakened their confidence in Chinese Communist leadership. In fact, Ho Chi Minh himself, in the late '20's, advocated the creation of separate Southeast Asian Communist parties as distinct from local Southeast Asian branches of the Chinese Communist Party, and this line was approved by the Comintern. How far removed the Vietnamese and the Chinese Communist leadership were from each other at that time is perhaps best evidenced by the fact that I was told on the record by one of Ho's closest associates that it was the French Communist Party's representatives in the Shanghai International Settlement who eventually put him in touch with the CCP upon Ho's return to China in 1934 after a two-year stay in Western Europe and Russia.

Inside Viet-Nam, the Communists hardly fared better. French political intelligence was excellent, and one Communist leader after the other disappeared in French jails. The Indochina Communist Party (ICP) was created in Hong Kong by Ho in January 1930, but after a bitter intra-mural struggle between three or four Communist factions—not to speak of the Vietnamese Trotskyite group, which showed surprising strength. The quarrels got so bitter that the Comintern intervened and admonished the Vietnamese leaders to the effect that "the division within the Communist groups and elements constitutes a grave error . . . There should be a unified party and the only Indochinese Communist Party."

The young ICP was immediately put to a severe test: under the weight of the world depression, rice prices were collapsing in Indochina and the Vietnamese farmers in Ho's own native province of Nghe-An rebelled against the French administration and set up peasant soviets. To this day it is not clear whether that move was planned by the ICP or whether, when faced with the accomplished fact, it simply decided that it could not abandon the cause. (I had a long conversation with North Vietnamese Communist leaders on that subject two years ago and they seemed even then of divided opinions on the subject.) The struggle was hopeless from the outset, and the ICP went down in defeat along with the peasants. Its then secretary general, Lê Hong Phong, was captured by the French, and executed; and so were other senior ICP leaders—except Ho Chi Minh, who had remained in Hong Kong, where he was later briefly jailed by the British.

What was left of the ICP now aligned itself on Moscow, or rather: on the French Communist Party. The Popular Front regime in France also liberalized political activities in the colonies, and Saigon was treated to the spectacle of a municipal election in which Communists and Trotskyites ran for council seats. The Communists, true to the prevailing frame of mind in Moscow, preferred to break with the Trotskyites and lose the election than to be elected with them; and the latter gained two seats on the council. One of the Trotskyites was murdered by the regular Communists in 1946.

110

The change to the "Dimitrov line," that is, of limited Russian co-operation with the Western democracies against the rise of the fascist powers—brought about a further temporary alignment between the ICP and Moscow; and, locally, between the French colonial administration and the Communist apparatus. That honeymoon, of course, ended in September 1939 when Moscow backed the Nazis against the French and British. The Hitler-Stalin pact at least permitted the ICP to resume its traditional anticolonial struggle against the French, but at the same time it felt that it could not forego completely the popular issue of the anti-Japanese struggle; thus, in its final communique before it went underground on November 13, 1939, it condemned both the "French imperialists" while promising to "Struggle against the aggressive designs of Japanese imperialism." At the same time, the ICP received yet another series of bloody setbacks at the hands of the French police: most of its senior leaders were arrested and many of them sentenced to death; an uprising in South Viet-Nam was crushed in September of 1940; and the surviving senior members of the party received orders to retreat into neighboring Nationalist China.

That is when the Vietnamese Communists renewed their contacts with the Chinese Communists. The latter had weathered their worst trials of the '30's and '40's, had reconstituted their bases, and had temporarily joined in the anti-Japanese struggle. Ho Chi Minh himself had joined the 8th Chinese Communist Route Army, and so had other senior Communist Vietnamese leaders. Late in 1940 Ho, accompanied by a Red Chinese mission under the later field marshal Yeh Chien-ying, arrived in the Indochinese border area to take in hand the dispirited ICP survivors. A meeting (the eighth) of the ICP Central Committee was held in May 1941, in the border area, in the course of which a new secretary-general of the ICP was elected. His own cover name was a whole program in itself: *Truong Chinh*—or: "The Long March." Now the powerful chairman of the Standing Committee of the North Vietnamese National Committee, Truong Chinh still is considered as the foremost exponent of the pro-Peking faction within North Viet-Nam. But the Chinese support for the ICP was at best tenuous: after all, Mao Tse-tung's bases were far away in the northwest and in Southwest China, Chinese Nationalist power was pre-eminent. When it became apparent that

111

the Vietnamese Communists were being uncooperative with the local Chinese warlords, one of them jailed Ho Chi Minh from August 1942 to September 1943—apparently without interference from the Chinese Communists.

From then onward until December 1949, when the Red Chinese arrived on North Viet-Nam's borders, the Vietnamese Communists fought virtually in *total* isolation from *any kind* of outside Communist aid. This must be underlined if one wants to understand the present frame of mind of the North Vietnamese leadership, as it apparently is once more faced with rather hesitant outside Communist help in its life-and-death struggle with overwhelming odds. Several times in its short life, the Vietnamese Communist movement has found itself abandoned or traded off by its erstwhile mentors or protectors. With cold realism, the Vietnamese Communist leaders under Ho Chi Minh turned toward the Chinese Nationalists and the United States Forces in China for help in setting up guerrilla movements in Indochina.

On December 22, 1944, a young doctor of history by the name of Vo Nguyen Giap, took a first platoon of 34 guerrillas into North Viet-Nam's Dinh Ca valley. Here again, a photograph has been preserved: it shows us a short pudgy man, wearing a rather formal Borsalino hat, knickerbocker trousers but no shoes, and a U. S. Army .45 caliber pistol. Ten years later, as commander of the Viet-Nam People's Army, he was to defeat the French at Dien Bien Phu and ten years later again, as Vice-Premier and Minister of Defense of North Viet-Nam, he was to face the United States in South Viet-Nam. The takeover of Viet-Nam by the Communists had begun.

Western shortsightedness and outright stupidity were to make things relatively easy. The Japanese-imposed Vietnamese regime was swept away by the guerrillas within a few days after VJ-Day, the Vietnamese Nationalists allied with the Chinese Kuomintang failed to re-enter Viet-Nam fast enough to get organized, and on September 2, 1945, Ho Chi Minh, from the balcony of the French municipal theater in Hanoi, proclaimed the independence of the "Democratic Republic of Viet-Nam." The Communists in Viet-Nam had won the first round without almost firing a shot. French mistakes were to make things only worse.

After an initially hopeful phase of negotiations, which permitted French troops to return to North Viet-Nam alongside with Communist (now called "Viet-Minh") garrisons; relations with Hanoi worsened as diehard colonial administrators refused to allow the reunification of South Viet-Nam with the rest of the Vietnamese state. A triple scission reappeared for a time within the Hanoi regime: one group advocated temporary collaboration with the Chinese Nationalists who occupied North Viet-Nam until March 1946 under the Potsdam Agreements, as a counterpoise to French encroachments; a second group (the majority under Ho) held to what was called the "Brest-Litovsk" line; that is, co-operation with the French as a palliative to the real hardship of a Chinese occupation. And yet a third group (notably General Giap) argued for a pre-emptive strike against the French before their military build-up was complete. Apparently, French unwillingness to provide Ho with a reasonable alternative precipitated the latter's decision to approve Giap's views, and the French (or First) Indochina War began on December 19, 1946.

The relations between the Vietnamese Communists and their fellow-parties abroad during the period were of an interesting nature. Moscow, to all appearances, was almost exclusively interested in Europe; the Red Chinese were once more fighting for their lives in northern China; and the French Communist Party was in the throes of a major chauvinistic binge, in the course of which its leader Maurice Thorez (then a vice-premier in General de Gaulle's provisional government) declared that the "Communist Party did not advocate the hauling down of the Tricolor wherever it flies." The reasons for this were very simple: in the French CP's view, it stood a better than even chance to gain power in France—in which case all French colonies would have acceded directly to Communism as well. Hence (and this was actually expressed by the French CP cell in Saigon to the local ICP leaders) Ho very much risked to find himself charged with "nationalist deviationism" —just as Tito was three years later. This explains why the French Communist leadership allowed the vote for the first Indochina War budget without a murmur, and began to agitate against the Indochina War as a *sale guerre* (a dirty war) only after it lost all chances, in March 1947, of gaining power in France. Here again, the fecklessness of Western Communist support was driven home to the Vietnamese leaders—as well as the cold indifference of the Soviet Union. The lesson surely was not lost on them.

Russian restraint with regard to the DRV perhaps had more practical grounds as well: Stalin had just gone through the disastrous experience of losing the Greek guerrilla movement and the Communist dissidents in Northern Iran. In 1948, Titoism added to his woes. Hence, there was little inclination in Moscow to espouse yet another guerrilla movement whose seeming chances of success were rather slim. Thus, when Ho's DRV made its bid for world recognition on January 14, 1950, Red China recognized her four days later, but Russia only on January 30, followed on the next day by North Korea and later on by the other Soviet satellites.

But again, that recognition meant very little at first, as only Red China was physically able of reaching the North Vietnamese guerrilla leaders in their jungle hideouts. However, Russian-donated equipment began to arrive via the Chinese pipeline—as well as much American equipment captured in Korea. While this help was important, it did not go far enough to make the victory over the French totally decisive—and, above all, it stopped short of giving the DRV full control over all of Viet-Nam at the conference table at Geneva in July 1954.

From then onward, the DRV's relations with the Soviet Union were, while cordial, not as warm as Hanoi thought they would be. Eastern European and Russian aid to North Viet-Nam was important and amounted over the next decade to somewhat less than a billion dollars. Diplomatically, North Viet-Nam received Russian support for its candidacy to a U.N. seat—but no more (and, in fact, less) than South Viet-Nam received on the part of the United States and France. In terms of military aid, the DRV received no high-quality equipment. In fact, it can be said in all candor that Soviet observance of the armament limitations of the 1954 cease-fire went far beyond that of the United States, as the present North Vietnamese lack of high-performance aircraft and antiaircraft missiles shows . . . although that situation could now, of course, change overnight.

But the greatest North Vietnamese disappointment with Russia must have been when Moscow did not, in July 1956, press the case for the reunification elections which, under the 1954 agreements, were to have taken place by then. As co-chairman with Britain of the 1954 conference, Russia made hardly more than a perfunctory show of protest over the unilateral abrogation of that election promise by Saigon. Here again, we witness the pro-Moscow wing of North Vietnamese Communist being ill-repaid for its fidelity.

One last open confrontation took place between the pro-Moscow faction and the pro-Peking faction in the late fall of 1956, precisely at the moment when Russia crushed the Hungarian rebellion: a too-slavish adherence to the Peking example in the field of land reform brought about a peasant uprising—whose center, like that of 1930, was Ho's own home province of Nghe-An. It was ruthlessly crushed by People's Army troops, but Ho used this for a temporary purge of the pro-Peking elements, including the party secretary Truong Chinh. Nonetheless, the succeeding years—particularly as North Viet-Nam's support for the South Vietnamese Viet Cong guerrilla movement became more overt and concrete military and political outside support for Hanoi's position became necessary in case of a confrontation with the United States—saw a distinct shift toward Peking taking place. It came to a climax during the Communist Party Congresses of 1961 and 1962.

Hanoi now embarked on a careful navigation between party lines in which the old President and party leader, Ho Chi Minh, still showed his customary skill in spite of his advanced age (he is now 75). A succession of Soviet and Chinese missions to Hanoi, from Ho's old guerrilla friend Yeh Chen-ying to Liu Shao-chi and Soviet premier Kosygin, produced a series of communiques which all successfully averted definitive breaks with either side.

Perhaps the Liu Shao-chi-Ho Chi Minh communique of May 1963 reached the height of that North Vietnamese fence-straddling, when it simultaneously managed to reaffirm Hanoi's faithfulness to Marxism-Leninism (the Peking line) and also warned against "dogmatism" (Moscow's charge against Red China). But the realities of the war in South Viet-Nam impeded more and more in Hanoi's freedom of maneuver: after all, Peking showed itself willing to aid it in its "Liberation War." Moscow, for all its

115

good words, was still holding back. And liberation war it was going to be.

When I was in Hanoi in 1962, I was able to interview both Ho Chi Minh and Pham Van Dong, the North Vietnamese Prime Minister, on their views of the South Viet-Nam situation and Pham Van Dong consented to state his views on tape for me—which was probably a Western "first" in that field. It has thus far never been heard in public.

That line has substantially remained the North Vietnamese view to this day, although there are indications that American pressure on North Viet-Nam may have given Hanoi some second thoughts. For example, General Giap, on March 10, 1965, released an interview with Japanese TV, in which the departure of American forces from Viet-Nam no longer appears to be a *prerequisite* to a conference—but the cessation of U.S. air operations in North Viet-Nam is. It remains to be seen whether we are dealing here with one of the "signals" the U. S. Government has spoken of in recent weeks; or whether this merely translates a real intention of being willing to settle the Viet-Nam problem on something less than Hanoi's terms.

In sum, then, Hanoi's position between Peking and Moscow is one of imperfect balance, in which Peking, for a variety of reasons, hold several high cards. As seen from Hanoi, Moscow's attitude toward a basically pro-Western and openly pro-Russian Communist Party, has been one of almost callous indifference. Repeatedly, the Vietnamese Communist leaders have been literally "sold out by Moscow" for small tactical reasons, which (as France's wrecking of EDC in 1954) turned out to be of no ultimate benefit even to Russia. This, of course, gives Peking's arguments a great deal of persuasiveness in Hanoi these days—save for a few small but hard facts: one of them is that Peking is in no position to help Hanoi in case of an aero-naval confrontation with the U.S. (as was clearly shown in the Tonkin Gulf incidents of last summer, which the Chinese prudently sat out), and the other is that the Vietnamese, no matter what their political color, don't trust the Chinese—no matter what *their* political color . . .

It is this historical reality which gives some substance to the assertions made by some writers that, given a chance, Hanoi

116

would turn to some form of "national communism" along Tito lines. But, so goes the rebuttal, the best proof of such "Titoism" would be that North Viet-Nam abandons the South Vietnamese guerrilla cause, just as Tito abandoned the Greek guerrillas. And whether Hanoi still is in a position to make such an agonizing choice, after having abandoned the conquest of the South once before in 1954, is very much open to question. Rather it might well resort to the anonymous artillery haulers who once before had brought victory against the airplanes and other modern weapons of the adversary.

U.S. Policies in Indochina
1940–1960

⟨∞⟩

THE WORD "Indochina" is used here advisedly; for, as events tend to show more and more, it is impossible to conceive a coherent policy for, say, Cambodia or South Viet-Nam that does not affect Laos or North Viet-Nam as well.

In the case of American diplomatic operations in the area, the term is likewise appropriate, as this paper will show. Contrary to popular belief (and the argument is used as an excuse by people who should know better), American diplomatic, political, and military involvement in Indochina is almost a *quarter of a century* old.

Briefly, American policies toward Indochina can be subdivided as follows:

1. Anti-Vichy, 1940–45;
2. Pro-Viet-Minh, 1945–46;
3. Non-involvement, 1946–June 1950;
4. Pro-French, 1950–July 1954;
5. Non-military involvement, 1954–November 1961;
6. Direct and full involvement, 1961—

While the paper will touch upon most of those points (some of which are self-evident) it will concentrate on the 1940–1954 period, since the latter is least known even to the specialist.

Lecture delivered at International Conference on Asian History, University of Hong Kong, September, 1964.

118

1. Indochina in World War II

When the French mainland was overrun by the Germans, in the spring of 1940, and France signed an armistice with the Third Reich, on June 25, 1940, Indochina could no longer count on any help from France. Although a loose coordination of defense measures in the Far East had been agreed upon by the British and French during talks in June 1939, and similar talks had taken place with the Dutch, the loss of both France and Holland and the dire straits of Britain after Dunkirk ruled out the possibility of an effective defense of Southeast Asia against Japanese aggression.

There always remained the possibility of an alliance with the only other major democratic power in the Pacific—the United States. But in the summer of 1940, the United States still clung to its policy of noninvolvement. On June 30, 1940, Under Secretary of State Sumner Welles told the French Ambassador in Washington:

> . . . considering the general situation, the Government of the United States did not believe that it could enter into conflict with Japan and that, *should the latter attack Indo-China, the United States would not oppose such an action.*

This policy was apparently based on a State Department estimate of the situation, according to which it was doubtful that the Japanese, involved as they were in mainland China, were ready to take on additional military commitments; in other words, Washington believed that Tokyo was bluffing. This explains the statement a few days later by Sumner Welles's chief, Secretary of State Cordell Hull, that America's policy in Southeast Asia should be limited to encouraging "countries like Indochina . . . to delay and parlay [sic] and hold out to the last minute against Japanese demands [since] Japan would not dare make a military attack at this time."

General Douglas MacArthur, who then commanded the American and Filipino forces in the Philippines and had a keener appreciation of the ultimate dangers to his own position if the French and Dutch were forced to yield to Japanese pressure, had intervened in their behalf with his own superiors in Washington, but he had been turned down. On September 15, 1940, a last request was made by General Martin, the French commander in Tonkin, to the Commander of U. S. Naval Forces in the Philippines for a naval demonstration in the Gulf of Tonkin when Japanese pressure became intolerable. This, too, was not acted upon.

With the Vichy government of Marshal Pétain under the thumb of Japan's German ally, and Indochina totally isolated from outside help, the outcome of the next round was never in doubt.

On June 19, 1940, as France's government lay dying—it had just fled Paris and was incommunicado for several days until it could be installed in Bordeaux, only to flee that city a few days later as Nazi tanks approached—Japan addressed an ultimatum to the French governor general, General Catroux, demanding joint control of the Tonkinese border. (Tonkin, with its Yünnan railroad, was Nationalist China's "iron lung," pumping in supplies from the outside world.) When, in the absence of orders from Paris, Catroux acceded to the Japanese demand, the moribund Third Republic relieved him of his command—on June 25, the very day France signed an armistice with Germany—and replaced him with tough and able Admiral Jean Decoux, who, when faced with similar Japanese demands, told his home government that he would rather fight and die than see Indochina "reduced to becoming another Manchukuo."

Historians have failed to record, however, that Catroux's hands were tied not only by France, but also by the United States and Britain. Prior to his assent to the Japanese conditions, Catroux had sent a purchasing mission to the United States with orders to acquire 120 modern fighter aircraft and modern antiaircraft artillery to be supplied out of the sizable orders France already had placed, and paid for, with American manufacturers—only to be informed that *delivery of that equipment to Indochina had been forbidden by the U. S. Government.* And Donald Lancaster, a British diplomat turned historian, pointed out in his excellent *The Emancipation of French Indochina:* "When he had completed this bleak assessment of his resources and had made every effort to get American or British help, Catroux had no alternative but to accept the Japanese demands."

Catroux's own feelings are perhaps best indicated by the fact that he left Indochina to join the Free French and fought with them gallantly in North Africa and the Middle East. His successor still had to face the insatiable Japanese military. In the best tradition of Cordell Hull's formula of "delaying and parlaying," Decoux told the Japanese to take up the problem with the government in Vichy. Before Vichy agreed to make some concessions to the Japanese, its ambassador in Washington once more beseeched the United States to strengthen France's hand. On August 22, 1940, Sumner Welles let Vichy know that the United States was unable to come to the aid of Indochina but that it "appreciated the difficulties with which the French Government was faced and did not consider that it would be justified in reproaching France if certain military facilities were accorded Japan."

On August 30, 1940, Vichy signed an accord with Japan that recognized Japan's "pre-eminent position" in the Far East and granted the Japanese in principle certain transit facilities in Tonkin, subject to agreement between the military authorities on the spot. This qualification gave Decoux one more opening for further "delays and parlays." The Franco-Japanese negotiations, conducted by Generals Martin and Nishihara, began on September 5 at Hanoi and dragged on for weeks. Martin still expected American naval support and thus delayed the talks in the hope that an American naval demonstration might induce the Japanese to scale down their demands. That outside support failed to materialize, and the Japanese, growing impatient with the progress of the negotiations, decided to give the French a graphic demonstration of their own power: Without warning, on September 22, Japanese troops stationed in neighboring Kwangtung and Kwang-si suddenly attacked the French border forts at Lang-Son and Dong-Dang, while Japanese aircraft bombed Haiphong and, on the evening of the twenty-fourth, began to land troops. Outnumbered and outgunned, the border forts fought to the last cartridge, losing 800 men in two days of fighting. Further fighting broke out in Haiphong when Japanese troops attempted to occupy several airfields.

By now, the Japanese had made their point. General Nishihara termed the whole matter a "dreadful mistake"; Vichy wired Decoux to accept the Japanese demands without further delay, and Decoux told Martin to stop the useless heroics and get on with the negotiations. Even so, the determination of the French field commanders had bought time for Nationalist China and also had reduced

121

Japanese demands substantially. In the end, only three airfields in Tonkin were occupied. The permanent Japanese occupation force was limited to 6000 men. No more than 25,000 Japanese were authorized to transit through Indochina.

To Decoux and the French in Indochina, however, their abandonment by everybody (including their own home government) had been a rude awakening. They knew that henceforth no course was left to them but to "play ball" with the Japanese. They had had their own miniature Pearl Harbor a full fifteen months before the United States, and the only outside attention the event attracted was a tongue-in-cheek editorial in an American newspaper entitled: "Who Wants to Die for Dear Old Dong-Dang?" The answer, apparently, was obvious.

It was obvious that French sovereignty over Indochina had become a farce. The Japanese now "negotiated" over Decoux's head, directly with the Vichy regime (that is, they told the Germans what they wanted, and the Germans saw to it that Vichy fell into line). In a further agreement on July 29, 1941, Japan acquired *de facto* control of all vital airports and port facilities. On the night of the strike against Pearl Harbor, Japanese troops surrounded all the French garrisons, and Decoux was faced with yet another ultimatum: to stay put and cooperate with the Greater East Asia Co-Prosperity Sphere, or face the immediate destruction of his garrisons as well as the loss of even nominal French sovereignty. Decoux yielded, thus saving 40,000 of his countrymen from the immediate ordeal of Japanese concentration camps and saving for France at least the appearance of being in command of the local population.

Perhaps one of the most important but least-known facets of the struggle to keep Indochina from falling into Japanese hands is the last-minute intervention of the United States. It would not be an exaggeration, in fact, to say that, in July, 1941, Indochina became the watershed that separated peace from war in the Pacific. Until the Japanese occupation of French airports in South Viet-Nam, Washington had clung to its non-committal attitude, but on July 26, 1941, when it became obvious that Vichy would no longer resist Japanese demands, the President ordered the freezing of all Japanese assets in the United States and an embargo on petroleum exports to Japan. Japanese views of those events are now available, and they shed much light on subsequent events. In his memoirs, the then Foreign Minister of Japan, Togo Shigenori, tells of a meeting on July 24 between Admiral Kichisaburo Nomura, then Japan's Ambassador to Washington, and President Roosevelt, in which F.D.R. proposed the complete neutralization of Indochina in exchange for a guarantee of Japan's "right of acquisition . . . of supplied and raw materials therefrom on a basis of equality." But that solved neither of Japan's two desperate problems: her need for oil (obtainable only in Indonesia) and the necessity to cut off the Haiphong-Yünnan life line through which American equipment sustained the Chinese Nationalists. The issuance of the Executive Order on July 26, before Japan's reply was received, hardened the Japanese Navy's insistence upon an attack on Southeast Asia before its petrol supplies were totally exhausted.

Indochina's role in Japanese-American relations during the crucial days before Pearl Harbor became even more evident in the last round of negotiations, in November, 1941. On November 26, Secretary of State Hull handed Japan a note that, in effect, was a draft for a mutual declaration of policy. In Paragraph 2 of Section II, the "Hull Note" proposed negotiations between the British, Chinese, Japanese, the Dutch government in exile, and Thailand, in order to guarantee Indochina's neutrality and to provide "for each of the signatories equality of treatment in trade and commerce with French Indochina." The remarkable aspect of that part of the Hull Note was that it simply sidestepped the fact that there still existed a French administration in Indochina itself and the Vichy government in France, with which the United States had diplomatic relations at the ambassadorial level.

It is not without a touch of irony that Japan brought up this point in its notification of a state of war, delivered to the Department of State on December 7, 1941, a few hours after Japanese bombers had attacked the U.S. naval base at Pearl Harbor. Tokyo asserted that the Hull Note's provisions with regard to French Indochina would be tantamount to establishing a six-power protectorate over the country and, further, that "apart from the fact that such a proposal totally ignores the position of France, . . . [it was] unacceptable to the Japanese Government," which considered it merely as an extension to Indochina of the open-door policy. In those historic hours when what had been a European conflict turned into World War II, President Roosevelt addressed one last message to the Japanese Emperor, offering Japan a nonaggression guarantee in exchange for the evacuation of Indochina. That, in Togo Shigenori's words, was "the only concrete subject touched upon in the President's message."

As will be seen in the following pages, President Roosevelt's preoccupation with Indochina and the attitude of the French there did not abate to his dying day. And, considering the negligible role that Viet-Nam, Laos, and Cambodia played throughout World War II, they probably absorbed more of the President's attention than they deserved. Indochina thus became the object of several high-level decisions of fateful importance to its postwar development—decisions that might perhaps have been better adapted to local realities had they been made at a lower level. Admiral Decoux, however (and in all likelihood, his superiors in Vichy), was hardly aware of what those decisions were, and operated in a frame of reference that was as much divorced from reality as that in which the decisions regarding Indochina were ultimately made.

Later, Decoux was to say with a measure of pride that, thanks to his action, France's was the only Allied flag not to have been struck in the whole Far East. That, in retrospect, is nonsense. While Decoux's acts were wholly defensible (and even commendable) up to July, 1941—just as Pétain's rule was defensible until the Nazis overran the so-called Free Zone of southern France, in November, 1942—the maintenance of French rule beyond that point merely gave rise to personal and political ambiguities that weakened France's position with her allies and certainly did not enhance it with the natives of Cambodia, Laos, and Viet-Nam.

But the key question in appraising the situation must be whether or not the situation in Indochina hampered the Allied war effort. In terms of active military cooperation with Japan, no French units fought against Allied troops, as Vichy troops did in Syria or Morocco. In terms of passive cooperation, Indochinese raw materials went to Japan, just as those from Manchuria, the Philippines, and Malaya did, as long as Japanese shipping was available (i.e., until June, 1944). The assertion that French resistance to the end and direct Japanese administration of the area would have required the immobilization of large bodies of Japanese troops does not hold water.

Postwar research has shown that the Japanese held their occupied territories quite thinly, and the continued presence until March, 1945, of 50,000 armed French troops compelled the Japanese to maintain a far larger force "in being" in Indochina than would have been required had those forces been destroyed once and for all in September, 1940, when all the other Allies were sitting on their hands. Those are the objective facts of the situation; they do not make the French attitude look particularly heroic or moral—but in eminently practical terms (and those were the terms under which the situation should have been considered at all times, instead of the high-level emotionalism that did prevail), it served the Allied cause in the Far East a great deal better than has been admitted.

But despite the relative merits of the Decoux regime, it was in most respects a carbon copy of its Vichy masters: It was anti-Semitic, anti-Masonic, anti-Gaullist, and pro-Axis—although the warmth toward the Axis was greatly tempered by the racially based anti-Japanese bias. There was also a dim realization, as the war turned against the Japanese, that it was they who were going to be the real engineers of France's downfall in the Far East, and not the "predatory Anglo-Saxons."

As a small footnote to history, Pierre Boulle, the French author of *Bridge on the River Kwai,* was an officer on Admiral Decoux' staff. It is very likely that Decoux served as a model for the ill-fated Colonel Nicholson who thought he was serving his country by working for the Japanese.

2. The American View

Of all this, very little was known on the Allied side, but this did not prevent the rapid formulation of an American policy on Indochina and its postwar fate. Even after the refusal of the United States to help Indochina to defend itself, American concern for the area was expressed repeatedly to the Vichy authorities. Thus, on July 19, 1941, when Vichy was readying itself to sign the treaty of July 29 with Japan, the American Ambassador to Vichy, Admiral William D. Leahy, transmitted an oral message from President Roosevelt stating bluntly "that if Japan was the winner, the Japanese would take over French Indochina; and if the Allies won, *we* would."

The statement was delivered to Pétain and Number Two man Admiral Darlan, at a time when the United States was still six months away from war with Japan.

Once the United States became involved in the war with Japan, a subtle process of "double-think" took place, which was superbly described by one of America's greatest contemporary diplomats, George F. Kennan, in his remarkable *Russia and the West under Lenin and Stalin:*

> There is, let me assure you, nothing more egocentrical than an em-battled democracy. It soon becomes the victim of its own war propa-ganda. It then tends to attach to its own cause an absolute value which distorts its own vision on everything else. Its enemy becomes the embodiment of all evil. Its own side, on the other hand, is the center of all virtue.

Far from admitting that American impotence in the Western Pa-cific, and America's repeated refusals (in 1931, 1934, and 1937) to join Britain and France in an anti-Japanese alliance to protect the area, were in good part responsible for the disaster that engulfed Southeast Asia, American policy-makers—often contradicting their own statements of the year before—now began to heap scorn on the French in general and their rule in Indochina in particular. The Indochinese situation, especially in the eyes of President Roosevelt, became the scapegoat for all of America's woes in the Pacific. As Hull noted in 1943:

> The President . . . himself entertained strong views on independence for French Indochina. [It] stuck in his mind as having been the springboard for the Japanese attack on the Philippines, Malaya, and the Dutch East Indies. He could not but remember the devious con-duct [of the French], the right to station [Japanese] troops there, without any consultation with us. . . .

The fact that this view was patently wrong on almost every count—i.e., neither the Philippine invasion nor the East Indies invasion was launched from Indochina (the Malayan invasion was backed by aircraft based in Saigon), and Washington *had* been repeatedly con-sulted with regard to Japan's encroachments in Indochina—did not prevent F.D.R. from sticking to it throughout the war and formulat-ing American policies accordingly. Evidently, Roosevelt did not feel himself bound by Welles's promise in August, 1940, not to "re-

proach France if certain military facilities were accorded Japan."
F.D.R.'s profound aversion to French actions in Indochina came to
the fore repeatedly, in front of both his own entourage and foreign
heads of state. Thus, while en route to the Casablanca Conference
F.D.R. told his son Elliott:

> The native Indochinese have been so flagrantly downtrodden that
> they thought to themselves: Anything must be better than to live un-
> der French colonial rule! . . . Don't think for a moment . . . that
> Americans would be dying tonight, if it had not been for the short-
> sighted greed of the French, the British and the Dutch.

This is indeed an amazing interpretation of why World War II
broke out in the Pacific, an interpretation that well-nigh absolved the
Japanese of any wrongdoing. Needless to say, modern historians and
the Japanese Government files that became available after the end of
World War II do not bear out such an oversimplified view of
world affairs. Nevertheless, that view prevailed at the various summit
conferences that determined the fate of postwar Southeast Asia—
just as similarly simplistic views about Europe determined the fate
of Poland, Hungary, and Germany. There is only one difference: In
the case of Eastern Europe, the fallacy of those premises has now
been openly admitted. In the case of Indochina, the evidence has
remained buried in the scattered files of various government departments or in the memoirs of the participants—and the American
public has remained largely unaware and uninterested in this important area of the world in which their country has been actively
fighting for more than twenty years.

Once it had been decided that France had "misruled" Indochina,
the next logical step was to prevent France from reasserting her
sovereignty over the area and to substitute another administration.
The idea of substitution was first officially broached at the inter-
Allied level during a White House conference on March 27,
1943, in which the President suggested to British Foreign Secretary
Anthony Eden that a trusteeship be established for Indochina. The
President also instructed Hull to present the trusteeship idea to the
Russians at the October, 1943, Moscow Conference, and he himself
spoke of it to Turkish and Egyptian representatives and to Chiang
Kai-shek during his brief stay in Cairo in November, 1943. Accord-
ing to General Joseph W. Stilwell, the U.S. commander in the China

Theater, F.D.R. had in mind a trusteeship under three commissioners—an American, a Chinese, and a Briton.

As the recently published secret documents on the Cairo and Tehran conferences show, F.D.R. did his best to convert Stalin (who was present at Tehran) to his own views on Indochina in order to outvote the very reluctant Churchill. According to the record (kept on the American side by Charles Bohlen, now U. S. Ambassador to France), F.D.R. stated that the first necessity "for the French, not only the government but the people as well, was to become honest citizens"; to this, Stalin replied that he was in full agreement and "went on to say that he did not propose to have the Allies shed blood to restore Indochina, for example, to old French colonial rule . . . and that the French must pay for their criminal collaboration with Germany."

President Roosevelt "said he was one hundred per cent in agreement with Marshal Stalin and remarked that after one hundred years of French rule the inhabitants were worse off than they had been before . . ." The State Department record shows in a footnote that Churchill objected to these assertions, but that F.D.R. cut him off with a curt: "Now look, Winston, you are outvoted three to one." (The "three" included Chiang Kai-shek, present at Cairo but absent from the Tehran Conference.)

As the sorry record of the Tehran Conference unfolds, one is struck by the unrealistic world views held by both Stalin and F.D.R. The latter, among other plans for postwar France, proposed to "eliminate from the future government of France anybody over forty years old" whereupon Stalin remarked that Charles de Gaulle was "of little importance as a real factor in political or other matters." And all this was said while Free French soldiers were fighting and dying side by side with their Allies from the North Atlantic to Cassino, and while inside France 400,000 French men and women (including an impressive number of people "over forty") were marched off to Nazi death camps, torture chambers, and execution posts. Only Winston Churchill preserved his full sanity during this interchange. Having heard the postwar plans of his fellow-summiteers, he stated simply that "he could not conceive of a civilized world without a flourishing and lively France. . . ."

Churchill came away from this conference gravely perturbed, and on January 3, 1944, the British Ambassador to Washington, Lord Halifax, asked Cordell Hull for further clarification of America's Indochina policy. President Roosevelt took up the matter personally with Halifax around January 20, 1944, and informed Hull on January 24 of their conversation:

> I saw Halifax last week and told him quite frankly that it was perfectly true that I had, for over a year, expressed the opinion that Indochina should not go back to France but that it should be administered by an international trusteeship.

And F.D.R. then repeated what by now had become his *leitmotiv* on the subject: that the French had been in control for a hundred years and the natives were worse off than ever before, that the French had milked Indochina dry, and that the people "are entitled to something better than that."

The trusteeship idea went through several other evolutions. For a time, when Chiang Kai-shek's fortunes were at a low ebb and there was some risk of China's dropping out of the war altogether, F.D.R. had offered China *all* of Indochina (including the "Hinduized" states of Cambodia and Laos!) as an outright grant. It is to Chiang Kai-shek's honor (or an indication of his political realism) that he turned down the gift. Mindful of China's previous experience with the Vietnamese—of which the President and his advisers seemed unaware—Chiang explained his refusal by pointing out that the Indochinese were "not Chinese. They would not assimilate into the Chinese people."

The trusteeship question was again brought up at Yalta in February, 1945. By that time, Roosevelt was willing to include one or two "Indochinese" and even a Frenchman in the Indochinese Trusteeship Council but insisted they be counterbalanced by a Filipino, a Chinese, and—a Russian ("because they are on the [Pacific] coast"). But this time, apparently, Churchill vetoed the whole scheme. F.D.R. decided to leave things as they were, since he wanted Churchill's support on more important matters. But on his return to the United States aboard the cruiser *Quincy,* F.D.R. vented to the journalists present his disappointment at having been foiled: "Stalin liked the idea. China liked the idea. The British don't like it. It might bust up their empire. . . ."

It is a further indication of how little Roosevelt understood either the French or de Gaulle that during a personal meeting with de Gaulle, the President offered him Filipino experts and advisers to help France establish "a more progressive policy in Indochina." De Gaulle, the record says, received the offer in "pensive silence." (It is likely that the word "icy" would have been more appropriate.) Almost to his dying day, F.D.R. found time to turn his thoughts to the Indochina problem. In the words of his son Elliott, F.D.R. held that Indochina, "liberated in main part by American arms and American troops, should never simply be handed back to the French, to be milked by their imperialists."

3. The Japanese Coup

This, however, still left the bothersome question of what to do with the French resistance in Indochina. Here, Washington followed the logical implications of its decision to evict the French from the country. On October 13, 1944, the President addressed a memorandum to Secretary of State Hull, stating that it was his "judgment on this date that we should do nothing in regard to resistance groups or in any other way in relation to Indochina." And on November 3, 1944, this instruction was implemented with another to American field commanders in Asia, enjoining them from giving "American approval . . . to any French military mission being accredited to the Southeast Asia Command." Translated into actual military terms, those instructions meant an automatic death sentence for any French attempt at organized resistance in case of Japanese attack, and that is exactly the way it turned out.

On March 9, 1945, at 2130, the Japanese struck without warning. One by one, the French garrisons had been surrounded by Japanese troops, and French senior commanders, almost without exception, were captured in their own homes or in those of Japanese officers with whom they were dining. The French underground movement bungled its operations miserably; having operated more and more in the open, its members were for the most part well-known to the Kempetai, the Japanese secret police, and were as easily arrested as the army. Only in Tonkin did Generals Sabattier and Alessandri get wind of what was afoot through their own intelligence and placed their troops on alert status. They broke through to the Thai mountain areas, established themselves around the airfields of Dien Bien Phu and Son-La, and began calling for Allied supplies and air support.

In South Viet-Nam, some smaller groups withdrew into the roadless swamps of Camau and began guerrilla warfare. In Laos, French resistance probably was the most effective. Some French troops, with the help of the Lao (including Prince Boun Oum, Premier of Laos in 1960–62), harassed Japanese communications along the Mekong until VJ-Day, receiving airdrops and reinforcements from British Force 136 teams throughout.

But in much of the rest of Indochina, particularly in the vital Tonkin area, Japanese action was brutal and effective. In Ha-Giang, they used the French women and children of the garrison as shields when they stormed the French fort. At Fort Briere de l'Isle, the whole garrison was machine-gunned to death, singing the *Marseillaise*. And ill-fated Lang-Son was again the center of a tragedy. The fort had secretly been rebuilt after its capture by the Japanese in 1940, and its defenders gave a good account of themselves. When the Japanese brought the captured military governor, General Lemonnier, and the civilian resident, Auphelle, under the walls of the fort and told them to ask the garrison to surrender, both men refused and both were beheaded by their enraged captors.

In the meantime, the nearest American field commander, General Claire L. Chennault, the famous father of the "Flying Tigers" and commander of the 14th U. S. Air Force in neighboring Yünnan, had moved into action. Following his own generous instincts, he had immediately sent liaison officers with small aircraft to make contact with Sabattier's forces. They had made a rapid survey of the most urgent needs of the French and arranged for airdrops and coordination of air support—and then had again vanished into Yünnan. No major airdrops materialized and many urgent radio messages simply went unanswered. Doomed Lang-Son also was calling for air support. The last message from the garrison that Sabattier's headquarters received said: "Still holding three-fourths of citadel— No water— Request air support and supply drops— Where are the Americans?" The garrison was massacred by the Japanese; only one man survived, after having been left for dead among the heaps of bodies thrown pell-mell into an open ditch.

What had happened to the 14th Air Force and General Chennault? After the war, Chennault provided the answer:

> . . . orders arrived from theater headquarters stating that no arms and ammunition would be provided to French troops under any circumstances. I was allowed to proceed with "normal" action against the Japanese in Indochina provided it did not involve supplying French troops. . . . General Wedemeyer's orders not to aid the French came directly from the War Department. Apparently it was American policy then that French Indochina would not be returned to the French. The American government was interested in seeing the French forcibly ejected from Indochina so the problem of postwar separation from their colony would be easier. . . .

While American transports in China avoided Indochina, the British flew aerial supply missions for the French all the way from Calcutta, dropping tommy guns, grenades, and mortars.

Through recent first-hand research in documents of the 14th Air Force stored at the U. S. A. F. Historical Branch at Maxwell Air Force Base, Alabama, I think that it is possible to show that General Chennault did not obey his orders as literally as the above passage implies; for example, on March 13, 1945, four P-51's and three P-40's of the 51st Fighter Group attacked Japanese positions near Lang-Son, while the 27th Troop Carrier Squadron carried out supply drops to the retreating French through May, 1945.

At theater level, however, General Wedemeyer unflinchingly adhered to the policies set by Washington, although he, too, apparently had some misgivings about them, as shown in the following passage of his memoirs:

> [March, 1945, visit to F.D.R.] I had not seen the President for several months and was shocked at his physical appearance. His color was ashen, his face drawn, and his jaw drooping. I had difficulty conveying information to him because he seemed in a daze. Several times I repeated the same idea because his mind did not seem to retain or register. He evinced considerable interest in French Indo-China and stated that he was going to do everything possible to give the people in that area their independence. . . . He admonished me not to give any supplies to the French forces operating in the area. [At a lunch with Secretary of War Stimson.] Mr. Stimson asked me about my conference with the President and I recounted the instructions I had received concerning the French. He expressed surprise and suggested that I mention this to General Marshall, which I did at the earliest opportunity.

In view of the foregoing, it seems clear that F.D.R., in his personal instructions to Wedemeyer, apparently went beyond what had been the agreed policy in his desire to eliminate the French from Indochina at all costs. This explains Stimson's surprise and his urging Wedemeyer to take up the matter with General Marshall. What the latter's instructions were on the subject has never been made clear, but it seems probable that he somewhat softened the President's admonition. Wedemeyer's testimony adds considerable weight to my view that, to the last, President Roosevelt accorded Indochina —and, in particular, French activities there—an importance far out of proportion to its actual position within the scheme of things; his preoccupation amounted almost to a fixation.

Meanwhile, the battle was continuing in Washington, where the Free French Military Mission pleaded daily with the American military to release Chennault's supply-loaded aircraft to support of Sabattier's forces. The telegrams the French Government sent to its diplomats in the United States at that time tell again and again of the bewilderment and shock that assailed the French officials concerned with the problems. They could not bring themselves to believe that such American inaction was deliberate (since they were unaware of F.D.R.'s decisions on the subject) and continued to believe that the absence of American support was due simply to an incredible ignorance of the desperate plight of the French troops in Indochina. In the meantime, the last surviving French troops in Viet-Nam could watch, thousands of feet above their heads, the condensation trails of hundreds of American bombers flying imperturbably on "normal" operations against the Japanese in Borneo, Bangkok, and Saigon —but not against Lang-Son or Japanese columns near Son-La.

It was only at the end of March—after the last organized French units in Viet-Nam had been destroyed and Sabattier's troops were reduced to haggard bands of disease-ridden stragglers—that Admiral Leahy succeeded in obtaining the President's permission to release Chennault's aircraft for support missions in Indochina. But by that time, the Japanese had settled the whole problem in their own way.

Of the approximately 13,000 French troops who were not immediately overwhelmed by the Japanese attack, 200 officers and 4000 soldiers were, according to de Gaulle's memoirs, killed or massacred

133

in the course of the fighting retreat to China. A total of 320 officers, both French and Vietnamese, and 2150 European and 3300 Vietnamese soldiers survived the 800-mile trek to Yünnan. In his inimitable style, de Gaulle took the long view of the whole affair:

> As painful as that development was locally, I must say that from the point of view of national interest, I willingly envisaged that hostilities would commence in Indochina . . . in view of our position in the Far East, I thought it essential that the conflict should not end without us having become, there also, [involved as] belligerents . . . French blood shed on Indochinese soil would give us an important voice [in later settlements]. Since I did not harbor the least doubt as to Japan's ultimate aggression, I desired that our troops should fight, no matter how desperate their situation.

Inside Viet-Nam, the Japanese administration had taken things in hand: All male Frenchmen were herded into concentration camps, some of which, such as Hoa-Binh, gained a reputation as sinister as Dachau's. Other less lucky Frenchmen, and Vietnamese known for their pro-French sentiments, were locked up in the infamous "monkey cages" of the Kempetai.

On March 10, 1945, the Japanese Ambassador to Saigon came to Hué and announced to Vietnamese Emperor Bao-Dai that his country was not "independent." On the following day, after deliberation with his Cabinet ministers, Bao-Dai repudiated the protectorate treaty of 1885 and expressed the "confidence of the Government of Viet-Nam in Japan's loyalty and its own determination to collaborate with [Japan] within the framework of the Greater East Asia Co-Prosperity Sphere."

France's rule over Viet-Nam had lasted a few months less than 60 years. Considering Viet-Nam's 2200 years of recorded history, it had been a very brief interlude.

4. The Viet-Minh Honeymoon

VJ-Day set the stage for the Viet-Minh takeover in Hanoi and Saigon and for the arrival of American military missions in the Indochina area (largely Hanoi).

The first such mission was as OSS team lead by Major Archimedes L. Patti. Patti adhered strictly to the set policy of no contact with the French, many of whom were still in Japanese prisons and

134

still guarded by Japanese. The Chinese occupation forces which followed in accordance with decisions taken at Potsdam, occupied Laos and Viet-Nam to the 16th parallel, came into the area very slowly, pilfering it as they went along.

It is remarkable that the Americans in China at least were under no illusions as to the effect of that Chinese occupation on the local populace. Thus, a document which I found in the U.S.A.F. files (TPS 1/6 of 26 August 1945) simply stated: "There will be resistance by the Annamites (e.g. Vietnamese) to any attempt at occupation by Chinese troops." If such hostilities failed to materialize, this was largely due to the iron will of Ho Chi Minh, the Communist leader of the Viet-Minh, who had clearly realized that he could not simultaneously fight against all comers and preferred to conserve his strength for the ultimate showdown with the French. The latter, with the help of Britain which occupied Indochina south of the 16th parallel, had brought with them the prestigious armored forces of General Leclerc and clearly were the greater long-term menace.

He also sought to open avenues of support in the West—particularly American. Thus, when an American liaison staff under Major General Philip E. Gallagher was attached to the Chinese forces, the Viet-Minh set to woo it with a will.

Successfully hiding their Communist background, the Viet-Minh leaders managed to make it appear, not only to the populace, but to the French and Chinese as well, that they had been "recognized" by the United States. General Gallagher was heard on the local radio addressing his good wishes to the local regime; and the Viet-Minh leaders, whenever possible, saw to it that they would be seen (and photographed by foreign press reporters) with Americans in uniform. In actual fact, however, no official recognition had taken place, and the Viet-Minh soon saw that for all their kindness, the local Americans were unlikely to be very helpful.

Whether this was due to a deliberate policy in Washington or, conversely, to an absence of policy, is not quite clear to this day. As relations between the Viet-Minh and the West worsened in late 1946, two State Department officers, Messrs. Moffat and Landon, were sent to Hanoi, where they saw Ho Chi Minh several times, were impressed by him as a person, but apparently recommended against American support for his regime.

135

Thus, Ho was left face to face with the returning French Army. The Indochina War broke out on December 19, 1946. The United States, preoccupied in Europe, ceased to be a diplomatic factor in Indochina until the outbreak of the Korean War.

5. *Support for France*

With the outbreak of the Korean "police action" the Administration clearly realized that Indochina had become intimately connected with its own efforts further north: support for the Viet-Minh's forces by Red China represented a drain which to a certain degree affected the volume of the Red Chinese commitment in Korea—and, as will be seen, vice-versa. Thus, within a week after the outbreak of the Korean War, a first token shipment of U.S. military supplies arrived in Saigon, soon followed by a military advisory group and an economic aid mission. By the time the war ended in July 1954, France had received close to $1 billion in U.S. equipment and aid, and the U.S. was irrevocably committed to the defense of the peninsula. Although it has not been stated publicly that the two allies exchanged formal agreements guaranteeing that neither would conclude a peace without the other, it has nevertheless been admitted by highly reliable French sources (and, at least once, mentioned before an American Congressional committee) that the United States would coordinate her Korean policy with developments in Indochina. The recent volume of memoirs published by President Eisenhower adds extremely significant evidence on that point: he clearly admits that with the cessation of hostilities in Korea the burden of Red China's military efforts fell on the French in Indochina.

The arrival of a new French commander in chief, General Henri Navarre, in July 1953, coupled with promises of extensive American aid, gave rise to a new wave of euphoria both in France and in the United States. Much space was devoted in the press of both countries to the so-called Navarre Plan, which John Foster Dulles, then Secretary of State, explained to a Senate committee as being designed to "break the organized body of Communist aggression by the end of the 1955 fighting season." That, of course, like much that has come out of Washington about Viet-Nam since, was wildly wishful thinking. Navarre himself, once he had taken stock of the situation in his widely dispersed command, was a great deal less sanguine. In a secret report addressed to his government in 1953 and published in 1956 in his memoirs, Navarre stated that the war simply could not be won in the military sense (just as the Korean War could not, without drawing Red China into it) and that all that could be hoped for was a *coup nul*—a draw.

And even that draw required an immediate reinforcement of the French Expeditionary Corps in such key fields as artillery and mobile infantry, merely to keep pace with the rapid build-up of Communist forces, thanks to the inflow of Chinese instructors and American equipment obtained in Korea, which had been at peace since July 1953. Little has thus far been disclosed publicly about the agreements reached in 1952–53 between the United States and France regarding coordination of military strategy in the Far East. It is nevertheless known that the two allies realized that the Korean and Indochinese theaters of operations were interdependent battlefields, since in both, the enemy forces drew upon Red China for their major support.

But after years of inactivity on the Indochina scene, the United States began to assert itself more energetically as the pace of the war increased. Far from espousing a policy of French disengagement, the Eisenhower Administration embarked upon an effort to cajole the French to stay in the fight as long as possible, "with the obvious intention," as a *Le Monde* observer stated, on November 12, 1953, "to avoid giving France any pretext for putting an end to the conflict. As an American diplomat recently said jokingly: 'We are the last French colonists in Indochina.'" The Eisenhower Administration was about to reap, in Indochina, the bitter fruits of its foreign-policy promises during the 1952 electoral campaign. Having branded the Democrats a "war party" and made the slogan "Peace in Korea" its major foreign-policy drawing card (along with such other phrases as "rolling back the Iron Curtain," and "unleashing Chiang Kai-shek"), it had virtually ruled out even the threat of force—much less the use of force itself. Thus, the President and Secretary of State Dulles were compelled to walk a diplomatic tightrope; Dulles continued to sell a "hard" policy to America's allies abroad, while the President at the very same moment faced the delicate task of explaining those statements to Congress and to an anxious American public without openly contradicting Dulles.

Thus, after Dulles, on January 14, 1954, launched the concept of "massive retaliation," backed by the sending of 200 U. S. Air Force technicians to Viet-Nam to service French combat planes, the President, at his press conference of February 10, declared that he "could conceive of no greater tragedy than for the United States to become involved in an all-out war in Indochina."

What ensued is probably one of the most confused chapters of recent American diplomatic history and one that, in spite of its importance, has thus far escaped the scrutiny of American political scientists. Before it closed, it had brought a humiliating defeat in Indochina and embroiled the American leadership—the President, Vice-President, the Secretary of State, and major Congressional leaders—in bitter squabbles. It also had created the first open rift between the United States and her major allies in Europe, a rift that was never really more than patched over until Secretary Dulles' successor, Christian A. Herter, took over the reins at the State Department.

6. Operation "Guernica-Vulture"

While the President had once more assured the country that American military intervention was unlikely, the Pentagon was feverishly working out the military implications of such an intervention. Here also, sharp disagreement occurred between the American top commanders. Admiral Radford, a strong advocate of carrier-based aviation, urged American air strikes on targets around Dien Bien Phu, perhaps on a "one-shot" basis, like that first used by German and Italian aircraft to destroy the Spanish town of Guernica on April 26, 1937. A Guernica-type, single large-scale raid, which could perhaps even be carried out at night and by American aircraft bearing French insignia, was considered the operation most likely to avoid severe diplomatic repercussions. With two American carriers, the *Essex* and the *Boxer,* already operating in the Gulf of Tonkin, and with American aircraft stationed in Okinawa and Clark Field in the Philippines, a Guernica-type raid had the added advantage of being feasible on a few days' notice. It was also likely to be of doubtful military value. General Matthew B. Ridgway, then Army Chief of

Staff, had sent his own team of experts to Viet-Nam, and their report had been negative: American intervention, to be of any value at all, would have to involve ground forces, and such an operation could very well unleash the Chinese Reds, just as it had done in Korea. Ridgway thus took the forthright position that the price of a Western victory in Indochina would be "as great as, or greater than, that we paid in Korea."

The conflict was resolved by the President himself in a characteristic compromise: He accepted the Radford plan of a Guernica-type raid—but only if the American position was supported by "other allies," i.e., the British and, if possible, one or two Asian nations. Eisenhower—mindful of the adverse legislative reaction to President Truman's "police action" in Korea—also desired that intervention in Indochina be backed by Congressional approval. The resultant secret briefing Dulles gave top Congressional leaders of both parties on April 3, 1954, reportedly left them "bug-eyed" and brought about an acrimonious debate on the Indochina question in the Senate on April 6, a debate that abounded with statements whose doubtful relation to the facts clearly showed how little was known about the problem even among Americans who had access to official briefings.

Thus, according to Senator John F. Kennedy, the French still "must give their consent to the sending of [Vietnamese] diplomatic missions to foreign countries." This, as has been shown, had not been the case since 1949. He then proceeded to blame much of the Indochina War on the fact that French demands upon Ho Chi Minh in 1946 had been unreasonable, and backed up his statement by citing the example of the March 1946 agreements on French troops in North Viet-Nam, which, said the young senator and later President, "did not set any date for the [cessation of] use of French facilities in that area." As the record shows, the March 6, 1946, agreements provided for the stationing of French troops in the D.R.V.N. for a maximum of *five* years. (In July 1946, the U.S. signed an agreement with the Philippines that provided for the continued presence of American bases in that country for ninety-nine years.) Senator Mike Mansfield provided the Senate with the statistic that the French Union Forces in Indochina numbered 591,000 troops against the

Viet-Minh's 290,000. In reality (including even the poorly armed Vietnamese, Cambodian, and Laotian national armies), French forces never exceeded the 350,000 mark, and the Viet-Minh could usually count upon at least as many troops—but in a guerrilla war a 12-to-1 superiority is required for the regular force just to "break even," and more than that to win.

The Republican side was not to be outdone. Senator Everett Dirksen informed his colleagues that the Red River Delta "exported" 500,000 tons of rice to Japan and was "the rice bowl which takes care also of Burma, Thailand, Cambodia, Laos, Formosa, Indonesia, and other countries." It should be remembered that the countries cited include all the world's largest rice *exporters* along with some potential consumers—none of whom had ever bought food from North Viet-Nam, much less from the delta area, which is traditionally short of food. And while Dirksen, along with Vice-President Nixon, and Senators Knowland and Jenner, did not, in his words, "share the anxiety and concern some feel about the danger of sending American troops to Indochina, other than technicians," Senator Alexander Wiley probably summed up the feelings of the majority of his Republican colleagues when he said: "Mr. Speaker, if war comes under this Administration, it could well be the end of the Republican Party." Noninterventionist feeling ran equally high among the often-burned Democrats. Senator Edwin C. Johnson of Colorado summed up the view of most of his party by saying that he was "against sending American GIs into the mud and muck of Indochina on a blood-letting spree to perpetuate colonialism and white man's exploitation in Asia."

In other words, the overwhelming majority of senators of both parties were *against* American military intervention in Indochina as early as mid-April 1954; and since President Eisenhower had made it clear in March that he would not involve America in combat operations in Indochina "unless it is a result of the constitutional process that is placed upon Congress," it was obvious that any American policy that ran against both Congressional opinion and the advice of at least part of the Joint Chiefs of Staff was pure rhetoric, if not worse. In any case, the facts do not square with the self-serving assertions in the Dulles-sponsored "brinkmanship" article in *Life* two years later:

140

. . . the policy of boldness impressed the Communists. Dulles had seen to it that the Chinese and the Soviets knew that the US was prepared to act decisively to prevent the fall of Southeast Asia . . . Thus, instead of negotiating from the extreme and undisguised weakness of the French position, Mendes-France and Eden found themselves able to bargain from Dulles' strength. . . .

It is certain that the Communists were at least as aware as Sir Anthony Eden of the real hollowness of the Dulles position in the matter, since Eden, even before Dulles' arrival in London on April 11 to discuss "united action," set down his own view as follows:

I cannot see what threat would be sufficiently potent to make China swallow so humiliating a rebuff without any face-saving concession in return. If I am right in this view, the joint warning to China would have no effect, and the coalition would then have to withdraw ignominiously or else embark on warlike action against China.

Eden then argued that the same threat had had little if any effect on Red China's intervention in Korea, but might give China "every excuse" to invoke its alliance with Russia and thus precipitate a world war. The position the British then adopted did not exclude a warning to China at a later date, but the British felt that for the time being the best should be made of the forthcoming Geneva Conference. They maintained that position throughout the ups and downs of the conference over the next ten weeks, despite Dulles' attempts to shake it. As it turned out, it was the British position that proved to be the right one—for reasons having little to do with Indochina. Because Russia was trying to strike a bargain with Pierre Mendes-France (who had taken over the premiership on June 19 from Laniel and acted as his own Foreign Minister at Geneva) over France's membership in the European Defense Community, the Viet-Minh accepted a cease-fire on conditions a great deal less advantageous than those it could have obtained on the strength of its military successes. The fact that Mendes-France, though more liberal than his predecessors, immediately airlifted troop reinforcements into Indochina and ordered tropical inoculations for two French divisions in Germany (including, for the first time, draftees) also added to the credibility of a stiffening Western position, to which the threat of American intervention gave further weight.

7. Rift at Geneva

But the British refusal, in Eden's words, "to endorse a bad policy for the sake of unity," gave Dulles and the Eisenhower Administration a convenient avenue of escape from the cul-de-sac of military intervention they themselves had constructed; as James Shepley was to show in the *Life* article, the whole failure of united military action was blamed on Britain. In a speech in Seattle on June 10—that is, in the middle of the Geneva Conference—Dulles alleged that "some of the parties had held back," and he proceeded to compare the situation to a "rebuff" the United States received in 1931, when it tried to bring about united action against Japan in Manchuria. For months after Dulles' speech, every major American news weekly, quoting "authoritative" sources (usually unattributed statements by the Secretary of State himself), came out on one side or the other of the issue, thus adding to the confusion of conflicting assertions that will not be fully unraveled until the publication of official American documents. According to one of the best American press reports, written by Chalmers M. Roberts for the Washington *Post* of June 7, 1954, the later Eden version, as well as *Life*'s, was substantially correct. In other words, the United States *was* prepared to intervene militarily in Indochina. Dulles himself, when questioned about the accuracy of the *Life* article in a press conference on January 18, 1956, specifically confirmed that the statements attributed to him "did not require correction from the standpoint of their substance." In a debate on the Senate floor on July 9, 1954, however, two Republican senators, Homer Ferguson and Alexander Smith, solemnly denied that the subject of intervention had come up in Dulles' briefings to them; and *U.S. News & World Report,* in a headline article of August 9, quoting a highly authoritative source, asserted that "the official records show that the U.S. never was on the verge of a shooting war with Communist China over Indochina." (This did not prevent its publisher, David Lawrence, from endorsing the *Life* article two years later in a statement that the latter publication used in its advertisements.)

Yet on January 13, 1960, after Eden's memoirs had appeared, President Eisenhower contradicted both Eden and his late Secretary of State by telling a press conference that "there was never any plan developed to put into execution in Indochina" and explained Dulles' statement to the contrary by saying that Dulles had been "a very forceful man. He could very well talk about possibilities that might by then be considered as proposals, when they were not meant as that at all."

It is precisely this Janus-faced quality of presenting at times a forceful posture on the home front while being conciliatory abroad, or of being cautious at home while taking a tough stand in the councils of the world, that produces confusion about American policies in general, and on Viet-Nam in particular. The new Viet-Nam crisis that began to boil in 1961 gave a few more choice examples of that lack of a consensus based on a coolheaded estimate of the facts.

By the time the dust settled in Geneva, it was clear that "Operation Vulture"—the official designation for the Guernica-type air strike—had failed to come off not only militarily, but also politically. Its failure had left a sour taste in the mouths of all U.S. allies involved, particularly the British, who had borne the brunt of the diplomatic battle and felt ill-rewarded when they found themselves blamed for what some Americans were comparing to another Munich or, at best, a Dunkirk. But as James Reston wrote in the New York *Times* of June 13:

> This picture, omitting any reference to Congressional or White House opposition to using force in Asia . . . is one of the most misleading oversimplifications ever uttered by an American Secretary of State, but it allocates blame and furnishes an alibi.

The last days of the Geneva Conference did not go any better than the earlier days. The Eisenhower Administration, after the failure of massive retaliation and united intervention, had found a diplomatic line of retreat in such slogans as "Peace with Honor," which the President himself translated at his June 30 press conference as "Coexistence Without Appeasement," adding that the United States would not be "a party to any agreement that makes anybody a slave." That new line seemed also to include a clear-cut dissociation of the United States from the cease-fire negotiations, reinforced by the fact that Dulles himself did not reappear at the conference and finally agreed to permit the American delegation, led by the very able Under Secretary of State Walter Bedell Smith, to remain only after Mendes-France and Eden pointed out that the United States would not escape its obligations (or save the Vietnamese from "slavery") by not participating at Geneva.

Thus, during the last few days of the negotiations, it was Eden and Mendes-France, aided by a not too unreasonable Molotov and a not totally uncooperative Chou En-lai, who had to carry the ball alone. In fact, some observers felt that the absence of Dulles (who had consistently acted as if Chou were made of thin air) considerably "unbristled" the head of the Chinese delegation. The terms finally obtained by Mendes-France were well within the minimum limits set out earlier by Dulles and were definitely a diplomatic success under the circumstances.

Therefore, the American delegation's announcement that it would not sign the final declaration was not greeted as good news by the other Western allies. In Eden's eyes, "since Dulles had been at least as responsible as ourselves for calling the Geneva Conference, this did not seem to me reasonable." But Molotov brought Chou En-lai around to accepting a separate declaration by the United States, on condition that the United States would also be included in the heading of the final declaration.

Thus, when his turn came to sign the final declaration, Under Secretary Smith read a declaration, according to which the United States took

> . . . note of the agreements concluded at Geneva [and] declares with regard to the aforesaid agreements that (i) it will refrain from the threat or the use of force to disturb them . . . and (ii) it would view any renewal of the aggression in violation of the aforesaid agreements with grave concern and as seriously threatening international peace and security.

The American statement went on to say that the United States was in favor of the principle of free elections under United Nations supervision and that all three Indochinese countries should be permitted to determine their own future.

If any delegation was in a more confused and ambiguous position than that of the United States, it was that of Bao-Dai's state of Viet-Nam. Bao-Dai himself managed to antagonize everybody by following the proceedings from his Chateau de Thorene, near Cannes (save for a two-day trip to Evian), and the change of govern-

1. Preparing to fire a 175-mm. gun.

2. Camp J. J. Carroll taken from landing zone.

3. Army officers observing artillery fire with Bernard Fall.

4. Close-up of The Rockpile.

5. Marine emplacements on top of The Rockpile taken from an H-34 helicopter.

6. Soldier sighting a 106-mm. recoilless cannon.

7. Watchtower

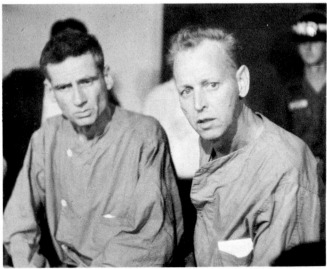

8. Returned U.S. prisoners being interviewed.

9. Bernard Fall interviewing a Viet Cong prisoner captured at the Iron Triangle.

10. Bernard Fall with Major Robert Schweitzer. (François Sully, *Newsweek*)

11. Prisoners being led away by Vietnamese soldiers. Picture was on film removed from Fall's mangled camera.

12. Marines firing at the Viet Cong on the Street Without Joy—from last film.

13. Marines firing from a dike into Viet Cong positions.

14. Bernard Fall with Mary McCarthy. (François Sully, *Newsweek*)

ment from Buu-Loc to Ngo Dinh Diem, which took place on July 7, in mid-conference, did little to help matters. In Viet-Nam itself, the worsening military situation was matched, on the Vietnamese nationalist side, by a slide into total unreality; various Vietnamese politicians (none representing anything more than a few close friends and family members) were making grandiloquent statements on how they would continue to fight on "to total victory," and hatching far-reaching schemes for this end; to these, the French replied with a blunt: "What do you expect to do? Continue the war alone?" It was obvious that the Vietnamese had no good counter-argument to that point, once it had become clear that the United States was not going to fight for Viet-Nam at this juncture, and since the South Vietnamese Government had no concessions to offer (the only position that would have given it some independent bargaining power would have been a willingness to deal with the Viet-Minh, and that it was unwilling to do), it was simply ignored by all concerned in the desperate rush of meeting the July 20 deadline for achieving peace that Mendes-France had set himself. As Tran Van Do, South Viet-Nam's dedicated Foreign Minister, cabled to Ngo Dinh Diem at the conclusion of the conference, whose declaration he also refused to sign:

> Absolutely impossible to surmount the hostility of our enemies and perfidy of false friends. Unusual procedures paralyzed the action of our delegation. . . . All arrangements were signed in privacy. We express our deepest sorrow on this total failure of our mission. . . .

And thus ended the first concerted international effort at saving Viet-Nam from Communism. It remained Senator Jenner's lot to perpetuate through the *Congressional Record* of August 14, 1954, a concise appraisal of what had happened at Geneva:

> The United States has been outthought, outtraded, and outgeneraled. . . .
> It does no good to say we did not physically sign the Geneva agreements. That is the old excuse of Pontius Pilate, who washed his hands to keep his conscience clear.

This was perhaps true in the short run; in the long run, however, the American and South Vietnamese refusal to sign at Geneva was to have beneficial consequences for the new administration abuilding south of the 17th Parallel: On the grounds of its nonsignature, South Viet-Nam refused to hold elections by July, 1956, since this would have meant handing over control of the South to Ho Chi Minh; and the United States, banking upon point II of its separate declaration at Geneva, could argue convincingly in 1962 that its military commitment in behalf of the Saigon regime was in response to North Vietnamese "renewal of the aggression in violation of the aforesaid agreements."

Another phase of the military and diplomatic struggle for Viet-Nam had drawn to an end. The struggle now began to rebuild a truncated land into a viable non-Communist Vietnamese state, around the new emerging leader, Ngo Dinh Diem.

8. From Partial to Full Involvement

With the French defeat at Dien Bien Phu and the ensuing cease-fire, the Indochinese peninsula became a largely American responsibility and separate policies had to be devised for the now-independent four Indochinese successor states—Cambodia, Laos, and the divided Viet-Nams.

As regards North Viet-Nam, the problem was simple: total non-contact, as in the case of East Germany and Red China. With regard to Laos and Cambodia, a certain ambiguity of policies persisted which was never resolved: in Laos, a fairly well-established pro-Western neutral regime was undermined in 1957–58 in favor of right-wing groups whose popular backing was nil and whose fighting ability non-existent. This led to the total destruction of the Western positions in Laos and the restoration of the self-same neutral regime—only much weaker.

In Cambodia, the ambiguity rested on the fact that the U.S. was simultaneously Cambodia's largest aid donor and the military ally of her biggest enemies, Thailand and South Viet-Nam. The Cambodian Government chose to remove that ambiguity by reducing contacts with U.S. to a minimum and by closing down U.S. aid activities in November, 1963.

This leaves the American commitment to South Viet-Nam. From the historian's viewpoint, the providing of alien cadre forces to national forces engaged in an "internal war" is nothing out of the ordinary. To cite but one example, French aid during America's Revolutionary War would fall within the category.

What gives rise, however, to some questions in the *diplomatic* and political frame of reference within which that commitment to South Viet-Nam was made: is it part of the "containment" policy; the "falling-domino" theory; or of a Southeast Asian Monroe Doctrine? Apparently, it is a part of all of them—although this has never been made quite clear to the American public or, for that matter, to the American fighting men who were killed or taken prisoner in Laos and now in South Viet-Nam.

9. Conclusion

A) American policy in the Indochina area, though a quarter-century old, has thus far not been able to produce a coherent frame of reference within which to operate.

B) For reasons never made quite clear, the U.S. failed to put on France in Indochina the pressure she put, for example, on The Netherlands in Indonesia, to come to a peaceful arrangement with local nationalists. France in 1947–48 was in no position to resist such pressure.

C) The ambiguity of the Eisenhower-Dulles policies of pursuing peace in Korea while providing first the French and then South Viet-Nam and Laos with the material base for a "die-hard" attitude in Indochina was *not* resolved by the change of administrations. The Kennedy Administration purely and simply took up where the previous administration had left off. In fact, it hardened its unconditional commitment to an anti-Communist South Viet-Nam by assigning increasing amounts of combat advisers to the area without asking for a commensurate share in the political decision-making.

D) A last-minute "flexibility," injected into that policy by announcing a large-scale American withdrawal from Viet-Nam by 1965, was annulled by the Johnson Administration in mid-December 1963 and March–April 1964.

E) Thus, one of the permanent traits of America's Indochina policy seems to have been a certain rigidity in adapting policies to local changes and a pursuit—until far too late—of policies based on theories not verified by the facts on the terrain (*viz.,* the "popularity" of Diem; the "successes" of counterinsurgency; the farmers' "love" for the Strategic Hamlets, etc.). But recent changes of personalities in Saigon as well as among American officials dealing with Viet-Nam may well bring about some policy changes that may eventually change the whole picture.

Viet-Nam:
The Quest for Stability

ⲒⲱⲒ

AS THIS WRITER STATED a year ago in *Current History,* "the Second Indochina War seems to grope its way slowly to a Korean-type 'meatgrinder operation' that nobody wants." The events in all of Viet-Nam during 1966 seem to have confirmed this estimate: the influx of North Vietnamese regulars, and the unabated ability of the National Liberation Front (N.L.F., or in Western parlance, Viet Cong) to recruit new manpower, left hostile forces at the unprecedented level of 283,000 men. On the non-Communist side —referred to, in Saigon parlance, as "Free World Forces"—the American build-up exceeded 350,000 at the end of the year and was likely to climb to over a half-million late in 1967.[1] The government of Viet-Nam had 705,000 men under arms, roughly one-half of whom were South Vietnamese army (A.R.V.N.) regulars, while other foreign contingents—notably the South Koreans (50,000) and the Australians (4500) and symbolic contributions from New Zealand, Thailand, and the Philippines—rounded out the picture.

In the military field, the year had seen a tremendous escalation of aerial bombardment, both in the North and in the South;

Reprinted by permission and first published in *Current History,* January, 1967. Copyright © 1967 by Current History, Inc.
[1] The New York *Times,* November 9, 1966.

and a consequent inability on the part of the Viet Cong to mount a coordinated offensive—assuming that it had actually had the intention of doing so. Much had been made in Western circles of a possible "monsoon offensive" in the course of which the Viet Cong would attempt to cut South Viet-Nam in two, either in the northernmost part below Hué, or further south around Road 19, between Pleiku and Qui Nhon. That offensive did not materialize in 1966, but several major Viet Cong units, described as being "in fact mere ghost outfits, decimated by battle losses and unfit to fight,"[2] put in a great deal of heavy defensive fighting at the end of the year. As 1966 turned into 1967, the over-all military effort of 1966 had succeeded only in breaking even at a higher plateau: the military collapse of South Viet-Nam had become impossible and some coastal enclaves—notably around the Marine bases in central Viet-Nam—had become more secure. But the initial modest target of 2000 pacified villages (out of a total of 13,211) was not in sight. By mid-September, 1966, only 195 previously Viet Cong-held villages had been integrated into the "revolutionary development" program.[3]

On the negative side, the following points are worth noting: (a) enemy strength went from 106,000 men in January, 1965, to 241,000 men in January, 1966, and to an all-time high of 284,000 men in September, 1966 (it was to decrease to 280,000 later in the year); (b) that strength was achieved in spite of only 50,000 infiltrators from North Viet-Nam and a 12-month alleged loss rate of 54,000 killed, close to 100,000 wounded and 7,200 prisoners[4]; (c) the Viet Cong in fact succeeded in tightening its vise around the greater Saigon area, sinking merchantmen and warships in the narrow shipping channel and finally shelling downtown Saigon on November 1, 1966, in the midst of the South Vietnamese government's celebration of the overthrow of Ngo Dinh Diem in 1963; (d) the South Vietnamese army desertion rate, which had reached a total of 93,000 "absentees-without-leave" [the word "desert" implies

2 Joseph Alsop, "Order of Battle," The Washington *Post*, September 30, 1966.
3 The White House, Report to the President by his Special Assistant for Pacification, Robert W. Komer, generally referred to as the *Komer Report*, September 13, 1966, p. 41.
4 Alsop, *ibid.*

passing over to the enemy, which most of the time did not occur] in 1965, maintained a roughly equal rate in 1966.

It is clear, however, that none of these points is likely to weigh heavily in the outcome of the military aspects of the war: reinforcements of American troops to the half-million level and beyond, and further widening of the firepower base already deployed will see to that. But a viable political balance is apparently going to be more difficult to achieve.

Southern Politics

The year began with an unfulfilled promise by the Ky government, made on December 8, 1965, to appoint a constitution-drafting committee of 70 to 80 members. But since the Nguyen Cao Ky government seemed particularly weak at that moment, there seemed no particular hurry among South Vietnamese politicians to commit themselves to such a body.

All this changed, however, with the Honolulu Conference between United States President Lyndon Johnson and Generals Ky and Nguyen Van Thieu (Thieu in his capacity as Vietnamese chief-of-state) on February 6–8, 1966.* By associating himself personally with the South Vietnamese generals, the American President committed the prestige of his office not only to the continued support of the southern regime, but to that of its leaders as well. The follow-up visit to Saigon of Vice-President Hubert H. Humphrey with an important suite of experts, in the course of which he declared that the National Liberation Front "was unfit to be part of any [South Vietnamese] government," further reinforced the feeling of the South Vietnamese leaders that they had been personally endorsed by Washington.

The immediate result of this view was a clear-cut "toughening" of the junta toward its internal noncommunist opposition. On March 25, General Ky announced that South Viet-Nam would be given a new constitution "within two months"—a promise that was, to be sure, not kept—and at the same time he began to take measures to oust General Nguyen Chanh Thi, the popular commander of I Corps in Danang, from his command. Thi had

* For the text of the Honolulu Declaration, see *Current History*, April, 1966, pp. 238 ff.

for years been the "stormy petrel" of the Vietnamese army; he was deeply implicated in the rebellion of November 11, 1960, in which the A.R.V.N.'s parachute brigade tried to murder Ngo Dinh Diem.[5] After residing in exile in neighboring Cambodia until Diem's death three years later, Thi returned to the A.R.V.N. and assumed increasingly important commands, in which he acquired a reputation of being anything but soft on Communism and neutralism.[6] But late in 1965, as Buddhist discontent with the increased devastation of the war began to grow and was eventually matched by similar moves among some Catholic groups, Thi acquired the reputation of being in sympathy with those elements who were in favor of a negotiated settlement of the war. The facts themselves are far from clear, as no concrete evidence to that effect was ever presented. Another version has it that Thi had become—far more so than the other three corps commanders—a law unto himself in I Corps, which contained the vital American base of Danang and the always fractious university city of Hué. The news of Thi's prospective removal sparked I Corps into overt mutiny late in April, 1966.

When Premier Ky announced on May 7 that he intended to stay in power for "at least another year," the Buddhist leadership in Saigon under Thich Tri Quang joined in appealing to the population for the overthrow of the Thieu-Ky regime. What followed was a show of determination on the part of Ky, with what may well have been the *de facto* cooperation of certain American military commanders before either the United States embassy in Saigon or the administration in Washington had fully evaluated the developing situation. Marine units protected an airlift of loyal A.R.V.N. troops sent to quell Danang's revolt and American artillery kept vital communication points covered until A.R.V.N. troops could take them over. In ten days of bitter street fighting— in the course of which there were at least 800 civilian casualties

[5] Stanley Karnow, "Diem Defeats His Own Best Troops," *The Reporter,* January 19, 1961.

[6] On March 19, 1965, three South Vietnamese (including Pham Van Huyen, a Catholic who, in Diem's government, had organized the refugee flow from North Viet-Nam) were expelled across the 17th parallel to North Viet-Nam for being what the Saigon press called "peacemongers." General Thi presided over the expulsion proceedings, accusing the three of being men who "eat our rice while worshipping Communist ghosts." Cf. *Saigon Post,* March 20, 1965.

—Danang was retaken by A.R.V.N. forces on May 24. The fall of Hué on June 10 settled another assiduously-maintained myth: the alleged pro-Communist leanings of the Buddhist leadership. As Danang agonized, the well-organized and armed students of Hué had ample time to form a temporary alliance with the Viet Cong, of the kind which the Hoa-Hao and Cao-Dai sects had maintained with it between 1958 and 1963.[7] In the end, however, they (and with them the Venerable Tri Quang) opted for the certitude of Saigon detention camps,[8] in preference to the total chaos of a three-cornered civil war.

One byproduct of General Ky's victory was that his position was significantly strengthened. Already on May 16, when the Danang battle was going his way, Ky announced that a constituent assembly would be elected on September 11—a date he eventually kept. And on July 13, he brought some civilian ministers into his cabinet, after having appointed (on July 5) a "civilian-military council" of 60 civilian and 20 military members whose powers remained obscure, but whose sentiments became apparent when it voted a motion on August 31 advocating a "counteroffensive north of the 17th Parallel," e.g., an invasion of North Viet-Nam —an opinion repeatedly expressed also by Generals Thieu and Ky.

The Elections

The decision to hold elections for a constituent assembly met with a great deal of skepticism in Viet-Nam as well as abroad. The least critical defenders of American policies in Viet-Nam found that part of Viet-Nam's past problems lay in the fact that "Diem was responsible, prematurely [sic], and sincerely . . . for introducing the idea of democracy in his talks and constitutional endeavors."[9] Ambassador Henry Cabot Lodge warned that the forthcoming electoral contest was the first the young nation had experienced (though, in reality, ten other elections had taken place

[7] See, for example, U. S. Mission in Saigon, Joint U. S. Public Affairs Office, "A Note on the Vietnamese Sects," May, 1966.
[8] At the end of 1966, there were between 500 and 3000 Buddhists awaiting trial.
[9] Frank N. Trager, *Why Viet Nam?* (New York: Praeger, 1966), p. 157.

there since 1946); according to Washington reports, Lodge was somewhat wary of the whole idea. But here again, the outsiders had failed to take the full measure of the Saigon junta and *its* set of advisers.

On June 19, 1966, the first anniversary of the creation of the Ky-Thieu government, the junta promulgated an electoral decree whose ironclad provisions were designed to eliminate all neutralists, pro-Communists, or other possible opposition elements from the competing slates. In addition, Article 20 of the decree saw to it that even this heavily-screened assembly would be subject to a minority veto: if the government opposed a given article, the assembly had to be able to muster a two-thirds majority (78 votes out of 117) in order to overrule the government's veto. Another seemingly innocuous provision replaced the absentee ballot by a measure which permitted soldiers to vote *en masse* in the area in which they were stationed—and it was always easy to switch a 1700-man regiment into a doubtful electoral district, if necessary.

Irregularities occurred: "In Bien Hoa Province near Saigon," reported The Washington *Post* on September 4, 1966, ". . . there is evidence that one of the candidates is attempting to buy votes with money and, moreover, is being successful." In II Corps, General Vinh Loc, the commander and a prince of Viet-Nam's former royal family, "instructed local police, army officers and other functionaries to take opponents of the election into custody."[10] And since the Liberation Front in turn announced that it was engaging in a drive to keep people away from voting, the whole election simply turned from a vote on politically meaningful representatives to a numerical competition—whether the Saigon government or the Viet Cong could enforce its writ more effectively on more Vietnamese. As a Saigon-based diplomat later put it: "It wasn't a victory for democracy. It was surely a victory for government organization."[11]

It was indeed, as the official figures revealed. When the polls closed on September 11, a total of 4,274,812 voters were said to have passed through the polling booths—slightly over 80 per

[10] The Washington *Post*, September 11, 1966.
[11] *Ibid.*, September 13, 1966.

cent of the total electorate of 5,288,512 registered voters. The provincial election figures, which the American press failed to publish, were even more surprising: not one province—including the most heavily Communist-held areas of the mountain tribal zone or of the Plain of Reeds or of Camau Peninsula—showed attendance records of less than 72 per cent. Formerly rebellious Hué came in with 87 per cent and Danang with 81 per cent, while Saigon, with its many foreign journalists watching the polls, showed only 74 per cent of those eligible voting.[12]

What is surprising, of course, is that none of the major American news media went through the simple arithmetic which would have shown the apparent inconsistency of these figures. According to the *Komer Report* of September 13, 1966, "it is estimated that secure population had increased to almost 8,300,000, or over 55 per cent of the population." In Viet-Nam, as in most underdeveloped countries, it can be safely accepted that one-half of the population is below 18 years old. That would, on the basis of the Komer figures, leave about 4.15 million Vietnamese of voting age in government-controlled areas. If 80 per cent of those 4.15 million actually *did* vote, this would have given a total voting figure of 3.32 million—not 4.2 million.

To be sure, the Diem regime, in an election so badly faked (it took place on September 27, 1963, in the midst of the Buddhist crisis) that most newspapers failed even to mention it, managed to obtain a voting record of 92 per cent of 6.8 million voters.[13] Only in that sense can it be understood why *The New Yorker*'s able Viet-Nam reporter, Robert Shaplen, while admitting that "a certain amount of exaggeration . . . is widely suspected," claimed that the 1966 election "was still without a doubt the fairest election ever held in South Viet-Nam."[14]

It was considered a good omen that only 20 of the 117 members were from the military (there had been widespread fears of a

[12] Radio Saigon, September 11, 1966, 1200 GMT (midnight, Saigon time). The incredible rapidity with which the votes were collated and computed in a wartorn country is worthy of note.

[13] U. S. Operations Mission, Saigon, *Public Administration Bulletin*, No. 8, October 14, 1963.

[14] "Letter from Saigon," *The New Yorker*, October 1, 1966, p. 191.

"khaki [uniform] party" within the assembly), but the assembly suffers from one unsurmountable flaw: in a country in which regional and even village allegiances are paramount, all but 44 of the 117 members lived originally *north of the 17th parallel!*[15] How this escaped the American experts who were heavily involved in the preparation of the elections—assuming that they thought this to be important—is incomprehensible. And the results were evident when the Ky regime once more drew heavily on its "credit" of American endorsement after the October, 1966, Manila conference by shedding its most responsible "southern" ministers (notably Au Truong Thanh, an excellent economist) and by planning, late in November, the removal of two of the army corps commanders.

At the same time, the assembly, which had let three (of its six) constitution-writing months go by in futile wrangling, decided to take on the junta over Article 20. But everyone knew that this was merely a procedural fight: what was at stake was whether or not the assembly, at present the only holder of a semblance of legitimacy in Saigon, would gain power commensurate with its legitimacy, or would be a democratic adornment for an unreformed military regime. It should perhaps be remembered that, for example, in Laos in 1959, and in Indonesia in 1965, two completely handpicked legislatures turned against their creators and became, for a time, largely free agents. This may well still happen in Saigon—in which case all eventualities—including for the first time meaningful political contacts between the Vietnamese adversaries on the ground—may become possible.

Pacification

If the high-sounding principles of the Honolulu Declaration of February 8, 1966, and of the Manila Communique and Declaration of October 25, 1966, were to be the gauge of accomplishment in the field of socio-economic development in Viet-Nam, then the past year will have proven a regrettable failure.

[15] *Ibid.*, p. 193. Shaplen contradicts himself, since he asserts on page 191 that the "majority of those elected are natives of the provinces in which they ran" while two pages further he gives these figures.

According to the Manila Communique, "the conference was told of the success of the Government of Viet-Nam in controlling the inflation" of the past year. Indeed, the runaway inflation of last year, with its 200 per cent price rises, was checked for a time thanks to a devaluation overdue by at least five years. This was "paid" for in part (and vitiated, of course) by the establishment, with American gold, of a free gold market in Saigon in the midst of a war, a luxury which even the United States, with its incredible prosperity, has not been able to afford since 1933. In any case, by the time of the Manila conference, there had been two inflationary spurts of about 15 per cent each in two weeks in September and October. As a perceptive observer was to note,

> the inflation mounts and the economy pulls away from its old moorings on the uneven tide of new money. . . . The planners put their faith in pacification. [But] USAID still clings to its original brief for rural development as it teeters between its horror of overinvolvement and its fear of ineffectuality.[16]

One million refugees—mostly due to aerial and artillery bombardment, as former Assistant Secretary of State Roger Hilsman pointed out in congressional testimony—cluttered the coastal enclaves under South Viet-Nam's control and received a total of $11 million in cash aid during the 1966 fiscal year, or an incredibly low $11 per person yearly. In fact, it was the hapless refugees who accounted for the whole 5 per cent of the population said to have come under government control since last year, in addition to the 50 per cent who already had been under South Viet-Nam's control.

"Revolutionary development" (R.D.), as the pacification program is now officially called—it is also referred to as the "other war" in some of the press releases—came into its own in 1966, when 76 59-man R.D. teams were graduated from the cadre school at Vung Tau in May, to be followed by another 38 teams at year's end. The R.D. teams include specialists in all the skills required in a rural environment; they are also trained in the

16 Frances Fitzgerald, "The Tragedy of Saigon," *Atlantic Monthly*, December, 1966.

157

use of weapons and in psychological warfare and police interrogations. At the core of their activities is a so-called "census grievance" program in the course of which all the inhabitants of every community are to be periodically interrogated in isolation, so that they may feel free to air their "grievances," including what they think of their neighbors' political views. Other programs contemplated have an incredible resemblance to George Orwell's futuristic novel *1984,* since they include the possibility of installing in Saigon a central memory bank which will have on file all the information elements which can be gathered about every Vietnamese citizen, including even his "voice print."

A thorough perusal of the *Komer Report,* which is by far the most complete public record of R.D. accomplishments during the first half of 1966, shows that R.D. has been more successful in the repressive aspects of police work than in physical improvement for the Vietnamese—particularly those of the rural areas. Over a quarter-million tons of fertilizer were distributed to 700,000 farmers for almost 2 million acres (which works out to 0.3 tons per farmer); hog production is said to have grown from 1.7 million in 1963 to 3 million in 1965 (which leaves without explanation the chronic meat shortages and high meat prices in the cities); and off-shore fishing more than doubled, from 165,000 tons in 1959 to around 400,000 tons in fiscal 1966 (the above observations on availability and prices prevail here also). The number of hamlet school teachers reached only 3,800 at the beginning of 1966—one for every four hamlets. An additional 3,400 were trained by September. A brief period of high optimism, encouraged by the President himself in the late summer, was followed by far more pessimistic estimates by Secretary of Defense Robert McNamara in October, and by somewhat of an innovation in South Viet-Nam: reports emanating from Vietnamese authorities which were far more pessimistic than those of their American advisers. General Ky suddenly asserted that pacification was lagging behind; and on October 20, 1966, on the eve of the Manila conference, it was Major General Nguyen Duc Thang, the able "super-minister" (he controls several related departments) for revolutionary development, who bluntly stated that "although rural institutions go by the name of 'New Life' hamlets, the truth of the matter is that they have not provided a new life for the peoples in the hamlets."[17]

Indeed, a glance at a map of "returnees" (*Chieu-Hoi*) from the Communist side, amply bears out this view. The *only* areas in Viet-Nam where there have been significant increases in "returnees" are in the areas where American-Korean multidivision operations have literally smothered the opposition: of the total of 9728 returnees for the first six months of 1966, a full third (3394) returned to the South Vietnamese side in the two coastal provinces of Binh Dinh and Phu Yen [see map], which had been the object of vast search-and-destroy operations and were under tight military control. The conclusion which seems to have been drawn from this by the military is that "pacification" and ideological competition with the Viet Cong have failed and should yield to straightforward saturation with troops, regardless of the short-range costs to Viet-Nam or to the United States (the latter indirectly in the form of casualties or budgetary burdens). As Ward Just, the careful observer for The Washington *Post* in Viet-Nam, wrote recently:

> . . . there is now increased certainty that the war effort, despite public homage to "the other war" and the "hearts and minds of the people," is more thoroughly military than ever—and more thoroughly American.

The Adversary Stands Fast

On March 8, 1966, columnist Joseph Alsop averred that "Hanoi's current reinforcement of the [Viet Cong] is . . . clearly a one-shot proposition—a last high rise in the game." That turned out to be an incorrect view of the situation, but it was shared by many top-level advisers in Washington. By July, the inflow of North Vietnamese regulars and the internal recruitment of Viet Cong draftees had reached unprecedented heights.

But the increased bombing in North Viet-Nam also made the burden heavier to bear in Hanoi. Economically, the five-year plan terminated in 1965 was not followed by a new five-year plan, but simply by a two-year emergency program designed to switch

---

[17] The New York *Times*, October 20, 1966.

from large-scale industries relying on another efficient large plant for materials and supplies, to highly-dispersed small industrial units capable of carrying on production with the help of local products and primarily for the satisfaction of local needs—just as they had done in the jungle during the eight-year war against the French. The big cities—some of them, contrary to American affirmations, had been badly hit, notably Nam-Dinh, Vinh, and Thanh-Hoa—were rapidly being drained of their excess civilian population. By late 1966, Hanoi had 200,000 inhabitants, out of an original population of almost 800,000.

On July 17, after the bombing raids on the oil storage areas of Haiphong and Hanoi, North Viet-Nam began to call up its trained reserves, and President Ho Chi Minh warned his people that the "war may last another 5, 10, 20 years or longer. Hanoi, Haiphong and other cities and enterprises may be destroyed, but the Vietnamese people will not be intimidated."

Nevertheless, the impact of the American air offensive began to make itself felt in the cities. By late September, 1966, Jean Raffaeli, the surprisingly free[18] reporter of *Agence France-Presse* in Hanoi until late in the year, observed food lines in Hanoi and reported that announced food rations were in part not available. The progressive destruction of all surface communications by bombing brought about the influx of 50,000 Chinese railway and road construction personnel and, probably, some Chinese flak** batteries for the protection of the communication lines they are rebuilding.[19]

But the real strategic change which occurred in North Viet-Nam during the past year, and which reestablished stability at a higher level of escalation, was the massive arrival of Soviet military aid, particularly in the form of antiaircraft artillery and the sophisticated guidance systems necessary to make it highly effective. North Vietnamese flak, as the French and American pilots who flew at

[18] In an interview while on vacation in Paris, Raffaeli stated that North Viet-Nam observed a strict *internal* censorship but did not tamper with his outgoing press reports.

** *Flak,* a German abbreviation for *Fliegerabwehrkanone* (antiaircraft gun), has become a standard international expression for that type of ordnance.

[19] The Washington *Post*, November 13, 1966.

160

Dien Bien Phu can attest,[20] was excellent even then. By 1966, it was, in the words of General John P. McConnell, the United States Air Force's chief-of-staff (in re the Hanoi area), "the greatest concentration of antiaircraft weapons that has ever been known in the history of defense of any town or any area in the world."[21]

But that military point, while important, was not crucial. What makes it so is the fact that it brings closer to reality the possibility of an *American-Russian confrontation at a level of danger* (since Russian flak already is killing American pilots, and American flak interdiction surely kills Russian guidance, gun or missile crews working alongside with the North Vietnamese) *perhaps exceeding that of the 1962 Cuban confrontation.* Such side-effect agreements as the Russian-American accord to fly tourists from New York to Moscow, and vice-versa, have about as much political influence as the German-Russian economic accords of 1939–1941 (they were scrupulously carried out to the last day) on the outbreak of the German-Russian war. On October 17, 1966, the Warsaw Pact members, meeting in Moscow, promised North Viet-Nam $1 billion in nonrefundable aid,[22] and on October 25, using a long-standing American formulation on the very day of the Manila conference, North Vietnamese Premier Pham Van Dong vowed that there would be no sell-out peace in Viet-Nam: "Never Munich again, in whatever form."

Conclusion

There is, then, a dangerous possibility—unless a real step forward is taken by the United States away from sterile and ambiguous statements immediately contradicted by military action on the ground[23]—that the next level of the Vietnamese War will involve the nuclear superpowers by sheer accident, if not by design. It

[20] See the author's *Hell in a Very Small Place: The Siege of Dien Bien Phu* (New York and Philadelphia: Lippincott, 1967).

[21] Sam Butz, "Our Pilots Call Hanoi 'Dodge City.'" *The New York Times Magazine,* October 16, 1966. Butz is the technical editor of *U. S. Air Force & Digest.*

[22] The New York *Times,* October 28, 1966.

[23] For an interesting study of past U.S. escalation moves and their coincidence with U.S. peace offers, see Franz Schurmann, *et al., The Politics of Escalation in Vietnam* (New York: Fawcett, 1966).

is particularly futile to count eternally on the Sino-Soviet dispute as a deterrent to Russian escalation in Southeast Asia: Mao's successors may see China's comparative isolation more clearly; the technocrats now in charge in Moscow may find themselves supplanted by air marshals perfectly willing to bomb *South* Viet-Nam "back into the stone age." And, after all, Soviet displeasure does not necessarily have to express itself at its weakest point, in Asia. Berlin or the Elbe may prove strategically far more convenient.

On the American side, also, there are considerable pressures to the effect that it is militarily and morally (in terms of the morale of the pilots and their families) unfeasible to accept indefinitely very high aircraft and pilot losses while leaving Russian ships free to deliver flak guns and SAM (surface-to-air) missiles to the port of Haiphong, or to leave unscathed the transshipment points of light materiel along the Chinese border. Yet any departure from such policies is likely to re-create overnight the deadly gambit of the worst day of the 1962 Cuban confrontation—the day before Soviet Premier Nikita Khrushchev, in Secretary of State Dean Rusk's words, "blinked."

In both Viet-Nams, then, 1966 has brought about a certain amount of totally artificial and highly ephemeral "stability"—but it was bought dearly in terms of human and material destruction for all of Viet-Nam, and American casualties and expense. It was also paid for by an all-around escalation of the tempo of the war and the range of its participants. And that in itself augurs ill for the future chances of a negotiated settlement.

Viet-Nam's
Twelve Elections

‿⟨✕✕⟩‿

[The Vietnamese] "never had elections on a national basis and a national question. It's never happened in their whole history."—AM-
BASSADOR HENRY CABOT LODGE, *Saigon, April 22, 1966*

SOMETHING LIKE a magic curse attaches to the use of elections
in settling Vietnamese problems. All along, both sides have paid
homage to the sacred principle of the free exercise of popular
will, only to corrupt it. And contrary to Ambassador Lodge, the
Vietnamese do *not* lack experience in elections. Quite to the contrary: A good case could be made for the assertion that the
Vietnamese have been *overexposed* to phony elections to such a
degree that they are terribly sensitive to the stage-managing which
is again likely to be going on in the name of insuring that only
the "good guys" get elected.

Under the French colonial administration, the Mekong lowland
areas of South Viet-Nam to the edge of the southern mountain
plateau formed the colony of Cochin-China, which voted for representatives in the French parliament. The colonial electoral process
was then about as badly twisted as in the American Deep South
before the 1965 Civil Rights Act, with the result that only about

5000 native Vietnamese participated in the election of a senator and a deputy. At the local level, however, the Vietnamese soon found out that a strong voice in the Saigon city council was an extremely effective way of getting a public hearing for the disfranchised colonials.

Officials in Saigon would do well to read again the best American account of that stormy period, written by Milton I. Sacks in Frank Trager's *Communism in Southeast Asia*. To the amazement of the colonial administration, Saigon left-wing elements as well as bourgeois nationalists coalesced in 1933 to put up an eight-man slate running as *Liste Ouvrière* (Workers Slate). For the first time, the Vietnamese "Uncle Toms" on the city council were faced with concrete democratic demands, from the right to vote and to strike, to lighter taxes and better housing. Two of the slate's members were elected by the lower middle-class voters who came out *en masse* for the first time. One of them, 30 years later, would be North Viet-Nam's minister of labor. By the time the next municipal elections came around in 1935, the left coalition (one of the few in the world at the time where Trotskyists and Stalinists would still cooperate with each other and with the Nationalists), gained a little further ground. Four of its members were seated.

Cochin-China's last pre-World War II elections for the colonial council—the assembly which voted the budget for the whole colony and which, in the guise of discussing budgetary matters, could handily embarrass many a colonial governor—were held on April 30, 1939. There Trotskyists were elected to it with 80 per cent majorities over French-supported candidates or competing Stalinists. Never again would Saigon hear such widely conflicting opinions confront each other in public debate, but many South Vietnamese are old enough to remember.

The destruction of the French colonial regime by the Japanese brought with it the creation of Ho Chi Minh's "Democratic Republic of Viet-Nam" in September, 1945. Within a year, Ho's regime organized elections for a legislative assembly whose first job would be to write a constitution. The elections, which took place in January, 1946 throughout the whole country, from North to South and clandestinely even in those areas where returned French garrisons forbade them, were greeted with genuine enthusiasm. Of course, they were slanted in favor of the ruling Viet-Minh alliance, but two hard facts must be remembered: in the North they took place in the presence of Chinese Nationalist occupation troops, and in the South in the presence of British and French garrisons. An American writer who observed Vietnamese affairs very closely at the time, Dr. Ellen J. Hammer, correctly observed that even by "the strictest of Western standards, a few more conservatives might have been chosen," but that the overall results would still have heavily favored Ho. And a highly-respected French observer who then was a young officer right on the spot, Philippe Devillers, noted later that, considering the times, the 1946 elections clearly reflected the realities of Viet-Nam. The 1946 Vietnamese elections were "on a national basis and a national question."

But it was again the turn of the French to default on their promises. A preliminary accord, signed between France and Viet-Nam on March 6, 1946, provided for an eventual settlement of the reattachment of Cochin-China to Viet-Nam by mutual negotiations; and an attempt by the runaway colonials to set up an "Autonomous Cochin-China Republic" contributed much to the outbreak of the Indochina War. When the French finally recognized the inevitable and decided to grant Cochin-China the right of free choice—they made the decision three years later, and in favor of the unpopular Bao-Dai regime—by the reelected Territorial Assembly of Cochin-China voted, on April 23, 1949, in the midst of the Indochina War, to join a unified Viet-Nam! The vote: 55 for reunification, 6 against, and 2 abstentions. On May 21, 1949, the French National Assembly in turn transferred the colony to the State of Viet-Nam. Again, Vietnamese (and South Vietnamese at that) had made a key political choice at the ballot box—and it again had been for reunification.

In 1953, a new attempt was made to elect, in the non-Viet-Minh zones, a first tier of municipal councils and village councils, to be topped off by elected provincial councils which, in turn, would elect a representative assembly. The French knew that the elections would go against them, but finally felt that an anti-French but palpably honest election would help their cause more than yet another phony operation. However, political rivalries among the non-Communist Vietnamese finally had the same result. In the North Vietnamese Red River Delta, the right-wing governor's *Dai-Viet* (Great Viet-Nam) Party managed to have only 687 out of 5861 villages declared as "secure" enough for voting, which immediately raised a storm of protest and resulted in a revision of the village lists. The same problem is likely to arise in any future election in South Viet-Nam. The elections nonetheless took place, were predictably anti-French and in perennially radical-minded Saigon (doesn't *anybody* realize by now that Saigon is radical-minded?) the Taxi Drivers Union got a Trotskyist elected to the city council. The provincial council elections took place also and brought forth some strong regional leaders: Catholic bishops from the North, Cao-Dai Buddhist leaders from the South, etc.

And in October, 1953, Bao-Dai's regime, French-dominated though it was, had to face up to yet another crucial decision: a treaty with France which would seal Viet-Nam's membership in the French commonwealth structure. Bao-Dai convened a congress in Saigon of Vietnamese politicians and spiritual leaders as a substitute legislature. The congress included open neutralists who advocated an end to the fighting and United Nations supervision of national elections. The chief advocates of that line then were not the Buddhists, but the left-wing Catholic groups around Ngo Dinh Nhu. Predictably enough, the congress, on October 16, 1953, voted against Vietnamese membership in the French Union. Again, Vietnamese had made an important political choice in the midst of a war, and one that went against the desires of their own government and the expectations of its major foreign ally, France.

With the end of the fighting at Geneva in July, 1954, two separate Vietnamese states emerged with their own political institutions. In North Viet-Nam, Ho's republic now became a full-fledged "people's democracy." The 1946 parliament had, over the war years, shrunk from over 400 members to about 220. It had met only once during the Indochina War—in December, 1953—to approve the new land-reform program, but its "standing committee," like the Supreme Soviet, continued the appearance of legislative control. The legislative elections in the North, held in 1960 and 1965, returned predictably 99 per cent Communist legislatures, but here again, total silence has not yet set in, at least in such technical fields as budgeting and the allocation of resources. And in Hanoi, a few stubborn Socialists and Democratic Party members keep on voting their own ticket and electing one or two members to the Hanoi parliament.

A Rubber-Stamp Legislature

In the South, the Ngo Dinh Diem regime also tried its hand at elections. On October 23, 1955, a plebiscite dethroned ex-emperor Bao-Dai and made South Viet-Nam a republic with Diem its first president. Donald Lancaster, then a British Embassy official in Saigon, stated later in his excellent *The Emancipation of French Indochina* that the elections were run with "cynical disregard for decency and democratic principles"; and *Life,* in an otherwise wholly laudatory article on Diem, remarked innocently on May 13, 1957 that Diem's American advisers had told him that a 60 per cent "success" would have been quite sufficient, "but Diem insisted on 98 per cent." In fact, in Saigon Diem got 605,025 votes for a total of 450,000 registered voters. The South Vietnamese legislature elected in March, 1956, was, of course, as much a rubber stamp as its North Vietnamese counterpart. By 1959, the regime shed all its pretenses: it had dissolved elected village government in 1956 (thus exposing the appointed unpopular village chiefs to immediate guerrilla reprisals) and even Catholic candidates running without the regime's approval were the object of hounding and harassment. When one lone American-trained loyal opposition candidate was finally elected in spite of the fact that 5000 government troops were trucked into his district to vote, he was finally barred from taking his seat on charges of vote fraud.

But again the Vietnamese showed that they had understood the election mechanism better than they had been given credit for. In 1961, Diem again ran for the presidency in the face of token opposition by two put-up candidates, one of whom was a faith-healer and the other a business associate of Diem's brother. By his own reckoning, Diem lost *one million* votes since 1955 (although Viet-Nam had gained two million people in the meantime); and in Saigon, where the foreign press watched some of the polls, he got 354,000 votes out of a total of 732,000, or 48 per cent of the vote.

167

As the whole dynastic house of cards was collapsing under the impact of the awakened Buddhist masses, the Diem regime in October, 1963 once more went to the polls to "elect" a legislature. With one-half of South Viet-Nam under guerrilla control, the regime simply invented election statistics: 6.8-million voters allegedly registered for voting and 92 per cent allegedly voted. The 123 "elected" legislators were a perfect cross-cut of the oligarchy which has never ceased to run things in South Viet-Nam: 31 "civil servants on leave," 19 lawyers, 17 teachers and professors, 15 landowners, 14 "businessmen and farmers" (!), 8 doctors, etc. There was not one factory worker, rubber plantation tapper, Buddhist leader or labor union official in the lot. The Diem regime misunderstood its people to the last.

The one thus far civilian-dominated regime since the November, 1963 coup promulgated a Provisional Charter which provided for a measure of civil rights, but whose Article 5 stated that "freedom of speech may not be abused . . . to make propaganda for Communism and neutralism." And that wasn't idle talk: four respectable non-Communist Vietnamese who had spoken of a neutralist Vietnamese solution in terms which President Johnson would not have disavowed, found themselves expelled across the 17th Parallel to North Viet-Nam, after several worse fates had been initially contemplated for them. Yet, on May 30, 1965, municipal elections again were held throughout South Viet-Nam. Of 9-million voters termed "eligible," 4.5 million actually were said to have registered for voting, and of those, 73 per cent voted. Liberation Front interference was minimal, but the effect of the war was clearly visible by the fact that there were, for example in the IIIrd Army Corps area, which surrounds Saigon, only 144 candidates for 87 posts, i.e., many posts went uncontested. Many of the local and provincial councils were never installed as the new military regime of Generals Thieu and Ky, which came to power on June 12, 1965, began a new round of administrative changes, abolished the Provisional Charter of 1964 to replace it with a brief "Convention" on June 19, which does not even mention rights of citizens; and set about ruling the country without benefit of popular advice. The illusion that this could continue *ad infinitum* without challenge (and it was an illusion which the South Vietnamese military

168

were not alone in holding) was rudely shattered somewhere between Honolulu and Danang, a few weeks ago. And once more—for the twelfth time, by actual count—the poor, war-weary, harassed South Vietnamese people are being asked to settle their own fate via the ballot box. Providing, of course, that they vote exactly as they are expected to.

The Real Issue

But there, precisely, lies the problem. The South Vietnamese no longer even know *what* is expected of them; or, rather, *who* expects what from them. If they were to believe voices heard in Washington, nothing would please anyone more than if the good South Vietnamese would vote themselves a government which would ask for an end to the war; call for direct talks with the Viet Cong; and request a gradual departure of American troops to be replaced (optimally) with the Southeast Asian equivalent of an Inter-American Peace Force; or (minimally) would at least keep the "Yankee Go Home!" signs off the walls until the last GI has reembarked.

That program might sound terribly tempting to Americans—and not only of the "dove" variety—but it happens to be against the law in Viet-Nam. For there is Decree Law No. 004/65 of May 17, 1965, on the books, which makes a crime, punishable by jail from one to five years (more in some specific cases) of ". . . All moves which weaken the national anti-Communist effort and are harmful to the anti-Communist struggle of the people and the armed forces. All plots and actions under the false name of peace and neutrality. . . ."

By that definition, the State Department's 14-Point program of January, 1966 would fall within the definition of such a "plot." And what the fate of a "peace and neutrality" candidate would be under such circumstances is hardly open to question. Yet, there is no evidence thus far that it is being clearly understood that this election, like the democratic system in the American Deep South, will entirely hinge on the *electoral process*. For it is the latter which will control whether the *real* issue—the question of war and peace in Viet-Nam—will be something on which the South

169

Vietnamese will at long last be able to express themselves, or not.

Let there be absolutely no mistake on this. The great definitions of who can vote; what issues can actually be discussed in the electoral campaign; which parties can or cannot run; whether the competing candidates will or will not get radio time on the entirely government-controlled broadcasting system; whether or not they will obtain travel space on government aircraft (for the woefully inadequate "Air Viet-Nam" is booked months ahead and in most places one can no longer engage in surface travel)— all these very simple nuts-and-bolts requirements of the basic democratic process must be present in Viet-Nam if the promised election of a constitutional convention is going to be more than yet another sham foisted on a war-weary people and an uninformed and unsuspecting foreign audience.

And those optimists who already see peace-via-the-ballot-box around the corner in South Viet-Nam, along with an honorable disengagement for the United States, would do well to remember that the contemplated elections would (or could) be limited to the election of a *constitution-writing* body. The regime then in existence could well deny that body legislative powers, let alone an "advise-and-consent" function in the field of foreign policy. In subsequent elections, a real legislature would have to emerge which, in turn, would form the new government. That process takes time and tranquillity under the best of circumstances. In South Viet-Nam, both items are excessively scarce. It would be a miracle if it took less than a year to run its course if everyone were hell-bent to make it work. Yet last week General Ky already had warned that the August 15 election deadline would have to be pushed back to October. Or later, perhaps. Preferably after victory. In a way, perhaps General Ky is logical. What is the point of going through this whole elaborate ceremonial as long as the problem of what to do with the Liberation Front—the Viet Cong—has not been solved? The Pentagon itself estimates the adversary at 80 per cent *South* Vietnamese. The VC may simply ignore the whole thing, as they have done in the past, and go on fighting while we breathlessly admire the South Vietnamese as they go for the twelfth time through an election process which allegedly "never happened in their whole history."

And while we engage in yet another round of self-congratulations on how smoothly the Vietnamese learned the rudiments of Western electioneering which they allegedly had never seen before (who advised them on the 1955–1965 elections?), the grim little people in the thick jungles of "Zone C" and their mentors in Hanoi may well be in the process of preparing South Viet-Nam's twelfth election—one which will no longer be ours to inspire or to guide, and which will foreclose the future of all of Viet-Nam for a long time.

Viet-Nam
in the Balance

∽✕✕∾

IT MAY WELL BE the opinion of future historians that the small but fierce engagements which in late 1965 pitted newly-arrived American troops against the *Chu-Luc* (Main Force) units of the Viet Cong and of North Viet-Nam were the First Battle of the Marne of the Vietnamese War. The Battle of the Marne in September 1914 halted the seemingly irresistible onslaught of the Kaiser and thus foreclosed the possibility of an immediate end of the war through a collapse of the French; but the Great War, with its immense human and material losses, still ground on for four years and the enemy would often again come close to victory. The same happened in World War II before Moscow in the winter of 1941, or at Guadalcanal a few months later: no "turning point" as yet, but a halt to the runaway disaster.

In South Viet-Nam, after being stopped at Chu-Lai, Plei-Mé and the Ia-Drang, the Communist regulars lost enough of their momentum for the time being not to be able to bring about the military and political collapse of the Saigon government late in 1965—a situation which would have altogether closed out the American "option" of the conflict. But just as at the Marne 52

172

years ago, or before Moscow a quarter-century ago, nothing had been decided as yet. Years—perhaps a decade—of hard fighting could still be ahead. And the political collapse of the government in Saigon is still a distinct possibility. It is, however, important to assess in detail the military and political elements on which this precarious balance rests and what *real* possibilities for maneuver (as against wishful thinking on one side or party rhetoric on the other) exist at present in the Viet-Nam situation.

II

On the American and South Vietnamese side, two main events dominated the scene between the first deployment of major American combat units in September of 1965 and the Saigon government's attempt at providing itself with the beginnings of a representative base in September 1966: the government of Air Vice Marshal Nguyen Cao Ky, by surviving for more than one year, provided planners both in Saigon and Washington with a political "peg" on which to hang some of the reform programs deemed essential to any counterinsurgency effort worthy of the name; and also the increasing effort by the United States to shift the whole main burden of the war as far north as possible. The latter was being achieved by committing the bulk of the American forces to the Central Vietnamese mountain and coastal areas under the jurisdiction of the South Vietnamese II Corps, and by "raising," in the words of President Johnson, "the price of aggression" which North Viet-Nam would have to pay for her participation in the war. What this meant became clear on June 29, 1966, when American bombers attacked oil storage depots within the city limits of Hanoi and Haiphong and unleashed an air offensive outstripping in intensity most of the bombing operations of World War II.[1]

The decisions which led to this situation were based on the clear realization in Washington that, earlier optimistic predictions to the contrary notwithstanding, the South Vietnamese were in the process of being defeated in an operation which was a carbon

[1] According to Secretary of Defense McNamara, the 1966 "bombing plan" for Viet-Nam involves an expenditure of 638,000 tons of aerial munitions. In comparison, the whole Pacific theater expended 600,000 tons throughout all of World War II.

copy *not* of the French defeat of 1954 but of the Chinese Nationalist defeat on the mainland in 1948–49. And exactly as in the case of China, it was American prestige which now was at stake. Opposite views were strong even within the American military, however, where advisory support for friendly local ground troops was considered with favor over the commitment of large American ground forces. As late as August 1964, that viewpoint was clearly expounded as official policy in a pamphlet jointly issued by the State and Defense Departments, which explained the Viet-Nam problem in question-and-answer form. The answer to the then hypothetical question as to why no American combat units were committed to Viet-Nam reads in full as follows:

> The military problem facing the armed forces of South Viet Nam at this time is not primarily one of manpower. Basically it is a problem of acquiring training, equipment, skills, and organization suited to combating the type of aggression that menaces their country. Our assistance is designed to supply these requirements.
> The Viet Cong use terrorism and armed attack as well as propaganda. The Government forces must respond decisively on all appropriate levels, tasks that can best be handled by Vietnamese. U.S. combat units would face several obvious disadvantages in a guerrilla war situation of this type in which knowledge of terrain, language, and local customs is especially important. In addition, their introduction would provide ammunition for Communist propaganda which falsely proclaims that the United States is conducting a "white man's war" against Asians.[2]

That perceptive statement of the basic liabilities involved in using massive numbers of white troops is beyond doubt as true today as it was in 1964. One can, therefore, only guess at the sudden deterioration inside South Viet-Nam—or the suddenness with which the worsening situation was finally perceived in Washington—which compelled the Administration to do in 1965 what it felt was unwise only six months earlier. But the decision was made to commit large American forces to the land battle as being the lesser of the two evils: 300,000 were in Viet-Nam by September 1966, and another 100,000 could be there by the end of the current year.

[2] Department of State Publication 7724 (Dept. of Defense, Gen.-8), *Viet Nam: The Struggle for Freedom.* Washington: Government Printing Office, 1964, p. 21.

The immediate net result of that American influx was that the brunt of the major encounters was now to be borne by the American troops instead of the South Vietnamese, just as on the other side infiltrated regular units of the People's Army of Viet-Nam (P.A.V.N.) now assumed the larger part in engagements in the II Corps area and the northern section of III Corps. The argument that South Vietnamese forces still suffered heavy casualties —they suffered 11,000 dead and 21,600 wounded in 1965—must be modified to include the fact that the bulk of the South Vietnamese Army (A.R.V.N.) casualties are suffered passively, i.e. by units garrisoned in forts or ambushed on roads rather than engaged in offensive operations.[3] A 1965 net desertion rate of about 93,000 out of about 600,000 troops, which by all accounts further increased during the first half of 1966, also indicated that the A.R.V.N. has yet to become a stabilized force, let alone a diplomatically stabilizing factor in the way the South Korean Army became during the negotiations of 1952–53. How much indeed the war had become "American" is also shown by the relatively high casualties suffered by the U.S. combat forces in the field: out of a total of 240,000 troops in Viet-Nam in the spring of 1966, about 50,000 at most were actual combat troops. Yet they had suffered, in less than one year, the bulk of America's 4,000 dead and 21,000 wounded. Losses of combat leaders were even more severe, as shown by statistics covering 1965 only, when it turned out that the officer death rate was 23 per cent, as against 5 per cent for U. S. Forces during the Korean and Second World Wars,[4] while the French officer death rate during the Indochina War amounted to about 3 per cent.

On the civilian side, a thorough perusal of the testimony given by senior Administration officials before various Congressional committees shows that, like Abbé Sieyès during the French Revolution, the Saigon government had survived but had done little else besides. To be sure, some particularly optimistic observers already felt a

[3] According to the *Weekly Summaries* prepared by the Department of Defense, the average number of A.R.V.N.-initiated battalion-size operations has slightly decreased over the past year while the number of Vietnamese under arms went from 493,000 to 640,000. At the same time, the number of U.S.-initiated battalion-size operations has trebled.
[4] The New York *Times,* January 19, 1966.

year ago, a bare three months after Ky's rise to power, that "there is genuine enthusiasm generated by the imaginative programme worked out by [the government's] civilian advisers," and that "a social, economic, and political revolution" was finally under way.[5] The hard statistics and observed facts paint a somewhat different picture. Economically, the country experienced a 130 per cent inflation in less than a year, which finally led to a strong devaluation of the South Vietnamese currency in an effort to keep prices from rising uncontrolledly. And while there are, as in the past, hopes of future improvement, they have as yet to materialize in Viet-Nam for anyone who is not in the war-economy circuit— that is, working for the big building contractors who construct runways and bases, or, for instance, serving as a barmaid. Land reform has never gotten off the ground; there have been at least four distinct reforms, all of which stalled, over the past decade or so. While the Diem regime expropriated a total 457,000 hectares (2.47 acres per hectare) and the French Government gave South Viet-Nam between 225,000 to 246,000 hectares of formerly privately French-owned land as early as 1958, only some 248,000 hectares have thus far been redistributed, according to a recent A.I.D. report,[6] i.e. the equivalent of the French-owned land. According to a recent American observer who was an adviser in Viet-Nam, much of the unredistributed land was kept under government control and "commonly put up for rent to the highest bidder."[7]

While it is obvious that the middle of a war is not the best place to start such reforms, it must be realized that in Viet-Nam the choice no longer exists, for the reforms are as essential to success as ammunition for the howitzers—in fact, more so, because the failures of land reform create an almost hopeless vicious circle. With only 25 per cent of the non-urban population under effective government control, a large mass of landless peasants stands to lose a great deal the day Saigon reestablishes control over the countryside and thus restores the old tenant-landlord relationship, as invariably happened in the past wherever government troops reoccupied a given area. (In fact, in some such areas the landlords

[5] P. J. Honey, "Viet Nam Argument," *Encounter,* November 1965, p. 69.
[6] *Congressional Record,* March 10, 1966, p. 5328.
[7] Stanley Andrews, "Red Tape and Broken Promises," *The Reporter,* May 5, 1966.

arrived in the supply trucks of the troops and some unit commanders could be persuaded to launch a clearing operation in an area where the returning landlords promised to share the proceeds with them.) Hence, the certitude of a genuinely "peasant-oriented" land reform, including a freeze on land holdings already distributed by the Viet Cong, would do more to change the allegiance of the peasantry than probably any other single counter-insurgency measure. And the much graver problem then arises as to whether the landlord-oriented leadership group in Saigon—regardless of whether it is made up of generals or medical doctors, as seems to be alternately the case—is *intellectually* capable of engineering that kind of revolution.

Finally, South Viet-Nam must face up to political problems which, even in the absence of the Viet Cong insurgency, would leave it in the precarious position of the Dominican Republic a year ago. To blame the French colonial legacy for all the present ills has become a sort of ritual to which every writer in this field pays automatic homage. It does not, unfortunately, explain why North Viet-Nam, similarly saddled with French colonial hold-overs, does not suffer from administrative disintegration; nor does it explain how twelve years of extensive public-administration training in South Viet-Nam—staffed and financed by America—has apparently made no dent in the problem. The reason is that South Viet-Nam's ills are of a more fundamental nature.

Regionalism in Viet-Nam is a fact of life which no amount of centralization can paper over. For some unfathomable reason, the decision was made in 1954 to replace what was on the whole a well-decentralized administrative system[8] by a truly French-patterned, highly centralized administrative structure. More and more power was heaped on the fragile shoulders of Saigon's central bureaucracy, while such "natural" units of government as the region or the district were either abolished or lost all effective power. The village, which had been the real cradle of a Jeffersonian type of representative government in the country (the French found a well-operating local election system and, like all colonial powers, left village life to its own devices), was deprived of

[8] *Cf.* the little-known but excellent study by Vu Quoc Thong, *"La décentralisation administrative au Viet-Nam."* Hanoi: Presses Universitaires, 1952.

its elected officials by Ngo Dinh Diem's fiat in June 1956 and for the first time felt the full brunt of central arbitrariness and maladministration without the relative compensations of a rapidly improving economic situation. On a broader plane, the Hoa-Hao and Cao-Dai sects were in a state of more or less overt anti-Saigon dissidence until Diem's murder in November 1963, and those two sects number about 3,000,000 people between them and live over a vast area north and west of Saigon. The mountain tribesmen of the vast plateau area which covers almost 65 per cent of South Viet-Nam were the object of political and economic oppression which American experts as early as 1957 considered tantamount to genocide. They formed an organization known as FULRO (*Front Unifié de la Lutte des Races Opprimées*) which, like "Black Nationalism" in the United States, has pathetic overtones of a curses-on-both-your-houses attitude, and which resulted in two major rebellions quelled in the nick of time by well-liked American advisers who found themselves in the strange position of being honest brokers between two "Vietnamese" ethnic groups.

But by far the most serious regional problem is that of Buddhism and Catholicism. The term "regionalism" is used advisedly, for in South Viet-Nam today Catholicism is largely associated with the North Vietnamese civilian refugees of that faith (almost 600,-000 out of a total of 850,000), while Buddhism, though practiced lackadaisically throughout Viet-Nam, finds its most fierce and tradition-bound adherents in the Central coastal area around the ancient imperial capital of Hué. People are rarely tolerant about their religion, and the Vietnamese possibly less tolerant than most. This, added to the fact that the Catholics, though only perhaps 11 per cent of the population, were in power under Diem for almost a decade and that the A.R.V.N.'s officers corps is over 50 per cent Catholic to this day, would be sufficient to create an explosive situation anywhere. In Viet-Nam, in the absence of a broadly accepted government, people of necessity must fall back on the *one* structure of society they can trust—their religion. It was a foregone conclusion, then, that the Buddhists would attempt to gain power, just as far smaller groups have previously done with great success.

The argument that perhaps the Buddhists are not "ready" to assume the reins of government is by-and-large irrelevant. After all, Buddhists as individuals—including Premier Ky, who is a North Vietnamese Buddhist—have been in positions of power all along. What is, however, true is that the Buddhist political organization in Saigon, grouped around the *Vien Hoa Dao* (Institute for the Implementation of the Dharma), has yet to find a political program which it can openly proclaim. That is meant in the literal sense of the term, for many of the Buddhists are known to be in favor of a negotiated solution to the war, but under presently-existing legislation any utterance to that effect is likely to earn its maker a prison term of up to five years. Not being able to stand openly on a platform of moderation or neutralism, the Buddhists are condemned to vague utterances about "social revolution," "true democracy" and other similarly noncommittal slogans. But that is not the kind of program likely to rally the war-weary Vietnamese 'round the flag for a supreme effort against the Viet Cong, or, for that matter, against Saigon. And perhaps the supreme refinement of the dilemma came last spring when the Central Vietnamese Buddhists were cornered by A.R.V.N. troops into abject surrender: at that time there were better than five North Vietnamese regular regiments in the I Corps area which, had the Buddhists and the mutinous 1st A.R.V.N. Division chosen to go over to their side, could have wreaked utter disaster in almost half of Viet-Nam, with incalculable consequences in Washington and Saigon, not to speak of the rest of the world. But the Buddhists chose the likelihood of political destruction and the detention of their key political and military leaders by Premier Ky as against the highly speculative possibilities of entering into an alliance with the National Liberation Front (N.L.F.), the political arm of what is commonly called the Viet Cong.

Yet the very extremism which the government of Premier Ky showed late in July 1966 when he suddenly resumed harping on a theme dear in 1964 to one of his predecessors, General Nguyen Khanh, *"Bac Tien!"* ("Let's March North!") may have a maturing influence not only on the Buddhist leaders but also on the moderate Catholics of Father Hoang Quynh and lead to an alliance between the two religious groups. This in turn could become a base of political power owing nothing either to an alien ideology or to the massive presence of foreign troops.

179

III

It is against this South Vietnamese backdrop of frustration and upheaval that the military effort which has been made over the past year now must be measured, and *not* simply against its own abstract yardsticks of increasing troops present, ammunition expended, enemy killed, "structures" destroyed, rice confiscated, weapons captured and weapons lost or acres of rice fields defoliated. Not that such indicators are wrong per se; but they are simply meaningless in terms of what is going on.

First of all, the war must be judged against its progress toward its initial objectives. If the objective was—as was contemplated in 1961—to "pacify" South Viet-Nam with the help of an eighteen-month counterinsurgency plan, then the operation already has failed. This is also true if Viet-Nam is judged against Secretary McNamara's target date, announced on October 2, 1963: "The major part of the United States military task [in Viet-Nam] can be completed by the end of 1965." If the next set of objectives was to nip the rising insurgency in South Viet-Nam merely with an increased American advisory effort and perhaps with the "antiseptic" help of American-manned airplanes and naval craft, that policy failed in 1964. The same can be said of such tactical measures as the bombing of North Viet-Nam. It first was explained as a retaliatory measure against a guerrilla attack on the American base at Pleiku, then as a measure designed to cut off the flow of North Vietnamese manpower and supplies to the insurgents, and, finally, as simply a political measure designed to bring the North Vietnamese to the conference table.[9] Since it was clearly admitted that the retaliatory aspect of the raids was at best a temporary rationale, only the two other criteria need to be judged. Secretary McNamara, in explaining the bombing of the storage depots near the former Hanoi and Haiphong "sanctuaries," stated that during the previous year of bombing Communist supply deliveries had increased by 150 per cent and troop infiltration by 120 per cent, and President Johnson, two days later at Omaha, stated that what hitherto had

[9] Secretary McNamara's press conference of June 29, 1966.

been jungle trails had in many places become fully motorable "boulevards."

Obviously, then, as with operations "Strangle" and "Choke" in Korea 15 years ago, air operations failed to effect decisive results in spite of a 1965 bomb tonnage (255,000 tons) far exceeding what had ever been used before on so small a target area. As for the political effectiveness of the air operations, the record is plain: more intransigence from Hanoi and a gradual increase in the Russian commitments to Hanoi, at least in the field of air defense.

All this could well delineate the conditions for a stalemate, were it not for the fact that, contrary to what happened in Korea, the American build-up in Viet-Nam is at the present moment open-ended. Neither budgetary nor manpower ceilings seem to have been arrived at and whatever limitations there are appear to be imposed more by the difficulties of finding suitable deployment areas and logistical support facilities than by a lack of will in Washington to provide massive reinforcements. Even so, man-power requirements are likely to become extensive this autumn: by late September, about 165,000 men now in Viet-Nam will have fulfilled their one-year tour; that, added to the 400,000-man strength considered desirable for the end of 1966, would mean that at least a quarter-million new troops must be moved to Southeast Asia fairly rapidly.

All this, of course, is perfectly feasible for the United States, and so are the many "search-and-destroy" and spoiling operations which are said to have prevented the Viet Cong from launching a "monsoon offensive." (Ironically enough, the North Vietnamese claim that the American "dry-season 'counteroffensive'" had like-wise met with failure.)[10] Enemy losses are heavy, and may well reach 60,000 dead this year; but the present infiltration rate may match this, and local recruitment inside South Viet-Nam still amounts to 3,500 men a month, while the total number of Viet Cong and P.A.V.N. forces rose over the past year from 110,000 men to 270,000. The present American pincer operations, with their net results of a few hundred enemy killed in return for a commit-ment of often more than 10,000 troops for ten days, are by and

[10] *Viet Nam Courier* (Hanoi), Nos. 60 and 61, May 26 and June 2, 1966.

large no more efficient than similarly large French operations were (the French using paratroop battalions where the United States uses helicopter-borne units). They are unlikely to achieve gains of strategic importance until a troop saturation ratio is attained which permits the permanent reoccupation of cleared areas in strengths which deter attack. Expert advocates of such tactics, notably Hanson W. Baldwin, feel that they can be the only logical conclusion of present policies and estimate that one million American troops would provide for an adequate saturation ratio. Interestingly enough, that view is likewise shared by the opposition. In an interview granted in January 1965 by the Chairman of the Liberation Front, Nguyen Huu Tho, he made the cogent point that "it is not bombs and artillery that win wars; it is infantry that can occupy territory."[11]

Let us then reconstruct the military-political landscape which the Communist planners in Hanoi or in the N.L.F.'s jungle headquarters might see before them. In spite of severe casualties, their troops and underground administrative structure have held on to much of what they held last year and, with minor tactical adjustments, they are still capable of attacking. Aerial bombardment, north as well as south, hurts but has yet to cut deeply into their supply and replacement system (they have Secretary McNamara's word for it). The American ground effort has foreclosed the chances of a headlong rush to victory, but is not yet of a size to make a Communist defeat certain. Saigon, for all the beautiful plans on paper, has yet to come through with effective reforms. And abroad, the dark outlines of more massive Soviet help (with a concomitant Russo-American worsening of relations) appear discernible.

If the Communist interpretation of the situation is *anywhere* near this estimate, as it is very likely to be, then it can be easily seen why both Hanoi and the N.L.F. would be highly reluctant to accept negotiations which offer them literally nothing but the complete and permanent dismantling of the whole South Vietnamese Communist apparatus in exchange for a minor share in an economic development plan which contemplates a total ex-

11 Wilfred Burchett, "Viet Nam: Inside Story of the Guerrilla War." New York: International Publishers, 1965, p. 240.

penditure equivalent to the cost to the United States of fifteen days of war in South Viet-Nam. Much depends, then, on whether Hanoi and the guerrillas in the south view the development of the war *exactly* in the same light, for the sacrifices they are expected to make at the conference table, as well as, for the time being, on the firing line, are of an entirely different nature.

IV

A major part of the whole Viet-Nam argument revolves around a clear identification of the character of the enemy—for it is that identification which pins the label of "aggressor" on North Viet-Nam (and thus justifies military action against it) or, conversely, makes the conflict largely a civil war, with the United States as the major foreign "interventionist."

A recent issue of *Foreign Affairs* presented an unusually well-argued and sophisticated case for the first view.[12] But precisely because it is so well argued, it unconsciously presents some of the arguments for the opposite viewpoint as well. And since it is almost impossible to discuss the possible rational outcomes of the Viet-Nam situation as long as the true character of the adversary is in doubt—it is this writer's own belief that it lies somewhere between the two extremes presented above—the nature of the Viet Cong must be explored further before it can be definitively dismissed as "faceless."

It can be conceded in advance that any Communist member of the National Liberation Front in South Viet-Nam is likewise a member of the *Lao Dong,* the Vietnamese Communist Party, and that North Viet-Nam, which had without a shred of doubt won the war against France in 1954, fully expected to gain control of South Viet-Nam as well either by the elections slated for July 1956 or at a later date. I am, however, inclined to doubt that Hanoi's decision to intervene in South Vietnamese affairs was prompted by any "increasing disparity between political life north and south." For it became obvious even to the blindest of optimists that, unfortunately, the political lives of both Viet-Nams, far from becoming "disparate," began to resemble each other as only two extremes can, with their

[12] George A. Carver, Jr., "The Faceless Viet Cong," *Foreign Affairs*, April 1966.

gradual falsification of representative processes and, finally, with their concentration camps and persecution of religious groups. The existence of a "Central Reunification Department" in Hanoi of which much is made is surely revelatory of something—until one becomes aware that West Germany, for example, has a Ministry for All-German Affairs to which, of course, East Germany and the Soviets ascribe equally sinister motives, even though it can be safely assumed that the *Ministerium für Gesamtdeutsche Fragen* is more innocuous than any Hanoi committee with the same purpose.

It is likewise very much open to question that the intervention of Hanoi was first evidenced by a terror campaign directed against small South Vietnamese officials. In actual fact, Diem began to become oppressive as early as January 1956, when a concentration camp ordinance (No. 6 of January 11, 1956) gave the regime almost unchecked power to deal with the opposition—and the non-Communist opposition, least inured to clandestine operations, was hit hardest. It took until May 1966 for a U. S. Government agency, the Public Affairs Office in Saigon, to state candidly what was a well-known fact all along—to wit, that some of the so-called "political-religious" sects provided the hard core of the early opposition:

. . . Ten of the eleven [Cao-Dai] sub-sects had opposed Diem, and their leadership fled to Cambodia or went into hiding. . . . The members of the other ten sects made up the bulk of the early NLF support, although the alliance was at all times an uneasy one . . .
. . . The [Hoa-Hao] sect in 1952 formed the Social Democratic Party as its political arm. It too challenged Diem, and its armies were smashed by ARVN in 1956. Like the Cao Dai, it was an early and major participant in the NLF, . . .
. . . The third of the esoteric sects of Viet Nam, the Binh Xuyen, which was also smashed by Diem, also worked with the NLF in its early days.[13]

The decision by Diem—probably his most pregnant in terms of its future consequences—to abolish elected village government in June 1956 (again before the July 1956 election deadline, at a time when the Communists were on their best behavior) did the rest. The hated appointees became a prime target for local resentment

[13] U. S. Mission in Viet-Nam, JUSPAO Planning Office, *A Note on the Vietnamese Sects,* May 1966, pp. 2–3.

and by March 1958 over 400 had been murdered by guerrillas who indeed, as Carver points out, "harped on local issues and avoided preaching Marxist doctrine." When it is remembered that there were enough "local issues" around to cause the South Vietnamese Army itself to try at least three times to murder Diem, it becomes understandable why South Viet-Nam appeared to Hanoi ripe for plucking. In other words, there can be no doubt but that Hanoi, or even South Vietnamese stay-behind Communist elements, took advantage of Saigon's glaring weaknesses after 1959. But the Communists can hardly be held responsible for the incredible stupidity of the Diem regime and the somewhat surprising blindness to its faults of its American advisers. And it is equally hard to deny that there was plenty of motivation *inside* South Viet-Nam, on the left as well as on the right, for a revolutionary explosion.

The next point which requires clarification is *not* whether the insurgency in South Viet-Nam is abetted, directed, and aided from North Viet-Nam (it is to a large extent), but whether such outside controls preclude the existence of *real* objectives which are specifically those of the insurgents rather than of their external sponsors. Here, the recent British revelations as to the truly enormous extent of the control of the French Resistance in France by the Special Operations Executive (S.O.E.)—the 1940–46 British equivalent of the Central Intelligence Agency—shows what is meant. According to the now-published official history of S.O.E. in France, "till 1944 the British had a virtual monopoly over all of de Gaulle's means of communications with France," and the French "could not introduce a single agent or a single store" without Allied permission and help, and "anything [they] planned with marked political implications was liable to be vetoed by any of the three major Western allies." Yet, having substantiated exactly what both the Vichy French and the Nazis had said all along, i.e. that the French Resistance was nothing but an "Anglo-Saxon conspiracy" and the resisters (this writer included) nothing but foreign agents, the official history makes the key point: "All these victories by and through resistance forces in France had a common basis: overwhelming popular support."[14]

[14] M. R. D. Foot, "SOE in France." London: Her Majesty's Stationery Office, 1966, pp. xix, 33, and 442–443, *passim*.

185

The hard historical facts which emerge from the French Resistance and which appear to apply to the Viet Cong are (a) that in spite of overwhelming technical control by the Allies, de Gaulle succeeded in winning political and military loyalty among the diverse guerrilla forces in France and (b) that even de Gaulle's own views and desires had to accommodate themselves to those developed by the internal resistance in its four-year fight, in which it bore the brunt of the struggle and suffered the bulk of the losses. The differences of view between Viet Cong leaders who have now been in the fight for six years (and some of them for twenty!) and the Hanoi theoreticians and conventional military commanders go in many cases far beyond normal internecine party struggles or mere tactical disagreements.

A glance at factual examples is interesting: there have been three changes of N.L.F. secretaries-general at times when Hanoi was in the throes of no purge whatsoever. There was the N.L.F. five-point manifesto of March 22, 1965, whose "jungle version" was rebroadcast later by Hanoi with 39 extensive amendments or text changes, softening some of the N.L.F. statements. There were the spontaneous reactions of N.L.F. leaders when faced with respected Western observers on neutral ground, openly explaining why they disagreed with the "narrow-minded commissars in Hanoi." And there is the fact that while the United States and Hanoi are now officially wedded to a return to a Geneva-type conference (and, presumably, its two-year election clause), the N.L.F. has thus far left Geneva out of its program, preferring a flexible formula of eventual reunification in negotiated stages.

It is easy to dismiss those differences as being mere camouflage (after all, some people believe that the Sino-Soviet split is nothing but a grand deception foisted on the easily-fooled West) and to believe the N.L.F. is indeed nothing but "a contrived political mechanism with no indigenous roots," as Carver avers. But in that case, the 220,000 Viet Cong who fight side-by-side with 50,000 P.A.V.N. regulars, and who over the past three years are said to have suffered almost 100,000 dead and 182,000 wounded, fight rather well for what must be a vast mass of remote-controlled and force-drafted recruits. Otherwise, desertion would be just as easy on the Viet Cong side as it is on the A.R.V.N. side, but thus far the VC desertion rate simply seems to keep pace with the increase of manpower on the Communist side.

That leaves, lastly, the argument of "facelessness": the N.L.F. leaders are men of little stature in their own society; they are unknowns. But four years ago only a few Vietnamese military men knew who General Ky was, and no one thought of him even two years ago as being of presidential timbre. Clandestineness is not attractive to the sort of men who are national figures: aside from Yugoslavia's Marshal Tito, it takes real expertise to recall the names of European resistance leaders. In any case, N.L.F. propaganda has seen to it that its leaders should not remain anonymous: at least forty senior leaders' biographies have been published, along with their photos.[15] Their background shows the normal social background of Vietnamese leadership in general, from medical doctors and pharmacists, to lawyers and even army officers (though the sprinkling of Montagnards and women is more typical of the likewise classic "united front" picture). And they have one remarkable common characteristic which thus far no Saigon government has been able to match: they are all from south of the 17th Parallel.

None of the foregoing justifies Hanoi's claim that the N.L.F. should be the "sole legitimate voice of the South Vietnamese people." But nothing justifies the opposite claim either, to the effect that without Hanoi's full support, the N.L.F. would disappear into thin air like a desert mirage. There can indeed be no quarrel with Carver's statement that "the Viet Cong organization is unquestionably a major factor in the South Vietnamese political scene." In that case, however, it must be treated as what it is—a political force in South Viet-Nam which cannot be simply blasted off the surface of the earth with B-52 saturation raids, or told to pack up and go into exile to North Viet-Nam.

There is one further consideration which argues against the likelihood of Hanoi being able (assuming it were willing, and it does not seem to be) to turn off the southern guerrilla movement like a water tap: Hanoi has, since March 1946, made four separate deals with the West at the expense of the South Vietnamese. The French-Vietnamese accords of March 6, 1946, provided for a Vietnamese "free

[15] Commission for Foreign Relations of the N.L.F., *Personalities of the South Viet Nam Liberation Movement*, n.d. [1963], 44 pp.

state with its own government, armed forces and foreign relations" but left South Viet-Nam proper (i.e. Cochin-China) under French control and, as it turned out, severe anti-Viet-Minh repression. The French-Vietnamese *modus vivendi* signed by Ho Chi Minh in Paris, September 14, 1946, further confirmed this seeming "abandonment" of the South. In the Geneva Accords of July 1954, it was South Viet-Nam which was left to the tender mercies of the Diem regime for at least two years, and we have Nguyen Huu Tho's own word in an interview with Wilfred Burchett to the effect that "there were mixed feelings about the two-years' delay over reunification." And when neither Hanoi nor Peking (nor the Soviet Union) made strong representations against dropping elections in 1956, it must have become obvious to even the most obtuse pro-Hanoi elements south of the 17th Parallel that the North Vietnamese Communists are somewhat unreliable allies.

V

These are simple historical facts, not extrapolations of obscure paragraphs in three-hour speeches of Communist leaders. They make it somewhat difficult to explain by the tenets of the all-out "aggression" theory why the same Communist leaders (in Hanoi and at least Peking) should have chosen in 1958 to fight a highly risky guerrilla war in preference to trying to win South Viet-Nam by a bitter political fight in 1956 (a call to the U.N. or for the reconvening of the 1954 Geneva Conference, or for the interpretation of the Agreements by the International Court of Justice; or simply by a vast propaganda offensive).[16] The fact of repeated abandonment goes a long way to explain why North Viet-Nam is somewhat reluctant to come to the conference table: Washington has sometimes seemed to feel that a sudden convening at a conference table might well bring about the collapse of the South Vietnamese government's spirit of resistance, for the South Vietnamese as a people know only too well what their military posture would be without all-out American help.

[16] It is totally forgotten today by those who support the "unilateral-aggression" theory that North Viet-Nam on March 7 and December 22, 1958, addressed two long notes to President Diem conceding the temporary division of the country and offering a 4-point program involving interzonal trade, travel and nonaggression. Saigon refused to reply to the notes.

But, vice-versa, in view of past performance, *any* peace conference in which Hanoi would once more speak for the southern insurgent elements and in the absence of their own full representation would raise among the Viet Cong the spectre of yet a fifth sellout of the southern guerrillas. Other countries too have "credibility gaps."

Yet it is precisely that symmetrical weakness which, in this writer's view, opens new perspectives on how to approach the Viet-Nam problem as a whole. And while lapidary formulations have in the past been more confusing than helpful, it would perhaps be useful to say that a major attempt must be made to "politicize" rather than to further "militarize" the Vietnamese conflict and to treat it as what it really is—a local conflict with outside support which has gotten out of hand, not the Stalingrad or El-Alamein of a worldwide cold-war confrontation.

There is no more reason to believe that a free-world "victory" in Viet-Nam is going to deter other revolutionary guerrilla wars than there was to have hoped that the Kaiser's defeat in World War I would teach Nazism a useful lesson in 1938; or to have expected that Communist guerrilla setbacks in Greece, Azerbaijan, the Philippines, Malaya, or the Congo would "teach" guerrillas something in Cuba, Venezuela, Laos, Burma, Thailand, or South Viet-Nam. If it "teaches" them anything at all, it may well be this: that unless the local regime undertakes a measure of true reforms, even the hugest military power in the world can be successfully stalemated for a long period of time by lightly-armed peasant guerrillas and the infantry of a tiny underdeveloped country. That point might well be left somewhat less substantiated than it has recently been.

In that case, the present balance, including the American and P.A.V.N. forces in South Viet-Nam, can be used to establish a political starting point from which to approach the whole problem anew, perhaps along the following lines:

1. Make the Saigon government and the Liberation Front leaders the center of all future negotiations, with the United States and North Viet-Nam in a back-up position, just as was the case with the Laotian factions and third powers at the Geneva Conference of 1961–62. (It will be recalled that the 1954 Geneva Conference on Indochina was a *military* cease-fire conference, like Panmunjom in Korea.)

2. Have the United States restate in less prolix language the promises contained in the State Department's 14-Point Declaration of January 1966, notably with regard to the non-permanence of American bases in South Viet-Nam and the disengagement of *both* Viet-Nams; and have this declaration filed with the United Nations as proof of good faith.

3. Prepare the Saigon government forcefully and publicly—just as Premier Ky informed the United States of his desire to carry the ground war to North Viet-Nam—for the coming *political* contest with a well-organized native left-wing minority which can neither be evacuated nor exterminated. (*Vide,* France and Italy in 1945–47 having to face the stark fact of heavily-armed Communist ex-partisan forces, which to this day in 1966 have not really surrendered all their weapons.)

4. Encourage Liberation Front leaders to commit themselves to specifically *South* Vietnamese political and economic options in preference to North Vietnamese desires (again as was the case of the West European Communists in the early 1950's, in relation to Moscow) in exchange for a legal participation in the political life of the country.

5. Encourage the eventual creation of a "piastre common market" (as advocated two years ago by Prince Norodom Sihanouk of Cambodia) which would include North Viet-Nam and thus satisfy its legitimate desire for contacts outside the Communist world, but which would include 26,000,000 people from non-Communist states as against North Viet-Nam's 19,000,000. Postwar international organizations—even the Warsaw Pact—have shown that small strong-willed countries succeed far better in holding their own within such organizations, even when they include a large predatory country, than they can individually.

6. On the basis of President Johnson's Baltimore speech, restate and expand the idea of a flexible area-wide rehabilitation program, taking into account the immensely increased destruction which has taken place since last year. Include proposals for political normalization, such as those which the United States implemented in Germany and Japan, Britain in Israel, and France in Algeria. In that case, Viet-Nam could set the pattern of a détente applicable to other divided countries as well.

None of the above is likely to produce a miracle cure for South Viet-Nam's ills. If Saigon is still grimly determined to botch its land reform or to falsify its elections, not even a million American troops can stop it from doing so. Of course those troops at least could crush the opposition even if it were at the price of which Tacitus spoke when he said of the Romans in Britain, "You have made this a desolation and you call it peace."

It would indeed be a pity if so much ingenuity, diplomacy, blood and treasure should have been spent on trying to persuade Hanoi to abandon the insurgents in South Viet-Nam, without a solid attempt ever having been made at getting the insurgents to modify their relationship with Hanoi in return for a specifically South Vietnamese solution that could be as honorable all around as it would be realistic. The only alternative to such an approach would be a further escalation both in terms of battleground and participating countries. And if Munich is not a good example of how to settle the Vietnamese conflict, neither is Guernica, or Sarajevo.

Viet-Nam:
The New Korea

ᗞᙡᗡ

> . . . American airstrikes and naval engagements against North Viet-
> namese fixed installations and warships have already taken place. . . .
> In actual military effectiveness, the worth of such operations is nil.
> . . . Primitiveness carries its own kind of invulnerability when
> matched against sophisticated weapons.

THE ABOVE PASSAGE, contained in this writer's article published in *Current History* for February, 1965, was written before round-the-clock bombing of North Viet-Nam began on February 7 of that year and therefore dealt with a hypothesis. The estimate of noneffectiveness, however, was made on the basis of earlier failures of similar operations in Korea[1] and during the French Indochina War,[2] and by December, 1965, was apparently confirmed by official American sources. "We had an assumption that North Viet-Nam was not going to reinforce the Viet Cong forces in South Viet-Nam, as it has done," was the view of a senior United States officer in Viet-Nam at the

Reprinted by permission and first published in *Current History*, February 1966. Copyright © 1966 by Current History, Inc.

[1] Robert F. Futrell, *et al., The United States Air Force in Korea 1950–1953* (New York: Duell, Sloan and Pearce, 1961).

[2] Bernard B. Fall, *Street Without Joy*, 4th rev. ed. (Harrisburg: The Stackpole Co., 1964).

end of year.[3] In actual fact, however, North Viet-Nam seems simply to have kept pace with additional American reinforcements at the average rate of two North Vietnamese regiments (about 3,000 men) for every American combat division (16,000 men). And thus, the Second Indochina War seems to grope its way slowly to a Korean-type "meatgrinder operation" that nobody wants.

It may, therefore, be useful to review some of the key events which have led to the development of the present situation. First of all, there are the Geneva Accords of July 20, 1954, examined in detail by a specialist in international law, Dr. Victor Bator, in his recent book, *Vietnam—A Diplomatic Tragedy*.[4] They are remembered in the main for a clause contained in the final declaration of the Accords—and not subscribed to by either South Viet-Nam or the United States—providing for reunification elections to be held on or before July 20, 1956. They, however, also contained other important provisions whose progressive violation by South Viet-Nam also contributed to a climate in which retaliatory violations of the cease-fire provisions by North Viet-Nam would become almost mandatory.

Two examples of such violations shall suffice. The Geneva Accords provided for the creation, in addition to the Indian-Canadian-Polish International Control Commission (I.C.C.), also known as the International Commission for Supervision and Control (I.C.S.C.), of a so-called Joint Commission (J.C.) under Chapter VI of the Accords. The J.C., composed of military representatives of the North Vietnamese army on one hand, and of the French Union forces—which then included the South Vietnamese army—on the other, was to set up, in turn, Joint Groups of an indefinite number. According to Article 33, the J.C. shall

> help the parties to execute the said [cease-fire] provisions, shall ensure liaison between them for the purpose of preparing and carrying out plans for the application of these provisions, and shall endeavor to solve such disputed questions as may arise between the parties in the course of executing these provisions.

[3] The New York *Times*, December 13, 1965.
[4] Dobbs Ferry, N.Y.: Oceana Publications, 1965. Also see pages 79 ff. and pages 113 ff. of this issue.

Similar joint groups made up of the two hostile parties have been working in Palestine under the supervision of the U.N.T.S.O. (U.N. Truce Supervisory Organization) since 1948. While they did not bring peace all by themselves in the Palestine case, and perhaps would not have in the Viet-Nam case, they nevertheless have permitted in Palestine the maintenance of certain working contacts between Israeli and Arab officials on the ground level where incidents are most likely to occur. In the case of Viet-Nam, the government of the late President Ngo Dinh Diem of South Viet-Nam unilaterally abolished the Joint Commission and its subordinate teams on May 18, 1958, and expelled from South Vietnamese territory the North Vietnamese who had belonged to it. One could speculate today whether the Viet-Nam war would have become the desperate hate-fight it now has become, had there been *some* channel through which South and North Vietnamese officialdom could have communicated.

A similar example is Article 23, which allows the "graves service personnel of the other party" to search for and remove the bodies of their fallen soldiers from the other party's zone. Existing war cemeteries of the other side were to be respected[5] and, in a protocol subsequent to the Accords, the French were even permitted to erect an ossurary for their thousands of dead at Dien Bien Phu. Here again, the Ngo Dinh Diem government allowed again the pathological hatreds of its leaders to get the better of its political judgment: North Vietnamese graves registration teams were expelled and existing North Vietnamese military cemeteries and memorials for their war dead (notably, from personal observation, the cemetery and monument in Qui Nhon) were destroyed.

In the case of North Viet-Nam, a Franco-Vietnamese graves registration mission composed of Captain Paul Belmont and Lt. Nguyen Van Sai had even been permitted to go to Dien Bien Phu in May, 1955; i.e., one year after the battle had ended, and had begun its surveys for the purpose of regrouping the war dead there into a permanent cemetery to be erected on the spot with a suitable monument. But that mission, and others, were expelled by North Viet-

[5] Article 15(d): "The two parties shall permit no destruction . . . of any public property. . . ."

194

Nam in reprisal against the measures taken by South Viet-Nam. To this day, those dead remain unattended and unrecorded. However, and again from personal observation in North Viet-Nam in 1962, the old French military cemeteries of Bach-Mai and Vinh-Yen (the latter dating in part back to the colonial campaigns of the 1880's) show no evidence of destruction or molestation.

A similar fate surrounded the *only written agreement* ever signed by North and South Viet-Nam without foreign advice from either side: the postal relations protocol signed in Haiphong (North Viet-Nam, then still a part of the French-held perimeter) on April 12, 1955. The postal protocol could have become the working model of a whole series of other *de facto* accords covering such fields as economic exchanges, telecommunications and even, under optimal conditions, a limited amount of interzonal travel beyond the simple refugee exodus. It is exactly those limited interzonal agreements which make the situation between the two Germanies somewhat less explosive, and which make even the equally senseless Arab quarantine of Israel (which at least has its Mandelbaum Gate in Jerusalem) a bit more bearable. North and South Vietnamese postal relations started out on the basis of postcards which were the direct verbatim copies (in Vietnamese translation) of the Nazi-imposed postcards used for correspondence between southern and northern France during World War II. But even this pitifully slender thread of interzonal relations was the object, on May 21, 1956 (i.e., before the July 20 election deadline) of a complaint by the North Vietnamese postal authorities to the effect that five announced shipments of cards had simply "disappeared" inside South Viet-Nam before delivery and others had been delivered with delays of several months.

Finally, another article of the 1954 Accords—14(c)—provided that both parties would "refrain from any reprisals or discrimination against persons or organizations on account of the activities during the hostilities and to guarantee their democratic liberties." Both sides obviously violated that article, but again it was the Diem regime that openly forbade the I.C.C., as of mid-1957, to investigate allegations that former resistance members (even those who had not been Communists) were being pursued and imprisoned; a fact which the

195

I.C.C. duly mentioned in its periodical activities report of November 4, 1957.

In other words, what augured ill for the future of the relations between the two Viet-Nams was not only the unilateral abrogation of the promise to hold reunification elections in 1956—per se an understandable point, since South Viet-Nam would have been certain to lose its existence in such an election—but the fact that Saigon had from the start hardly ever made an attempt to live up even to those articles of the Accords which would have somewhat sweetened the pill of North Vietnamese disappointment as it became clear in July, 1956, that reunification would not take place. It has been argued in some quarters that the North Vietnamese already "knew" at Geneva in 1954 that the division between the two zones of Viet-Nam would be of long duration, if not permanent, and that their clamor for elections in 1956 was one for the record only. While that argument has no legal standing, it is difficult to believe that the North Vietnamese, having just *won* the war against the French, were willing to see their victory recompensed by a permanent quarantine by their South Vietnamese brother state. As far as the two Germanies is concerned, they also, by virtue of the Allied wartime agreements, were not to become separate states, but did. A violation of a variety of solemn agreements did take place here also. But in the case of the two Germanies, good sense, some diplomacy (totally absent in the Far East), and, above all, the realization that the failure to achieve a *modus vivendi* would lead to a world war, contributed to a situation which, though far from ideal, appears viable. In Viet-Nam, also, basic violations of central agreements could have been overcome in all likelihood by creating acceptable peripheral conditions; and, above all, by preparing South Viet-Nam internally for the confrontation with the North that was bound to come.

That South Viet-Nam did not do this will have to remain a matter of eternal regret, as the country must now pay for this omission by a murderous war fought on its soil. That its government was not the object of the most emphatic pressure on the part of its main supporter, the United States, at least to make a good showing of compliance to the signed agreements (or, at least, their nonobjectionable parts), must remain a subject of further study by later historians to whom, hopefully, certain needed archives will become freely available.

As far as North Viet-Nam was concerned, the choice of alternatives was limited. It could resolve to abandon all prospect of future reunification without the slightest *quid pro quo* in the economic field and integrate fully with Red China—a prospect no Vietnamese relishes, regardless of political leanings. Or it could remain watchful for any sign of internal difficulty in South Viet-Nam in the hope of being able to exploit it at the right moment. South Viet-Nam did not fail to provide Hanoi with such an opportunity.

The Rise of the Viet Cong

It is axiomatic in the field of revolutionary warfare that the potential insurgent takes his source of power from a population which (in the words of the United States Army manual of *Counterguerrilla Operations* [FM 31-16]) has "become discontented with existing conditions which cannot be changed by peaceful and legal means." That is close to a perfect definition of what was to happen in South Viet-Nam *not*—contrary to some later appraisals —after 1960 or 1961, but starting in 1956.

There is strong evidence that the population of South Viet-Nam at first considered the Ngo Dinh Diem regime to be a vast improvement over the succession of French-backed non-Communist regimes which had preceded it. In less than a year after the cease-fire, by mid-1955, Diem had succeeded in defeating one by one the so-called "political-religious sects," i.e., the armed Cao-Dai and Hoa-Hao[6] units which had carved out quasi-feudal baronies in the South Vietnamese countryside. These sects were backed by the piratical Binh-Xuyen, who controlled the Saigon police, and even by a Catholic group, the *Unités Mobiles de Défense des Chrétientés* (U.M.D.C.), led by a Eurasian French colonel, Jean Leroy.[7] Diem unfortunately failed to realize that his victory over the sects was largely due to the fact that the population supported him—not that the South Vietnamese

[6] *Cf.* Fall, "The Political-Religious Sects of Viet-Nam," *Pacific Affairs,* September, 1955.

[7] Jean Leroy, *Un homme dans la rizière* (Paris: *Editions de Paris,* 1955).

army had suddenly developed a prowess and tactical efficiency it did not possess a few months earlier.

The same held true in the relations between the population and the stay-behind Communist cadres. There may have been about 6000 armed "Vietminh" who had stayed inside South Viet-Nam after the cease-fire and after about 100,000 other persons under Communist control had been transferred to North Viet-Nam (while 860,000 moved south). The purpose of those stay-behind cadres was twofold: if the reunification elections took place as planned in 1956, they would become the first on-the-spot authority of the returning Ho Chi Minh regime; if such elections did not take place, they would become the vanguard of a future insurrectional movement.

All Communist movements have a hard core of trained military or guerrilla cadres. Some of them may never have a chance to use their military or organizational skills; others do. It all depends on the *local circumstances,* and rarely vice-versa. Such Communist cadres will exploit occasions when they arise, but they are incapable of "creating" a revolution from scratch. It is Diem who created the movement of discontent in South Viet-Nam. North Viet-Nam and the Viet Cong fed on it.

Here again, the record is clear: the South Vietnamese regime began to take on highly-resented police state features long before the guerrilla threat justified the adoption of some of them for the purpose of restoring internal security. Thus, on January 11, 1956 (i.e., *after* the non-Communist sects had been crushed and long *before* the Communist guerrillas began their operations) Diem issued Ordinance No. 6 which stipulated that by

> decision of the President of the Republic upon proposal by the Minister of the Interior, may be sent to concentration camps . . . all persons considered dangerous to national defense or collective security.

And in June, 1956, the South Vietnamese government made perhaps its most fateful decision. In defiance of one of the most hallowed Vietnamese traditions, according to which the power of the central authorities stops at the bamboo hedge of the village,[8] the Saigon administration abolished by a stroke of the pen elected

[8] Gerald Hickey, *Village in Vietnam* (New Haven: Yale University Press, 1964), p. 182.

village chiefs and village councils and replaced them by appointive members.[8] In doing this, Diem outdid anything that either the North Vietnamese Communist regime or the French colonial administration ever attempted. The French (like almost all colonial powers) did not feel it necessary to interfere directly in village affairs; the Hanoi regime, while seeking to influence village administration, did so by the more indirect means of providing administrative *can-bo* (cadres) for the elected village chiefs. But the latter still were basically responsible to their villages.

In South Viet-Nam, elected village chiefs were replaced by centrally-appointed individuals who, in many cases, were not even native to the village and who, as insecurity grew, preferred to live in the nearby district town. This broke all normal feedback between the 80 per cent of the population which lives in village units of about 2000 people, and the South Vietnamese government. Once the traditional and homegrown village administrative structure had been destroyed by the South Vietnamese regime, the North Vietnamese and their sympathizers had found the chink in South Viet-Nam's armor. In a well-organized terror campaign involving massive assassination and kidnappings of local officials, they began to dismantle the South Vietnamese local administration and to replace it gradually with their own men.[9]

Here again, what is called "insecurity" or "insurgency" shows up most clearly in the compliance of the Vietnamese with their taxation system, as the latter represents a type of governmental activity which no state abandons lightly. A radical decline of taxation may also show an overall degradation in administrative performance. In South Viet-Nam, both insecurity and administrative degradation in the cities are clearly illustrated in the country's taxation system, as evidenced by a recent American survey of property tax assessments in that country.[10]

Of the 234 districts (*huyên*) into which Viet-Nam was divided in 1964, a total of 165 (or 71 per cent) failed altogether to respond to a central statistical tax inquiry. The remaining 69 districts (29

[9] "Vietnam: The Agonizing Reappraisal," *Current History,* February, 1965, p. 100.
[10] Ray E. Davis, *An Analysis of Property Tax Compliance in Vietnam* (Saigon: U.S.O.M., 1965).

per cent) filed some sort of acknowledgment, and of those, 51 provided useful data of some sort for the year 1964. Overall, the following appalling picture emerged from the survey:

South Viet-Nam Tax Delinquency

Year	% Delinquent
1960	44
1961	47
1962	51
1963	57
1964	74

The survey, moreover, showed that the urban areas which are mostly solidly under government control had, in 53 per cent of the cases, a higher delinquency rate than the rural areas—which, of course, could not be attributed to insurgency but was, in the view of the American tax experts in Saigon, due to the fact that possibly "some officials are using 'insecurity' as an excuse for their own incompetence. . . ."[11] Or, for example, in some well-documented cases, the tax funds simply disappeared in a welter of corruption. Here again, the figures are obvious: even at a time when Communist subversion and North Vietnamese infiltration were at a low level, in 1960, the Diem regime was hardly capable of effectively administering much more than half the country.

And the political alternative to Communism it offered at the center fully matched its performance in the countryside. One of Diem's most ardent defenders, Marguerite Higgins, was to say of him in 1965, when the record of his regime was clearly written all over the map of Viet-Nam:

President Diem had gone to the trouble of constructing a facade of democracy to placate the United States, whose aid was indispensable to him.[12]

And that is perhaps the Diem regime's best epitaph for almost ten years of misrule: it had "taken the trouble" to construct a democratic façade for the United States, but it had somehow never provided even a modicum of its reality to the South Vietnamese.

[11] *Ibid.*, p. 25.
[12] Marguerite Higgins, *Our Vietnam Nightmare* (New York: Harper & Row, 1965), p. 170.

All this, the stay-behind guerrillas watched with growing interest. But, interestingly enough, the initial armed resistance against Diem came from resolutely *anti-Communist* sect elements: four battalions of about 350–400 men each of the Hoa-Hao faith which refused to surrender after their chief, Ba-Cut, was taken prisoner by Diem's forces and guillotined during a truce. In the ensuing repression directed against ex-Viet-Minh elements who had returned to their villages,[13] many of the latter in turn went into hiding, sometimes collaborating with the Hoa-Hao,[14] and sometimes forming separate *maquis.* Faced with physical extermination, the ex-Viet-Minh elements had little choice but to face up to a second round of fighting, regardless of Hanoi's plans.

As Seen from Hanoi

Indeed, the Department of State's White Book of February, 1965, fully agrees with the North Vietnamese view (in fact, it uses it as "proof" of North Viet-Nam's aggression against South Viet-Nam) that the first statements dealing with support of a resistance movement in the South were made at the third Lao-Dong (Workers'— i.e., Communist) Party Congress in Hanoi in September, 1960. But neither North Viet-Nam nor the State Department explain the existence of guerrilla warfare in South Viet-Nam in the years from 1956 to 1960. That such guerrilla warfare indeed existed can be fully documented from South Vietnamese sources and was in fact so documented by this writer as early as 1958.[15] Here again irresponsible, across-the-board repression did the rest. On May 6, 1959, the Diem regime passed Law 10/59, which provided for a system of drumhead courts capable of handing out death sentences for even trivial offenses. Thus *all* South Vietnamese opposition—whether Communist or not—had to become subversive, and did. The South Vietnamese army resorted to putsches and coups (the first in No-

[13] According to *Tu-Do* (a Saigon newspaper) of February 28, 1959, the Saigon regime had arrested a total 39,909 "former communist cadres, . . . and sympathizers" in the preceding six-month period. The population of the province amounted to about 270,000.

[14] It took the overthrow of Diem in November, 1963, to get the Hoa-Hao battalions to return to the fold of the Saigon government. The Hoa-Hao sect now again controls the administration of three Mekong Delta provinces, which are the most peaceful of all of South Viet-Nam.

[15] "South Viet-Nam's Internal Problems," *Pacific Affairs,* September, 1958.

vember, 1960, even before the Viet Cong got started); the Hoa-Hao stayed in the *maquis;* and the Communists' turn also came. In a recently published book, the noted French Asian specialist, Jean Lacouture, describes the situation prevailing in 1959–60 in a few apt phrases:

> . . . new legislation was promulgated in Saigon that opened the great period of the "witch hunt"; four persons out of five became suspects and liable to be imprisoned if not executed. War generally entails extraordinary legislation; one can say that here extraordinary legislation entailed war. At that time Marxist organizations hardly took the lead. But, taken by the throat, they counterattacked.[16]

The same view of events was described earlier by Philippe Devillers as he portrayed the mood prevailing among the Viet-Minh cadres in the south of Viet-Nam in 1959:

> . . . The overriding needs of the world-wide strategy of the Socialist camp meant little or nothing to guerrilla fighters being hunted down in [South Vietnam]. It was in such a climate of feeling that, in 1959, responsible elements of the Communist resistance . . . came to the conclusion that they had to act, whether Hanoi wanted them to or not. . . . Hanoi preferred diplomatic notes, but it was to find that its hand had been forced.[17]

In March, 1960, a meeting took place somewhere in the depths of the South Vietnamese jungle, organized by a group that called itself "The South Viet-Nam Veterans of the Resistance Association," which launched a call for resistance against the Diem regime. And on April 26 of the same year, a group of highly respectable South Vietnamese Catholic and Buddhist leaders (including several who would in 1964–66 become ministers in the Saigon government) issued a proclamation to Diem, warning him of impending disaster. Neither of the two voices received the slightest hearing in Saigon's official circles, let alone in Washington.

But to Hanoi, the warning could only mean one thing—that the South Vietnamese government was simply and purely disintegrating under its own lack of support. In the typically conservative fashion of Communist regimes subsequent to the Greek and Filipino disap-

[16] Jean Lacouture, *Vietnam: Between Two Truces* (New York: Random House, 1966).
[17] Philippe Devillers, "The Struggle for the Unification of Vietnam" in P. J. Honey, ed., *North Vietnam Today* (New York: Praeger, 1962), p. 38.

pointments, Hanoi still hesitated to commit itself to the side of the guerrillas. Finally, on September 5, 1960, at the Hanoi party congress, Lê Duan, the Lao-Dong's party secretary and a former southern guerrilla leader himself, took official cognizance in his report of the "southern People's revolutionary struggle" and advocated the creation of a "broad national united front against the U.S.-Diem clique." Again, there was no automatic response from the southern guerrillas. But not long afterwards, on November 11, 1960, the elite paratroop brigade of the South Vietnamese army rebelled against Diem and had to be put down with tanks. Most of its leaders fled or were imprisoned, and another wave of mass arrests began throughout South Viet-Nam. Five weeks later, on December 20, 1960, the "National Liberation Front of South Viet-Nam" (N.L.F.S.V.) was proclaimed, and the Second Indochina War was under way.

Internally, by 1960 North Viet-Nam had succeeded in weathering the worst of what had been a botched land reform and had succeeded in building up a modicum of medium-sized industries. If a comparison with advanced European countries may be permitted, North Viet-Nam could expect to become, not a second Japan, but perhaps a second Belgium. It began to embark upon an ambitious five-year plan—it was the latter that was the main topic of the third Party Conference, and not the creation of the N.L.F.S.V.— whose targets it failed to reach but which nevertheless brought living standards up to a somewhat higher level than is usually realized. They are, however, lower than those of South Viet-Nam.[18] In the field of industrial development, progress up to the beginning of round-the-clock American air raids on February 7, 1965, was notable, thanks in large part to Soviet bloc and Chinese economic aid, whose total is estimated at over $1.3 billion.

In terms of politics, Hanoi was to feel increasingly the effect of the conflicting pulls of Moscow and Peking. The solid leadership of Ho Chi Minh successfully avoided a direct North Vietnamese commitment to either side in the dispute, although doubtless the increasing pace of the Second Indochina War made it at first appear that Hanoi would entirely rely on Peking. As it turned out, how-

[18] Fall, "North Viet-Nam: A Profile," in *Problems of Communism*, July–August, 1965.

ever (and, apparently, this is still the case), Peking was unwilling at first to commit its own power in a renewed confrontation along Korean lines with the United States in the absence of a Soviet commitment of full support.

Peking, furthermore, worked to prevent the Soviet Union from supporting North Viet-Nam in a decisive manner out of a fear, openly expressed by Chou En-lai prior to the abortive Algiers Afro-Asian Conference, that the Soviet Union would use her military leverage in North Viet-Nam for the purpose of compelling Hanoi to accept a compromise settlement with the United States—just as she had used her leverage on Cuba during the missile crisis of 1962. There is strong second-hand evidence[19] that the Soviet Union (at least in the spring of 1965) indeed did attempt to influence Hanoi in favor of a compromise settlement with South Viet-Nam and the United States; and that Hanoi—between late 1964 and May, 1965 —had made some attempts at making preliminary contacts with the United States.[20] The total failure of those alleged contacts still awaits full historical examination, but there can be little doubt that various miscues of both sides have now resulted in a climate of suspicion that have made further attempts at direct contacts between the major adversaries extremely difficult.

The Outlook

This leaves the Soviet Union in an extremely awkward position: it has become axiomatic in Washington that the U.S.S.R. prizes her good relations with the West in general and the United States in particular, above all, and will go to any lengths to preserve them. It also seems to be considered as axiomatic that the relations between Red China and the U.S.S.R. have gone beyond the point of no return. Any attempt on the part of the Soviet Union to provide effective help to North Viet-Nam (let alone to the Viet Cong inside South Viet-Nam) must bring in its wake a dramatic worsening of American-Soviet relations on a worldwide scale, with all that such a situation entails.

[19] Edward Crankshaw, "Peking Pushes Moscow to the Brink," *The Observer*, London, November 14, 1965.
[20] Fall, "The Year of the Hawks," in *The New York Times Magazine*, December 12, 1965.

The U.S.S.R. can, of course—in fact, Washington expects this—completely wash her hands of the Vietnamese affair, both in her role as the leader of the Communist orbit and as a cochairman of the 1954 Geneva Agreements, and let American technology reduce both Viet-Nams to rubble before reconstructing them under President Lyndon Johnson's Johns Hopkins speech program. Such an outlook on the Viet-Nam situation surely is more optimistic than the facts warrant. The Soviet Union has remained aloof from the Indochina area since the Laotian Agreements of 1962, but there are some very strong indications that this period of aloofness may well be at an end.

As for the American view, it curiously, if unconsciously, resembles the American view of Korea in September, 1950, in that very strange phase of relative stability after General Douglas MacArthur's Inchon landing had cleared South Korea of invaders, but before the Chinese "People's Volunteers" transformed the Korean War into the bloody three-year stalemate it later became. At that time also, as the authors of the *U.S. Air Force in Korea* point out in a chapter aptly called "Toward An Air-Pressure Strategy," it was advocated that a "massive strike" against the northern capital would cause the "tottering government" there "to listen more attentively to United Nations terms for ending the war." A later chapter is titled "Irrigation Dam Attacks Speed Truce Negotiations."

Both chapters may well have been replayed in Viet-Nam by the time these pages are read.

PART II

The Theory and Practice of
Insurgency and Counterinsurgency

⟨w⟩

1. The Century of Small Wars

IF WE LOOK at the 20th century alone we are now in Viet-Nam faced with the forty-eighth small war. Let me just cite a few: Algeria, Angola, Arabia, Burma, Cameroons, China, Colombia, Cuba, East Germany, France, Haiti, Hungary, Indochina, Indonesia, Kashmir, Laos, Morocco, Mongolia, Nagaland, Palestine, Yemen, Poland, South Africa, South Tyrol, Tibet, Yugoslavia, Venezuela, West Irian, etc. This, in itself, is quite fantastic. In fact, if a survey were made of the number of people involved, or killed, in those 48 small wars it would be found that these wars, *in toto,* involved as many people as either one of the two world wars, and caused as many casualties. Who speaks of "insurgency" in Colombia? It is mere banditry, apparently. Yet it has killed 200,000 people so far and there is no end to it. The new Viet-Nam war, the "Second Indochina War" that began in 1956–57 and is still going on, is now going to reach in 1965, according to my calculations, somewhere around the 200,000-dead mark. Officially, 79,000 dead are acknowledged, but this is far too low. These may be small wars as far as expended ordnance is concerned. But they certainly

Reprinted by permission and first published in *Naval War College Review.*

are not "small wars" in terms of territory or population, since such countries as China or Algeria were involved. These wars are certainly not small for the people who fight in them, or who have to suffer from them. Nor are they small, in many cases, for the counterinsurgency operator.

One of the problems one immediately faces is that of terminology. Obviously "sublimited warfare" is meaningless, and "insurgency" or "counterinsurgency" hardly define the problem. But the definition that I think will fit the subject is "revolutionary warfare" (RW).

Let me state this definition: RW=G+P, or, "revolutionary warfare equals guerrilla warfare plus political action." This formula for revolutionary warfare is the result of the application of guerrilla methods to the furtherance of an ideology or a political system. This is the *real* difference between partisan warfare, guerrilla warfare, and everything else. Guerrilla simply means "small war" to which the correct Army answer is (and that applies to *all* Western armies) that everybody knows how to fight small wars; no second lieutenant of the infantry ever learns anything else but how to fight small wars. Political action, however, is the difference. The Communists, or shall we say, any sound revolutionary warfare operator (the French underground, the Norwegian underground, or any other European anti-Nazi underground) most of the time used small-war tactics, not to destroy the German Army, of which they were thoroughly incapable; but to establish a competitive system of control over the population. Of course, in order to do this, here and there they had to kill some of the occupying forces and attack some of the military targets. But above all they had to kill their own people who collaborated with the enemy.

But the "kill" aspect, the military aspect, definitely always remained the minor aspect. The political, administrative, ideological aspect is the primary aspect. Everybody, of course, by definition, will seek a military solution to the insurgency problem, whereas by its very nature, the insurgency problem is militarily only in a secondary sense, and politically, ideologically, and administratively in a primary sense. Once we understand this, we will understand more of what is actually going on in Viet-Nam or in some of the other places affected by RW.

2. Recent and Not-so-recent Cases

The next point is that this concept of revolutionary war can be applied by anyone anywhere. One doesn't have to be white to be defeated. One doesn't have to be European or American. Colonel Nasser's recent experience in Yemen is instructive. He fought with 40,000 troops, Russian tanks, and Russian jets, in Yemen against a few thousand barefoot Yemenite guerrillas. The tanks lost. After three years of inconclusive fighting the Egyptian-backed Yemen regime barely holds the major cities, and Nasser is reported to be on the lookout for a face-saving withdrawal.

Look at the great Indian Army's stalemate by the Nagas. And who are the Nagas? They are a backward people of 500,000 on the northeastern frontier of India. After ten years of fighting, the Indian Army and government are now negotiating with the Nagas. They have, for all practical purposes, lost their counterinsurgency operations. In other words, (this is perhaps reassuring), losing an insurgency can happen to almost anybody. This is very important because one more or less comes to accept as "fact" that to lose counterinsurgency operations happens only to the West.

Very briefly, then, let me run through the real differences between, let us say, a revolutionary war and any other kind of uprising. A revolutionary war is usually fought in support of a doctrine, but a doctrine may be of a most variegated kind. It could be a peasant rebellion or it could be religion. For example, in Europe between the 1300's and the 1600's, as the feudal system evolved and then disappeared and was replaced by the early stages of the capitalist system, there were many peasant rebellions. Those peasant rebellions were fought, even though the people did not know it, for economic and social doctrines. The peasants were sick and tired of being serfs and slaves working for a feudal lord. Those peasant rebellions were in line with later socio-economic movements. This is why the Communists, of course, retroactively lay claim to the European peasant rebellions.

There were, of course, the religious wars in Europe—Protestant versus Catholic. Their doctrinal (ideological) character was self-explanatory. As soon as we run into that kind of war, not all the rich and not all the poor will stick together with their own kind.

211

Doctrine somehow will cut across all social lines. This is often misunderstood. We look, for example, at the Viet Cong insurgency in Viet-Nam, and expect that all the Viet Cong are "communists" of low class. Then we find out that there are intellectuals in the Viet Cong. There are Buddhist priests, Catholic priests, and minority people. Hence, this very oversimplified view of the enemy falls by the wayside; we are now faced with something which is much more complicated and multifaceted, and the enemy, of course, thanks to doctrine, cuts across all classes. Pham Van Dong, the Prime Minister of Communist North Viet-Nam, is a high-ranking Vietnamese nobleman whose father was Chief of Cabinet to one of the late Vietnamese emperors. One of his colleagues at school was Ngo Dinh Diem, a high-ranking nobleman whose father also had been Chief of Cabinet to one of the Vietnamese emperors. Ho Chi Minh was not exactly born on the wrong side of the tracks. His father had a master's degree in the mandarin administration. This is very important.

In a doctrinal conflict there are people on both sides who probably embrace the whole social spectrum. Athough Communists will always claim that all the peasants and workers are on their side, they find out to their surprise that not all the peasants or workers are on their side. On the other hand, neither are all the élites on our side.

Finally, we have the French Revolutionary War and the American Revolutionary War. There is a difference between the two. The American Revolutionary War was literally a "national liberation war." It did not advocate the upsetting of the existing socio-economic structure in this new country called the United States. But the American Revolutionary War brought something into this whole field which nobody really studied, and that is the difference in certain types of foreign aid that the United States received during its liberation war. What basically made the difference between, say, Lafayette and Rochambeau? Lafayette was an integrated military adviser, but Rochambeau commanded a separate military force. He commanded French forces fighting alongside the United States forces, whereas Kosciusko, Von Steuben, and Lafayette were actually the allied parts of the army that were sandwiched in (the new word for this in Washington is "interlarded") with the United States forces.

What would happen if American officers actually were put into the Vietnamese command channels—not as advisers, but as operators; or if a Vietnamese officer were to serve in the American Army like the Korean troops in the U. S. Army in Korea? Perhaps this is one approach to the problem of "advisermanship." There was a whole group of foreign officers in the American Revolutionary War army. Were they "mercenaries," and if so, who paid them? I don't know. Were they Rochambeau's men or not? Or, what was the difference between Lafayette and the mercenaries of the Congo? I don't quite know. It would be interesting to find out.

The American Revolutionary War was a national liberation war in present-day terms. The French Revolution was, again, a social, economic, doctrinal war—a doctrinal revolution. In fact, it is amazing how well the doctrine worked. The French had developed three simple words: *Liberté! Égalité! Fraternité!* And that piece of propaganda held an enormous sway. For ten years after the French Revolution was dead and gone, French imperialism in the form of Napoleon marched through Europe taking over pieces of territories in the name of liberty, equality, and fraternity. Millions of people throughout Europe turned on their own natural or home-grown leaders believing that this French concept of liberty, equality, and fraternity was carried around at the point of French bayonets.

To be sure, in many cases, Napoleon left behind a legacy of orderly administration, of such things as the Napoleonic Code, but certainly Napoleon did not bring independence any more than the Communists bring independence. He did bring a kind of Western order which was highly acceptable. To this day there are slight remnants of Napoleon's administration in the Polish Code. The streets are lined with poplar trees in Austria because Napoleon lined such streets 167 years ago.

One thing that Napoleon also brought with him was French occupation and the first true, modern guerrilla wars against his troops. For example, the word *guerrilla,* as we know it, comes from the Spanish uprising against the French. There were similar wars, for example, in Tyrol. The Tyrolians rose up under Andreas Hofer against the French. There were such uprisings in Russia also, although they were in support of an organized military force, the Russian army. In that case we speak of partisan warfare. We also had such things in Germany, the *Tugend-Bund,* the Virtue-League. This was sort of a Pan-Germanic underground which got its people into the various German states to work for the liberation of the country from French occupation.

Very interestingly we see the difference between Napoleon and some of the other leaders in the field of counterinsurgency. Napoleon tended to make his family members and his cronies kings of those newly created French satellite states. One of his brothers, Joseph, got Spain, and Jerome got Westphalia, a French puppet state cut out in the Rhine area. The population of Westphalia rose up against Jerome. He sent a message to his brother saying, "I'm in trouble." The answer returned was typically Napoleonic. It said, "By God, brother, use your bayonets." (Signed) Bonaparte. A historic message came back from Jerome to his brother saying: "Brother, you can do anything with bayonets—except sit on them." In other words: One can do almost anything with brute force except salvage an unpopular government. Jerome Bonaparte had the right idea, for *both* the right or wrong ideas about insurgency are just about as old as the ages. We have always found somebody who understood them.

What then, did Communism add to all this? Really very little. Communism has not added a thing that participants in other doctrinal wars (the French Revolution or the religious wars) did not know just as well. But communism did develop a more adaptable doctrine. The merit of communism has been to recognize precisely the usefulness of the social, economic, and political doctrines in this field for the purpose of diminishing as much as possible the element of risk inherent in the military effort. But if one prepares his terrain politically and organizes such things as a Fifth Column, one may reduce such risks by a great deal.

3. Insurgency Indicators

The important thing is to know how to discover the symptoms of insurgency. This is where I feel that we are woefully lagging in Viet-Nam. I will show you how badly mistaken one can be in this particular field. For example, I have a Vietnamese briefing sheet in English which the Vietnamese Government used to hand out. It is dated 1957 and is called *The Fight Against Communist Subversive Activities.* At the end of the last page it says: "From this we can see that the Vietminh authorities have disintegrated and been rendered powerless." Famous last words!

Here is a communication by Professor Wesley Fishal, who was the American public police adviser in Viet-Nam in the late 1950's. He said in August 1958, "Indeed, Viet-Nam can be classed as about the most stable and peaceful country in all of Asia today." I would underline the fact that in 1958 the Vietnamese were losing something like three village chiefs a day. But village chiefs were not considered a military target. They were not considered part of our calculations with regard to what makes a war. For example, the *Infantry Journal* of August 1960 stated:

> The Communist objectives, for the most part, have been thwarted by South Vietnamese military strength. Threats and actual attacks have been made on American advisers through their armed forces. The fact that these attacks have been made is a good indication that the American aid is effective.

What this seems to mean is that if American advisers get killed in Viet-Nam we are doing fine. *The Air Force and Space Digest* of June 1962 stated:

> There are a few things about the insurgent warfare that favor the use of air power and one of them is that the jungle rebels are not equipped with antiaircraft, so that air superiority is practically assured.

That would be good news to the helicopter pilots who represent the bulk of our casualties. In another *Air Force and Space Digest* article of August 1964 the following statement is made:

> The figures of 1963 in the Vietnamese theater indicate that the cost/effectiveness of the air effort is high. It is estimated that the Viet-Nam Air Force uses less than 3% of the total military personnel. . . . These planes account for more than a third of the total Viet Cong killed in action; that is 7400 out of 20,600.

The joke, of course, if you can see the point, is that if 3% of the Vietnamese personnel effects 33% of the casualties, a simple

215

tripling of that 3% of Air Force personnel would effect 100% of the casualties. Therefore, we need not send anybody else. But no one has considered that in all likelihood, of the 23,500 killed, a large part are noncombatant civilians. It is pretty hard to tell a Viet Cong flying at 250 knots and from 500 feet up, or more. This leads to the completely incongruous reasoning that if there are 100,000 Viet Cong in South Viet-Nam and the A.R.V.N.[1] kill 23,500 a year and maim perhaps another 25,000, and if we divide 100,000 Viet Cong by 50,000 a year the war should be over in two years. This meaningless equation probably accounted for 1963 estimates of victory by 1965. This is precisely where cost/effectiveness has its limitations.

Such reports point to a phenomenon which seems to conform to a pattern. Allow me to cite a report on the subject:

> There was little or no realism in the sense of appreciating facts and conditions as they really were or were going to be, instead of what was imagined or wanted to be. The cause was fundamental, consisting of an academic bureaucratic outlook, based on little realistic practice and formed in an environment utterly different to what we experienced in the war.
>
> In the case of the staff this environment was in the cool of an office or the comfort of the road, scarcely ever the rubber jungle with its storms and claustrophobic oppressiveness. All seemed good in a good world. There was no inducement to look below the surface or to change our appreciations.

The document is declassified now. It is a report of a British colonel whose regiment was destroyed in Malaya by the Japanese in 1941. This document is 23 years old. Yet it sounds like a U.S. adviser from yesterday. Then as now everybody likes to fight the war that he knows best; this is very obvious. But in Viet-Nam we fight a war that we don't Know Best. The sooner this is realized the better it is going to be.

When I first arrived in Indochina in 1953, the French were mainly fighting in the Red River Delta. This was the key French area in North Viet-Nam. The French headquarters city was Hanoi. When

[1] Army of the Republic of Viet-Nam.

I arrived I checked in with the French briefing officer and asked what the situation was in the delta. He said:

> Well, we hold pretty much of it; there is the French fortified line around the Delta which we call the Marshal de Lattre Line —about 2200 bunkers forming 900 forts. We are going to deny the communists access to the 8 million people in this Delta and the 3 million tons of rice it produces. We will eventually starve them out and deny them access to the population.

In other words, this was the strategic hamlet complex seen five thousand times bigger. There were about 8000 villages inside that line. This fortified line also protected the rice fields then, whereas now the individual strategic hamlets do not protect the same fields. "Well," I said, "do the communists hold anything inside the delta?" The answer was, "Yes, they hold those five black blotches." But at the University of Hanoi, which was under national Vietnamese control, my fellow Vietnamese students just laughed. They said that their home villages inside the Delta were Communist-controlled and had Communist village chiefs, and just about everybody else said the same thing; that both the French and the Vietnamese Army simply did not know what was going on.

Most of these villages were, in fact, controlled by the Communists and I decided to attempt to document that control. It was actually very simple: To the last breath a government will try to collect taxes. So I used a working hypothesis; I went to the Vietnamese tax collection office in Hanoi to look at the village tax rolls. They immediately indicated that the bulk of the Delta was no longer paying taxes. As a cross-check on my theory I used the village teachers.

The school teachers in Viet-Nam were centrally assigned by the Government. Hence, where there were school teachers the Government could be assumed to have control. Where there were none, there was no Government control. The resulting difference between military "control" and what the Communists controlled *administratively* was 70% of the delta inside the French battlelines! This was *one year before the Battle of Dien Bien Phu,* in May 1954. In fact, the military situation was complete fiction and had absolutely no bearing on the *real* situation inside the Delta. Of course, when regular

217

Communist divisions became available to attack the Delta in June 1954, the whole illusion collapsed. The area was solidly Communist-infiltrated and, of course, collapsed overnight. That is revolutionary warfare.

4. "RW" in South Viet-Nam

When I returned to Viet-Nam in 1957, after the Indochina War had been over for two years, everybody was telling me that the situation was fine. However, I noticed in the South Vietnamese press, obituaries of village chiefs, and I was bothered. I thought there were just too many obituaries—about one a day—allegedly killed not by Communists, but by "unknown elements," and by "bandits." I decided to plot out a year's worth of dead village officials. The result was that I counted about 452 dead village chiefs to my knowledge at that time. Then I also saw in the press, and here and there in Viet-Nam heard discussions about "bandit attacks." These attacks were not made at random, but in certain areas. That too worried me, so I decided to plot the attacks. I immediately noted in both cases a very strange pattern. The attacks and the village chiefs were "clustered" in certain areas.

I went to see the Vietnamese Minister of the Interior, Nguyen Huu Chau, who then was, incidentally, the brother-in-law of Madame Nhu, and I said to him: "Your Excellency, there is something I'm worried about. You know that I was in the North when the French were losing and I noticed the village chiefs disappearing and I think you now have the same problem here." He said, "What do you mean?" So I just showed him the map. He said, "Well, since you found that out all by yourself, let me show you *my* map." And he pulled out a map which showed not only the village chiefs but also the Communist cells operating in South Viet-Nam in 1957–58 when Viet-Nam was at peace and there was supposedly nothing going on. It was wonderful. We all congratulated each other. Yet, very obviously, to use a somewhat

218

unscientific term, the whole Mekong Delta was going "to hell in a basket," and much of South Viet-Nam with it.[2]

The insurgency cross-check was unexpectedly provided to me by the International Control Commission. They get reports from the Communists as well as from our side, but in this case what interested me was the alleged incidents inside South Viet-Nam. The Communists would report from Hanoi, through the ICC, that Americans or Vietnamese were doing certain things out in the villages which Hanoi alleged were "violations" of the cease-fire agreement. I said to myself, "If I plot out all the Communist reports about alleged violations on a map, and if they match high-incident areas, there may be a logical connection between the guerrilla operators and the intelligence operators who provide the basis for the ICC reports." Sure enough the same areas with the high incidents also had high reports. As of early 1958, I knew we were in deep trouble in Viet-Nam and I kept saying so.

In 1959 the Southeast Asia Treaty Organization gave me a research grant to do a study on Communist infiltration in the area. The results of the study showed that Saigon was deliberately *encircled* and *cut off* from the hinterland with a "wall" of dead village chiefs. President Kennedy, in his second State of the Union message on May 25, 1961, stated that during the past year (meaning April 1960–61) the Communists killed *4000 small officials* in Viet-Nam! This was one year before the Taylor Report which got the whole American major effort going. In other words, in 1960 and 1961 the Communists killed *11 village officials a day*. By the time we woke up and learned that we had a problem, the Communists had killed about 10,000 village chiefs in a country that has about 16,000 hamlets. This, gentlemen, is "control"—not the military illusion of it.

From then on, it was open and shut. One year later, in 1963, somebody discovered that my system of judging insurgent control from tax returns was applicable to South Viet-Nam also. A study produced by A.I.D. (The U. S. Agency for International Development) showed the extent of tax collection in South Viet-Nam. It reflected the situation for March–May 1963, six months before Diem

[2] *Cf.* Fall, "South Viet-Nam's Internal Problems," *Pacific Affairs,* September 1958.

was overthrown, and four months before the Buddhist outbreaks.

To make a long story short, there were only three provinces out of forty-five which reported no Communist tax collections.

5. The Erroneous Criteria of "Success"

I have emphasized that the straight military aspects, or the conventional military aspects of insurgency, are not the most important. Tax collections have nothing to do with helicopters. Village chiefs have nothing to do with M-133's except in the most remote sense, nor with the aerial bombardment of North Viet-Nam. What we are faced with precisely is a Communist, military-backed operation to take over a country under our feet. I would like to put it in even a simpler way: *When a country is being subverted it is not being outfought; it is being outadministered.* Subversion is literally administration with a minus sign in front. This is what I feel has to be clearly understood. Whether it is the Congo, Viet-Nam or Venezuela, is totally irrelevant. Whether we have the "body count," the "kill count," the "structure count," or the "weapons count"—these are almost meaningless considerations in an insurgency situation. We can lose weapons and still win the insurgency. On the other hand, we can win the war and lose the country.

We always hang on for dear life to the Malayan example, which, of course, is totally unworkable. The only thing that Viet-Nam has which resembles Malaya, is the climate. We don't give the Communists credit for making mistakes, yet Malaya was one of their big mistakes. They actually decided to take on the British in a straightforward military operation and, predictably, failed.

If revolutionary war simply were jungle war, every regular force could win it. Americans know how to fight jungle wars. One can fight a revolutionary war in Norway, or fight a revolutionary war in France. It doesn't take a jungle to fight a revolutionary war. One can take over villages not only in the highlands of Viet-Nam, but in the lowlands of Belgium the same way. This is, of course, the key point. Remember that the British fought in Cyprus, and Cyprus seemingly had everything in her favor. It is an island half the size of New Jersey. The Royal Navy, which can be trusted to do its job, sealed off the island from the outside. There were 40,000 British troops on Cyprus under Field Marshal Sir John Harding and his opponent, Colonel Grivas, had 300 Greeks in the EOKA. The ratio between regular troops and guerrillas were 110-to-1 in favor of the British! After five years the British preferred to come to terms with the rebels.

The French in Algeria learned every lesson from the French in Viet-Nam. The troop ratio there was a comfortable 11-to-1; the French had 760,000 men; the Algerians had 65,000. The French very effectively sealed off the Algerian-Tunisian border, and by 1962 had whittled down the guerrillas from 65,000 to 7000. But the French were winning at the expense of being the second-most-hated country in the world, after South Africa, in the United Nations. They were giving the whole Western alliance a black name.[3] At what price were the French winning? Well, 760,000 men out of about 1 million men of the French armed forces were tied down in Algeria. It cost 3 million dollars a day for *eight years,* or $12 billion in French money. No American aid was involved. The price also included two mutinies of the French Army and one overthrow of the civilian government. At that price the French were winning the war in Algeria, *militarily.* The fact was that the military victory was totally meaningless. This is where the word grandeur applies to President de Gaulle: He was capable of seeing through the trees of military victory to a forest of political defeat and he chose to settle the Algerian insurgency by other means.

Some of these wars, of course, *can* be won, as in the Philippines, for example. The war was won there *not* through military action (there wasn't a single special rifle invented for the Philippines, let alone more sophisticated ordnance) but through an extremely well-conceived Civic Action program and, of course, a good leader—Magsaysay.

Civic action is not the construction of privies or the distribution of antimalaria sprays. One can't fight an ideology; one can't fight a militant doctrine with better privies. Yet this is done constantly. One side says, "Land reform," and the other side says, "Better

[3] For example, when the French effected a reprisal raid on rebel bases in Tunisia on February 8, 1958, several senior U.S. leaders expressed shock and demanded the return to U.S. control of American-made aircraft used by the French.

culverts." One side says, "We are going to kill all those nasty village chiefs and landlords." The other side says, "Yes, but look, we want to give you prize pigs to improve your strain." These arguments just do not match. Simple but adequate appeals will have to be found sooner or later.

6. Conclusion

What, then, can be done in a warlike Viet-Nam? Does the West have to lose such wars automatically? I said at the beginning that even the non-Westerners can lose those wars. But, either way, one must attempt to preserve the essentials. The question in my mind is this: Can we in Viet-Nam, or anywhere else, save (or improve) the administrative or governmental structure? The answer is obvious, and there is no other effort really worth doing. We have tried this with the Strategic Hamlets and that literally failed. Out of 8500 strategic hamlets, about 1400 survived the effort. Some people have spoken of what is called the Oil-slick Principle which has been described as the holding of one particular area, one central area, and working one's way out of the center. That was fine when the French developed the concept for the Sahara, because in the Sahara there are obligatory watering points. If they have all the oases, those outside have to come in and get water. But Viet-Nam doesn't happen to be the Sahara or an oasis. Thus, the oil-slick method succeeds mostly in pushing the Viet Cong units into the next province. Of course, it looks good, at least, because for one week there will be a cleared province. For the time being this is considered adequate until something more imaginative is discovered.

The actual thing that can be done, and is also being done, is what the French call gridding.[4] One doesn't start from the center of something and work one's way out, but he starts from the periphery and works one's way *in*. The chances are that if it is done right, and if it is done in enough places at once, some Communist units will finally get fixed (as the army says) and caught. This may yet work, but this requires a high degree of manpower saturation not available in Viet-Nam.

[4] *Quadrillage.*

There are no easy shortcuts to solving the problems of revolutionary war. In fact, I would like to close with one last thought which applies, of course, to everything that is done in the Armed Forces, but particularly to revolutionary war: *If it works, it is obsolete.* In Viet-Nam and in many other similar situations we have worked too often with well-working but routine procedures and ideas. It is about time that new approaches and—above all— ideas be tried; since, obviously, the other ones have been unequal to the task.

"This Isn't Munich,
It's Spain"

⟨※⟩

". . . the whole country hates you, but at least they won't resist you . . ."

THE FOLLOWING PASSAGE is a quotation from a French book, *Revolutionary War and Christian Conscience,* prefaced by Msgr. Pierre Marie Théas, Bishop of Bardes and Lourdes, and bearing the imprimatur of a Jesuit organization in Paris, published by the French section of *Pax Christi* in 1963: *"Respect for Man means, above all, that the enemy (true or presumed guilty or suspect), is considered as a human being."*

Americans appear to have forgotten this in Viet-Nam. I have just returned from the war there and found it depersonalized and, to a large extent, dehumanized.

It is a brutal war. One million Vietnamese died in the long colonial encounter with the French—and already, in what may loosely be termed the "American period," the dead are near a quarter million, with perhaps another half-million people seriously maimed. And other Vietnamese people are dying because they are starving; there are vast areas where people starve because food cannot get through—food blocked off by our side so it won't get to the Viet Cong, or taken by the Viet Cong to feed their forces. If the present war were to last as long as the French war, another million people may well die in Viet-Nam.

There are two theoretical casualties in this war. One is the "war of national liberation" concept of the Communists, and the other is the American theory of "counterinsurgency." At the heart of counterinsurgency is the idea that people matter—that we are in Viet-Nam to get people to fight for something *they* believe in rather than something *we* believe in. The new mix of air war and of land and seaborne firepower in Viet-Nam is one of technological counterinsurgency—if you keep up the kill rate you will eventually run out of enemies. Or at least armed enemies. Of course, the whole country will hate you, but at least they won't resist you. What you will get is simply a cessation of resistance—an acquiescence in one's fate rather than a belief that your side and your ideas have really prevailed.

I don't think we are buying Vietnamese stability in the long run out of the present operation. What we are buying is an example—for Latin America and other guerrilla-prone areas. What we're really doing in Viet-Nam is killing the cause of "wars of liberation." And we may yet succeed.

The common explanation of America's Viet-Nam involvement is that the United States is being "tested"—that we have to stand up and stop Communism right here. The analogy of Munich is suggested here—the failure of the British and French to stand up to the Nazis. But the situation in Viet-Nam isn't Munich; it is Spain. There is in Viet-Nam a test of wills, of course, as at Munich—but above all, there is a test of military technology and techniques and military ideas. One side believes it can win with a combination of guerrilla warfare and political ideology. The other side believes it can win with the massive use of military power. America may be able to prove, as the Germans and Italians did in Spain, that superior firepower will carry the day in such a situation. One can find many people who will look at the last quarter-century in Spain and argue that if it took the Spanish Civil War with its one and a half million dead to produce a "stable" Spain for 25 or 30 years, then the war was worth it. And no doubt there must be Russians who now look at the crushing of the Hungarian rebellion of 1956 as a "necessary" step to the "orderly" liberalization that eventually ensued under Janos Kadar. It is not straining the analogy to suggest that there are now Americans who would make the same judgment of the war in Viet-Nam: it may be a nasty claw-and-nail war, but what the hell, it's worth it if we come out on top.

". . . their trees are dead . . ."

The impact of the war right now is not literally the killing of individuals by individuals—you do not often see heaps of the dead lying around. But what you do see is the impact on the countryside. In Asia vegetation is always lush, but now when you fly over parts of Viet-Nam you can see the dead, brown surface of the areas which have been sprayed with weed killers. You see the areas that were sprayed on purpose, and the places defoliated by accident. Ben Cat, a huge plantation near Saigon, was almost completely destroyed by accident; 3000 acres were transformed into the tropical equivalent of a winter forest. I visited a Catholic refugee village, Honai, along Highway 1 in South Viet-Nam. It was sprayed by mistake. All its fruit trees died. United States Air Force planes were defoliating the jungle along Highway 1, but the wind shifted and blew the killer spray toward the villages instead. In a supreme irony, the jungle now stands in the background, lush and thick, while the villages are barren.

When I was there, the villagers were chopping down the trees. The only resource they had left was the remains of their dead fruit trees, to be sold in Saigon for firewood.

The Overkill

Mao Tse-tung's theory that a guerrilla must live among the population like a fish in water worked in China against a politically and militarily ineffective enemy. This theory as a guideline for "wars of liberation" may be disproved in Viet-Nam. Mao's theory requires an effective political base in the country—but what is a political base against B-52's? The United States, by massive bombing, seeks to deprive the guerrilla of his population—the fish of his water. We want the population to flee to our side—after all, on our side you at least can get food, and get away from the bombing.

The statistics behind this strategy are as brutal as the reality. The Viet Cong are credited with killing or kidnapping between 15,000 and 16,000 village officials during the course of the war, and probably killing another 5000 in one way or another during the past year. American casualties are less than 1000 dead and about 3000 wounded. On the other hand, the official United States statistics of "enemy" killed since 1961 have now passed the 100,000 mark. In the week ending October 4, 1965, some 1067 Communists were said to have been killed in South Viet-Nam. At that rate, there will be 50,000 "enemy" deaths in Viet-Nam this year alone.

One of the great and crucial questions in this war is how many of these casualties are Viet Cong, and how many are civilians? It is generally estimated that there are two wounded for every one killed on the battlefield. Thus by the end of this year the Viet Cong or somebody in its area of operations must be presumed to have suffered upwards of 400,000 casualties. Since the entire Viet Cong force is estimated at between 150,000 to 160,000, this means that we have "overkilled" the Viet Cong about two and a half times. Obviously this isn't true.

Official figures set the number of infiltrators to the Viet Cong from North Viet-Nam at five to six thousand a year; yet, despite the tremendous firepower thrown at the Communists and the high casualty count, the Viet Cong does not appear to lose appreciably in strength. The conclusion that must be reached is that many of the people being killed are not Viet Cong, even though they may be listed as such. A truly staggering amount of civilians are getting killed or maimed in this war.

"An impersonal, an American war"

The Viet-Nam conflict has become an impersonal, an American war. I was with an American airborne unit operating strictly on its own. There was not one Vietnamese with that unit. It was going strictly by its own mark and literally by its own light. The "Skyraider," a World War II vintage bomber is used quite effectively in Viet-Nam. It is said to be the only airplane that carries its own weight in payload. An extremely solid and heavy plane, the "Skyraider" can withstand small arms and automatic weapons ground fire better than any other fighter bombers, including the jets. It is an amazing airplane—especially in the amount of destruction it can bring to bear. You have to know an airplane like this before you can really understand the tremendous impact of American firepower on the Vietnamese on the ground. This airplane can carry a bombload of 7500 pounds under its wings. It can unload a variety of bombs—750-pounders, 500-pounders, 250-pounders, 100-pound general-purpose bombs. It also can drop 260-pound fragmentation bombs, 120-pound fragmentation bombs, or 100-pound white phosphorous bombs and napalm. The "Skyraider" has four 20-millimeter cannon as well.

This was the airplane I was to ride in on a raid on a Vietnamese fishing village.

"A Raid On a Fishing Village"

Our "Skyraider" was loaded with 750-pound napalm bombs and 500-pound napalm bombs, plus our four 20-millimeter cannon. Our wing plane carried 7500 pounds of high explosive anti-personnel bombs, plus our four cannon. We were the lead plane going in. My pilot was Major John C. Carson.

We were airborne for one and one half hours before we reached our primary target. But as we came over the target the monsoon came down with quite incredible force and completely obscured the ground. Then a decision was made, in accordance with established procedures, to switch over to the alternate target which was described as a "Communist rest center" in the Camau Peninsula. A rest center may of course be anything, any group of huts, or it may be just a normal village in which Viet Cong troops have put down stake for, perhaps, 48 hours.

As we flew over the target it looked to me very much as any normal village would look: on the edge of a river, sampans and fish nets in the water. It was a peaceful scene. Major Carson put our plane into a steep dive. I could see the napalm bombs dropping from the wings. The big bombs, first. As we peeled back from our dive, there was an incredibly bright flash of fire as napalm exploded at the tree level. The first pass had a one-two effect. The napalm was expected to force the people—fearing the heat and the burning—out into the open. Then the second plane was to move in with heavy fragmentation bombs to hit whatever—or whomever—had rushed out into the open. So our wingman followed us in and dropped his heavy explosives. Mushroom-like clouds drifted into the air. We made a second pass and dropped our remaining 500-pound napalm bombs. Our wingman followed. Then we went in a third time and raked over the village with our cannon. We came down low, flying very fast, and I could see some of the villagers trying to head away from the burning shore in their sampans. The village was burning fiercely. I will never forget the sight of the fishing nets in flame, covered with burning, jellied gasoline. Behind me I could hear—even through my padded flying helmet—the roar of our plane's 20-millimeter cannon as we flew away.

"Awarding the 'Score'"

Behind us flew a small, very dainty-looking aircraft, an OF-1, otherwise referred to as a "bird dog." It is a spotter plane—used to find targets for the bombers and to determine whether the targets have been hit and—as the word goes in Viet-Nam—award you your "score." The "score" is usually worked out in numbers of structures hit and numbers of people seen dead on the ground. This information is reported to Air Intelligence, and eventually becomes part of the composite "score" for the week (the number of sorties flown plus what is called the "structure count" and the "body count"). These are the terms by which success is measured in the new Viet-Nam war.

There were probably between 1000 and 1500 people living in the fishing village we attacked. It is difficult to estimate how many were killed. It is equally difficult to judge if there actually were any Viet Cong in the village, and if so, if any were killed. The observation planes are called the FAC's (Forward Air Controllers). But it happens very often in Viet-Nam that, as a current joke goes, the FAC's have their facts wrong; that the raid information is stale; that

229

there may have been Communists in the village—but the day before. You may very often get the proper amount of structures awared to your "score," but you may not have hit any Communist structures. So it is difficult to say whether you hit a Communist or whether you just hit the village which, unwilling, may have been the host of a Communist unit for one night. Or maybe not at all. This has happened.

During our attack probably ten to fifteen houses were hit. There is at least one family per house, and Vietnamese families average from six to eight persons. In each of those houses there must have been people maimed or killed—no one knows how many. I read an official report later which described the village as a Communist rest center, and said it had been successfully destroyed.

Then something happened that was not part of the plan. One of our napalm bombs failed to drop off the airplane! Pilots are not supposed to land with bombs aboard for fear of the bomb exploding on the airfield and burning grounded planes (it happened at Bien Hoa and caused a major disaster). We had to get rid of our bomb or, if need be, bail out and let the plane crash. My pilot went into a steep power dive and pulled out brutally to force the bomb off its rack. It is an incredible experience as the force of gravity grabs your body. You cannot lift your arms except with enormous effort. I could see my face muscles being pulled into a horrible grimace in the side view mirror. Finally, the bomb dropped. The pilot pointed at an accelerometer: 4.8 G's. For a few instants my body had weighed 900 lbs.

It was a good thing for some Vietnamese peasants that we could find our secondary target and could get rid of our recalcitrant bomb, because if that target had been rained out or clouded over, we would have jettisoned our bombs in what is known as a "free bomb" zone. Now in a free bomb area you are authorized to drop your ordnance anywhere. Any target, any structure, any movement at all. The free bomb zones in South Viet-Nam change constantly, so it is difficult to give any accurate acreage for them. But, for example, the free bomb zone around Zone D adds up to something like 300 square miles. Anyone living in these areas is presumed to be the enemy. Or, at least, presumed to be "hostile" and therefore destroyable.

230

"The French Didn't Have the Bombs . . ."

The massiveness of American military superiority is overwhelming. When you compare it to the French Indochina military effort you see just how overwhelming. The raid I flew on was a small raid. But there are very large raids, very often, in Viet-Nam. It is quite normal to fly 150 air raids in one day. The French, at the peak of their Indochina campaign at the Battle of Dien Bien Phu, expended during the entire 56 days of battle less bomb power than the United States does in one single day. It is meaningless to compare the use of airpower by the French and Americans in Viet-Nam. When you resort to area bombing, you begin to frighten or to destroy the populace, and the French weren't effective at that because the French planes didn't have the range, and the French didn't have the bombs. The French aircraft total in all of Indochina—in North and South Viet-Nam, Cambodia, and Laos—was 112 fighters and 68 bombers. That is what the United States flies in a single mission.

One of the major mistakes that Europeans and many non-specialists make is to view the American military effort as only a multiple of the French effort. It is not a multiple, it is a geometric progression. This has to be clearly understood. For example, when I saw President Ho Chi Minh in North Viet-Nam in 1962, he told me that he thought that since he had been able to defeat the French in eight years, the stronger Americans could in all likelihood be defeated in 10 years. This is precisely the extent of the misconception. Anyone who believes the Americans are simply 20 per cent stronger than the French simply does not understand the strength of American power—and the willingness of Americans to use that power in such a war. The French, for example, never dared to send conscripts to Viet-Nam, nor did they increase the draft at home for fear of public opposition to the war. Viet-Nam was not considered by the French parliament, or for that matter the French people, as being a vital issue of French power. The United States obviously feels differently. This is reaffirmed every day in Viet-Nam.

The United States ground firepower is also extraordinary. Soldiers used to carry rifles with clips of maybe 8 or 10 rounds. Now, almost every American in Viet-Nam carries an automatic rifle which can shoot up to four or five hundred rounds a minute, if it has to. The Vietnamese are the only ones carrying single-shot or semi-automatic weapons. It doesn't even do the Viet Cong much good to capture American automatic weapons. A guerrilla force can't possibly sustain the supply of ammunition needed to keep those guns firing. Of course, the United States side can, indefinitely. And it does.

"No Respect for the Wounded . . ."

Then there is the South Vietnamese prisoner cage. I took a picture inside a camp where Americans were present. No attempt was made to hide the cage, an iron frame covered completely with barbed wire. About four feet high, it is used for bringing prisoners to "reason." I was not told what kind of prisoners are put in the cage, but no matter who they are, this is a pretty violent process. The prisoner cannot stand up or sit down—if he moves out of a crouch he falls against the sharp barbed wire; there is so much wire that his body is punctured all over. This makes Christ's Crown of Thorns look like a child's toy.

In this war, there is no respect for the wounded. A Communist prisoner had been shot in the back. He was bleeding when I found him lying on the floor in a Vietnamese Army Command Post. A journalist from a New York paper came in and asked to photograph him. The South Vietnamese officer in the room raised the wounded man matter-of-factly and propped him against a table leg for the photographer. The prisoner grimaced in pain.

I told an American officer who was with the unit that the man was wounded and should get some attention. His answer: "Yes, I know he needs help, but there isn't anything I can do about it. He's in Vietnamese hands. That is why I walked away, don't you see?" I saw. I also walked away and said nothing.

In this war, there is no respect for hospitals, either. I saw a South Vietnamese civilian ambulance which had been raked with machine gun fire by the Viet Cong. All four patients and the driver were killed inside. This sort of brutality has become normal on both sides: Joseph Alsop reported recently, unblinkingly, that there had been three Viet Cong hospitals destroyed in Zone D along with "vast stocks of medicine." This followed on complaints from the North, now verified by non-Communist outside observers, that at

232

least one hospital had been completely destroyed by bombers. Canadian officials who recently returned from North Viet-Nam also told me that the city of Vinh was "flattened." It used to have a population of 60,000. I can't believe that the whole city was a "military objective."

The answer to any attempt to raise the question of America's moral responsibility for such actions is the same excuse the Army officer gave me about the bleeding, unattended prisoner: the violation of rules is done by the Vietnamese. But that in itself is not an *excuse*. While it is true that South Viet-Nam is a sovereign entity, it is also true that it hardly operates independently of the United States. I spent 1946–48 at the Nuremberg trials as a young research analyst and in a number of cases I heard the Germans attempt to excuse atrocities as acts committed by troops of their allies. This wasn't considered an excuse and did not absolve the Germans of their responsibility. (By the way, both Viet-Nam and the United States have signed and ratified the 1949 Geneva Convention on War Victims.)

I have heard no questions of morality raised by American officials over the South Vietnamese treatment of prisoners. But many Americans have complained, on purely practical grounds, that the mistreatment of the wounded and captured has resulted in few surrenders by hard-core Viet Cong and has sparked reprisals against American soldiers by the Viet Cong.

But, contrary to what had been expected, the Viet Cong have treated American prisoners quite correctly. From all the accounts I received from Intelligence in Viet-Nam, there is no evidence of torture of American prisoners by the Viet Cong, and released United States prisoners have confirmed this.

The torture and terror utilized by the South Vietnamese is something else. It is, in the Pentagon phrase, "counter-productive." American officers in the field with Vietnamese troops make critical remarks about their behavior toward their own people—stealing, raping, burning down villages, generally kicking people around. In contrast to this random brutality, one of the most heralded of the Viet Cong's terror tactics, the selective assassination of village chiefs, could even be considered, in the military idiom, "productive." When Diem ended the 400 to 500 year tradition of the democratic election of village chiefs by each village, he made, to my mind, probably his most crucial mistake. He began making local appointments from Saigon, and the appointees—many of them outsiders—were met with open hostility by the villagers. Diem's men would have to go outside the village to the police post to sleep safely. Many of them were known to be gouging the villages. The hard fact is that when the Viet Cong assassinated these men, the Viet Cong were given a Robin Hood halo by the villagers.

The reality in Viet-Nam is that the international rules of war are not obeyed and, contrary to popular belief, the rules *do* apply to guerrilla wars as well. "War crimes" are recorded almost daily and sometimes by cameramen—the burning of villages, for example. There seems to be a predisposition on our side to no longer be able to see the Vietnamese as people against whom crimes can be committed. This is the ultimate impersonalization of the war.

"The worst is yet to come . . ."

The incredible thing about Viet-Nam is that the worst is yet to come. We have been bombing for a relatively short time and the results are devastating. The United States is probably only operating at 1 per cent capacity in Viet-Nam. Everything could be escalated vastly—in the North, major industrial targets, major towns, and then the irrigation dams; in the South, more powerful bombs on more vulnerable targets. (It is strictly a one-way operation in the South. The Viet Cong do not have a single flying machine. We can literally go anywhere and bomb anything. The possibilities of devastation are open-ended.)

Yet what America is seeking is not total victory over the Viet Cong. We are going for *total defeat* of the VC. The semantics are important, because what America should want to prove in Viet-Nam is that the Free World is "better," *not* that it can kill people more efficiently. If we would induce 100,000 Viet Cong to surrender to our side because our offers of social reform are better than those of the other side's, *that* would be victory. Hence, even a total military or technological defeat of the Viet Cong is going to be a partial defeat of our own purposes—a defeat of ourselves, by ourselves, as it were.

I think it is clearly established that the kind of American forces, in huge and growing numbers, are so enormous that the chance of an American Dien Bien Phu in Viet-Nam is nil. But I do not speak about military victory—rather I want to make it clear that military *losing* is no longer a question. But given military "unlosability," the big question remaining is what it will take to bring about a "stable" Viet-Nam. "Stability" is the great catchword these days, and the Pentagon is now using the phrase "stability operation" in lieu of "counterinsurgency." Most knowledgeable people will say that a ten-year "stabilization" period is not beyond the realm of the imagination, with the number of American troops in Viet-Nam reaching upwards of one million.

When Hanson Baldwin, the New York *Times'* noted military commentator, suggested last spring that one million Americans might be required in Viet-Nam he was greeted with general derision and disbelief. Now we can say that one million American troops is a quite possible figure, though it might be reduced if other nations send in troops. The United States is constantly on the search for allies.

If one accepts the 10-to-1 ratio of "stabilizing" troops to guerrillas, then at least 1.5 million men would be required in Viet-Nam. The South Vietnamese army now has 600,000 men with all para-military forces included, but has low morale and efficiency, and a high desertion rate—and is having a very hard time finding more men. Anyway, it is quite pointless in one sense to project a "stabilization" period in terms of years—the British had a 55-to-1 superiority in Malaya and it took them 13 years to win.

Neo-Machiavellianism

But in the way the war is now fought in Viet-Nam, the human element which, I feel, *must* be at the center even of a deadly conflict, recedes further and further into the periphery. Viet-Nam is simply a test case—on our side of "credibility" in resisting Communist penetration; on the Viet Cong side of the possibility of changing the world balance by leap-frogging (or burrowing under) the nuclear stalemate of the big powers. Or worse, Viet-Nam is simply a test bed of weapons and battle techniques. The armed

235

peasant versus Detroit and the "think factories." But what I really fear most, if this sort of situation drags on indefinitely, is the creation of new ethics to match new warfare. Indications are that a new ethic is already being created, and such influential men as former Secretary of State Dean Acheson have begun to provide its intellectual underpinning. Acheson said in a speech at Amherst College in December 1965:

"The end sought by our foreign policy . . . is, as I have said, to preserve and foster an environment in which free societies may exist and flourish. Our policies and actions must be decided by whether they contribute to or detract from achievement of this end. They need no other justification or moral or ethical embellishment. . . ."

That argument was answered in a way by French Cardinal Feltin in a Pastoral Letter issued on October 24, 1960 (in the midst of the Algerian war) to the French military chaplains. In it the Cardinal said:

"There cannot be a morality which justifies efficacy by all means, if those means are in formal contradiction with Natural Law and Divine Law. Efficacy, in that case, goes against the very aim it seeks to achieve. There can be exceptional laws for exceptional situations . . . there cannot exist an exceptional morality which somehow takes leave of Natural Law and Divine Law."

Looking back at the Viet-Nam I left, I can see the means only too clearly, and so can everyone else who is not altogether blind. But I cannot say that I have found anyone who seems to have a clear idea of the end—of the "war aims"—and if the end is not clearly defined, are we justified to use any means to attain it?

"You Can Tell 'Em, Buddy"

"LOOKS LIKE Tan Son Nhut got it again," said the Navy driver, as we drove off for Saigon's Tan Son Nhut airbase—the busiest in the world, allegedly, after O'Hare Field in Chicago. The airbase, though hardly four miles from downtown Saigon, has been repeatedly hit by the Viet Cong, despite acres of barbed wire, minefields, infrared detectors, etc. In fact, the Viet Cong, in accordance with its overall change of tactics of sticking close to American units in the hope of avoiding heavy aerial bombardment, now has units in close contact with the Saigon perimeter. This compels the American forces progressively to take over the defense of the Saigon area—an initial force of three battalions, to be eventually augmented to six or even nine, is devoted to this—or to fly heavy air strikes within easy earshot of the city, thus vividly driving home the close presence of the adversary. An ambitious operation dubbed *Hop Tac* (Cooperation) two years ago, which was to clear the provinces surrounding Saigon of all VC elements, was quietly closed down a few weeks ago, a failure. But this time, the base was not hit: just a few infiltrators had been sighted.

The military waiting room at Tan Son Nhut looks like the modern version of the Great Migrations. The U. S. Air Force runs a comprehensive airlines system throughout the country and to several "out-country" destinations (Bangkok, the Philippines, Taiwan, Okinawa). Not only do the American military travel on duty, as couriers, on leave, as replacements and what not, but the Vietnamese have caught on to the traveling frenzy and every planeload has its fair share of Vietnamese women (presumably, or hopefully, military dependents of one sort or another), traveling with tiny babies and indescribable packages. By a military subtlety which causes American Army Corps here to be known as "field forces" (reserving the word "corps" for the Vietnamese Army), these regular military flights are not known as "flights" but as "missions." The planes flying those routes usually are Lockheeds, C-123 "Providers" or C-130 "Hercules," brutes with magnificent short-takeoff characteristics but built by Lockheed in total and utter disregard of any possible human cargo. I have flown in military planes since 1944, but I believe that the C-123's internal noise level is far beyond the pain threshold. The maximum-density seating arrangement (back to back in the middle, and facing inward on the sides, with sagging cargo nets as seat backs), combined with the dismal lighting, give the whole interior an aspect of some incredible olive-drab slum. In the 99 per cent humidity of the Vietnamese air, the cooling system of the aircraft gives off a dense acrid mist. "Must be *Zyklon-B*," said the man from *Time* squeezed in next to me, referring to the gas used by the Nazis in the gas chambers. It rains steadily inside the aircraft, and from all sides at once, it seems, thanks to the speed of the plane. Here you can tell the old-timers from the new arrivals: The former have their raincoats handy; the others grimly settle down to getting soaked. A new item of equipment has appeared: black insignia of rank and service. The gold-and-silver ranks and metal badges worn only a year ago have given way to black silhouettes of their former selves, a grim homage paid to the VC snipers. This has now become a fad-in-reverse, as garrison troopers who never see combat also begin to wear the black combat insignia.

The first stop is Danang, the huge airbase in central Viet-Nam

238

with what seems like miles of airplanes parked in reveted alcoves. "Out-country arrivals check with U.S.A.F. Customs," says a big sign. In other words, the U. S. Air Force, not the South Vietnamese government, exercises customs-inspection prerogatives here. If a Vietnamese official was involved at all, he was invisible. The steady downpour still beats down. Contrary to popular mythology, there are *two* rainy seasons in Viet-Nam: a summer one in the south of the country and the mountain areas and the other (a winter monsoon lasting until February) along the coast and in the north, where it seriously hampers U.S. air operations. At Danang begins the zone of responsibility of the U. S. Marines. Here also, the subtleties prevail: the Marine units were first known as the "Marine Expeditionary Force" until somebody discovered that the French troops in Indochina had been known as the *Corps Expéditionnaire,* and thus the 60,000 Marines (a two-division reinforced corps) were rebaptized as the "Marines Amphibious Force" (MAF).

Further northward, beyond Dong-Ha, lies the 17th Parallel, with its no longer Demilitarized Zone (DMZ), its hapless inspection post of the Indian-Canadian-Polish International Control Commission (ICC), and more Marines. This is the realm of an all-pervasive red mud covering everything at least calf-deep. It is far colder here than in Saigon, for even in this tropical country there are marked changes of temperature with rising latitudes. A road sign along National Road No. 1 is a clear reminder how different things are up here: "Saigon—1,138 km, Hanoi—582 km." Dong-Ha is the base of the American forces, mostly from the 3rd Marine Division, blocking the 17th Parallel. They had borne the brunt of the year's heavy fighting in Operations "Hastings" and "Prairie," against People's Army Division 324-B and paid a heavy price for blocking its penetration into South Viet-Nam. That is, *if* it wanted to do that; for there are some military men here who think that the whole operation of the 324-B was a bit too overt, too blatant, for what the North Vietnamese or Viet Cong would usually do. What if the division simply had carried out a diversionary maneuver, deliberately designed to draw American troops and attention away from the more important areas deep in the South? The militarization of political thinking here (all lip service to "pacification" aside) makes

239

it only too easy to decoy everybody and everything into a wild-goose chase after troops in the hope of yet another high "kill count." Whatever the reason, 324-B took serious losses.

On the Roof

Marine headquarters in Dong-Ha is in an old French military post, with its ochre masonry walls, supplemented by American temporary barracks. "You're the guy who wants to meet all the Marines from Dallas?" says the Marine PIO (Public Information Officer). I assured him that I wasn't but that I wanted to go northward to a unit on the Demilitarized Zone for Christmas. The steady rain precluded the use even of helicopters—an interesting commentary on the foibles of airpower in this war—and the PIO suggested I try and hitch a ride with the Christmas mail truck. "But it's a hairy ride, I tell you." Before I left, I witnessed a brief ceremony in which Marines from the Reconnaissance Commandos (Recondos) were given medals. It was held in one of the French barracks which served as a chapel in the back, vertically stacked mortar shell containers gave a striking imitation of organ pipes. The Recondos stood at attention in the darkness as the general read the citation for their work inside VC territory. I am proud to be associated with you. . . . I know it's rough when we can't get to you as fast as we want to. . . ."

Out on the road at the checkpoint, two soggy MP's stood near a flimsy shelter covered with graffiti, one of which masterfully expressed the whole situation: "I can't relate to this environment." As flies assemble around exposed food, a handful of small Vietnamese children trooped around the checkpoint, begging. "Ho Chi Minh number 10," says a little boy in English, repeating an American-Vietnamese neologism according to which good things are "number one" and bad things scaled at 10. "Do you know where Ho Chi Minh is?" I say in Vietnamese. "No," says the child.

The mail truck. Red and yellow U.S. mail bags. Two GI's, young, one a Negro. As we leave the checkpoint, the driver passes his rifle and ammo clips back to me. "Sir, would you mind covering my side?" It's an M-14, looking very much like its older brother, the M-1. Familiar gesture of pulling back breech, inserting the first

240

round, learned two decades ago; of locking safety, of looking warily at jungle closing in on the road. On the right side, the other GI cradles his submachinegun on his legs propped up high on the dashboard as we pick up speed, rocking crazily on the washboard road. The roar of the engine does not entirely drown out the sound of Christmas caroling up front in the truck's cab:

> *Jingle bells*
> *Mortar shells*
> *VC in the grass*
> *You can take your Merry Christmas*
> *And shove it up your ass.*

In the mounting darkness, we begin to climb out of the bushes and trees into a flat expanse of shrubless ground completely churned up by the tracks of tires and tank treads. The sharp outline of a tank hull mounting twin guns whizzes by.

"Home," says a voice in the truck cab. "We done made it again."

As I climb out of the truck with my pack and hand back the M-14, the voice in the truck says: "And you can tell 'em, buddy. War is shit."

This was Camp J. J. Carroll, also known as "Artillery Plateau," probably the most incredible single assemblage of groundborne firepower anywhere in the country. Commanded by the Marines, but also including Army artillery outfits, it boasts having in its inventory every ground weapon deployed in the armed forces, from infantry weapons upward to the Marine "Ontos" with its six deadly 106mm recoilless cannon, the self-propelled and brand-new 175's with their 35-foot-long tubes, and even an eight-inch gun just a shade shy of the howitzers deployed in Europe which fire atomic shells.

Sandbag bunkers and acres of barbed-wire systems (even interior positions are sealed off with barbed wire to limit any possible penetration to one position) surmounted by the menacing tubes pointing in all directions for all-around support give the whole place a weird air of *déjà-vu:* that is the way the battlefield must have looked in World War I, and that was what some of the French strongpoints in North Viet-Nam looked like 12 years ago, minus the immense firepower. A Dien Bien Phu with solid American teeth.

241

On a Clear Day

The briefing officer, in his soft Southern drawl, soon reveals the essential feature of Artillery Plateau: "On a clear day you can see the South China Sea on your right and the Laotian border on your left." The concentric circles on the acetate map overlay, indicating the artillery's maximum "reach" for each caliber, show what is meant—not only is much of the whole South Vietnamese border zone within their range, but the DMZ and parts of North Viet-Nam as well. Did they shoot into North Viet-Nam?

"No. That's left to the bombers of the Navy and Air Force. A strange distinction, if you ask me."

But tonight, Christmas Eve, the truce had begun, and Camp J. J. Carroll (a Marine captain killed accidentally by American tanks last summer during "Hastings") was humming with its own Christmas activities in a subdued way, further emphasized by the fog-laden rain. At the mess tent, the menu was the standard hash potatoes and hamburgers known to army messes the world over. But outside, a Marine choir sang carols—most of the voices were very boyish. A Santa Claus in full rig, ho-ho-hoing through a loudspeaker, rode by on a Mechanical Mule (a sort of Marine mini-jeep), wishing all units a Merry Christmas.

"You know," said the officer next to me, "we're going to have a helluvva time sleeping tonight without the gunfire. We fire most of our H-and-I [Harassment-and-Interdiction] missions at night and we haven't known a quiet night since we arrived here last September."

Then a single cannon shot rang out thunderously.

"Oh, that. That's nothing. Since we don't include reconnaissance among the missions prohibited by the truce, we keep firing illuminating flare shells to be sure nothing crawls around out there." The single shots would keep on ringing out at irregular intervals throughout the two nights of the truce.

On the perimeter, where the bunkers stand intermingled with the tanks, the men on watch talked more easily than usual and were more relaxed. "On other days they can get darn' trigger-happy if you don't happen to have the password ready when they challenge you," said the platoon commander of one of the posts. But they were also pensive. "Here, we tell Sundays from the other days because that's the day we take our weekly malaria pills," a lance corporal said quietly. "It's not like Christmas at all, is it?"

The soldiers had built a stage with whatever materials could be scrounged, in the forlorn hope that one of the big touring attractions would come their way for Christmas. It did not, and the letdown could be clearly felt.

"The only guy who came to see us recently was one of those big-name writers that's touring the country, and he only stayed for about a half-hour. And, boy, *he* looked like he needed a fifth real bad."

By the morning of Christmas Day, the mud had deepened by another few inches, and the walk to the latrine, in combat boots and rain poncho, was exquisite agony. In the tent there was a mail call—the mail we had brought up the evening before—and our squad was entitled to one of those parcels made up by thousands of schools throughout the country. It contained nine sets of playing cards and about all the salacious pocket books that the neighborhood had been able to come up with. The accompanying form letter, signed by the mothers of Rosemont Elementary School in Minnesota, stated: "We hope that your effort will help the cause of democracy and help stamp out Communist aggression. . . ."

Sick call in the aid station tent. An earnest young doctor is closing a deep gash over an eye. The patient lies on a narrow table covered with an Army blanket, his boots still on his feet, under local anesthesia, as the doctor calmly stitches away under the light of a single, bare 40-watt bulb. "If they only could see me at medical school in Richmond," he says as he strips off his gloves a few minutes later.

But beyond Artillery Plateau which, with its various units, still gives the impression of spaciousness, there are other, more nightmarish places like The Rockpile and Khé Sanh. The Rockpile is a 1200-foot near-pyramid which, though overtowered by nearby mountains, commands a view of five valleys and cost the Marines dearly last summer when they had to dislodge determined VC machinegunners from it. Its top has enough flat space for two medium-sized dinner tables. Twenty Marines and two artillery FO's (Forward Observers) live on it for weeks at a time. Its helicopter platform is composed of a series of loose planks jutting out over a

243

900-foot sheer drop, and through what can only be called idiotic pride, the Marines insist on using their unwieldly H-34 choppers, whose tricycle landing gear prohibits settling down on the platform; rather than using the Army's "Hueys" whose landing skids accommodate themselves easily to it. On the day I went there, a Marine returnee nearly lost his grip as a gust of wind pushed the H-34 from its landing-hover stance. For some mad seconds the man hung on by his fingertips until the door gunner and I dragged him in by his clothes. Yet this was a "good" day, because the weather permitted the landing of a chopper.

"One of the FO's once stayed for 43 solid days on The Rockpile. By the time they picked him off, he was throwing rocks at the passing jets."

Throwing rocks is a favorite pastime on The Rockpile. Sometimes the VC crawls right past the sentries of Lima Company at the base of the mountain and throws rocks at the Marines. They, in turn, throw them back, "Finally, we threw a grenade every fifth time. *That* stopped them."

Some Other Problems

On so small an area, claustrophobia as well as boredom or the equally merciless sun or rain are real problems. The problem of what to do with the human excrement was almost insurmountable until a deep chimney was found to one of the uninhabited grottoes below. And then there are the monkeys, a thieving lot who often pilfer the meager rations. When the Marines routinely informed Lima Company below that they were going to shoot some of them, the reply came just as routinely. "Are they VC apes or friendlies?" Just before the truce, on December 22, the VC had made a determined probe against The Rockpile. It would not be the last.

Beyond The Rockpile lay Khé Sanh, another former French fort which had grown from a small Special Forces camp to a dug-in position with Marines and artillery. Sealed off from the outside world except for air transport, Khé Sanh had been isolated for five days around Christmas.

"Now *there's* real jungle," said a young artillery captain patiently awaiting a moment's clear weather to return to his outfit there. "On one patrol we had a man who had collected 80 leeches on his body. He died later from exhaustion and loss of blood. Another had a leech crawl through his penis into his bladder. Most of us are wearing prophylactics on patrol to prevent that, because it's painful as hell. How the VC can stay in there year in, year out, just beats me."

Hanoi Hannah, the North Vietnamese English-language radio announcer, recently informed the Khé Sanh garrison (naming units by name) that it would be destroyed. Recent intelligence reports show that elements of the 341st People's Army Division were on the move and that 17 elephants, possibly carrying heavy Soviet mortars, were somewhere near there in the deep jungle.

"All they need is a few days of bad weather when we cannot use our airpower, and we're in real trouble."

Christmas dinner included all the trimmings, but no turkey. Bad weather had upset that part of the logistics, apparently. Short Christmas services were held here and there by the chaplains before small audiences. A group of GI's was lustily singing:

> On the first hour of Christmas
> The VC came at me
> In one ambush
> With two hand grenades
> Three bugles blowing
> Four flags a-flying
> Five mortar rounds . . .

A few officers were discussing the war. Like the proverbial atheists who aren't supposed to be in frontline trenches, there wasn't a "hawk" among them. At 11 P.M. the message center brought a last "Merry Christmas" message from a parent unit further down along the coast. The drumming of the rain on the tents became louder as one by one the power generators closed down for the night.

At 7:15 A.M. on Monday morning, the ground started to shake as the heavy guns began to fire their first post-truce mission, unobserved H-and-I fire on targets deeply shrouded in fog, at $168 a shell.

One hour later, an enormous dull roar echoed back from the mountains to the north of us: the giant B-52 bombers from Guam had unloaded hundreds of tons of bombs on the Demilitarized Zone.

They had taken off for their mission five hours before the truce had expired.

Unrepentant, Unyielding

An Interview with Viet Cong Prisoners

୭ଉଙ୍ଗ

Lai-Khé, South Viet-Nam

TWO YEARS AGO, Lai-Khé was a tranquil place hardly an hour's ride from Saigon, and the home of the *Institut de Recherches du Caoutchouc du Viet-Nam,* a research institute jointly financed by the French rubber plantations in Viet-Nam. There was some rubber production as such, but the low, yellow-stuccoed laboratory building with its neat rows of glittering instruments and vats full of creamy latex, the clean native village of the rubber tappers, and the spacious villas for the French scientists and administrators, gave the whole place the air of a well-funded American agricultural college. The war changed all that, for Lai-Khé is at the edge of a forest complex situated between two rivers which eventually merge about 20 miles from Saigon, thus forming a triangle pointing at South Viet-Nam's capital. In a series of swift attacks on the Vietnamese Army posts at the edge of the forest in late 1964, the Viet Cong had completely dismantled the whole government civilian and military apparatus in the area and taken over the town of Ben-Suc, a pleasant little place inside a meander of the Saigon River, big enough to appear on most maps of Viet-Nam.

Reprinted by permission and first appeared in *The New Republic.* Copyright © 1967 by Harrison-Blaine of New Jersey, Inc.

Repeated attempts by the Vietnamese to retake the area failed (the stripped hulls of three American M-113 armored personnel carriers lost to accurate Viet Cong fire still lie near the road to Ben-Suc), and even a push by the U.S. 173rd Airborne Brigade in 1965 yielded no tangible results. Progressively, the 210 square miles of forest between Ben-Suc and Ben-Cat acquired its sinister reputation as the "Iron Triangle," said to contain not only crack VC elements, but also the command structure of MR-4, the Liberation Front's 4th Military Region covering the Saigon area. It was from the Iron Triangle that the repeated successful VC penetrations of Saigon's huge Tan Son Nhut airbase had come. As long as the Iron Triangle existed, Saigon itself would be exposed to the threat of attack. The decision was therefore made late in 1966 to destroy the Iron Triangle in the largest concentrated attack by U. S. Forces since the Viet-Nam war began. The operation, begun on January 8, opened with the 1st Infantry in position on the Iron Triangle's northern base, with the 25th Infantry Division 196th Light Brigade blocking all escapes on the left flank across the Saigon River, while the A.R.V.N.'s 5th Division and parts of the 173rd Airborne Brigade held the right flank. Other units, including the A.R.V.N. 8th Infantry which, the year before, had broken at Ben-Suc, further reinforced the assault units. In all, 28 combat battalions—over 30,000 men with their logistical support—and 35 artillery batteries (140 field guns) had converged on the Triangle. But the key actors, on the American side, were not the men, but the unleashed machines.

Bomb Carpets in the Jungle

For days before the actual attack, the windows of Saigon had been rattling from concentrated B-52 raids on the Triangle, at least 13 of them in eight days, unloading hundreds of tons of heavy explosives on every raid, plowing under the Viet Cong's incredibly extensive network of underground tunnels and depots. Thanks also to American technology, the Air Force cartographers are capable of providing the military with fantastically detailed photo maps *in color* within a few hours after the strikes. On these maps, the trails of the bomb carpets in the jungle look like the tracks of tiger claws on an animal's skin—claw marks that are three miles long and over

100 feet wide. Whenever the strategic bombers were not over the Triangle, artillery barrages and the hammering of the light fighter-bombers saw to it that no Viet Cong would try to break out from the hell that the Triangle had become.

But the newest weapon of them all and, in its own way, the most incredibly impressive for all its civilian normality, was an assemblage of perhaps 80 bulldozers, in many cases airlifted into the midst of the jungle by huge "Skycrane" helicopters or the somewhat smaller "Chinooks." Their job was simple: eliminate the jungle once and for all. By the third day of the battle, huge yellow scars had begun to be clearly visible in the deep jungle green as the bulldozers began to plow down the jungle as if some insane developer were suddenly hell-bent on covering Viet-Nam with Levittowns or parking lots. Such Viet Cong hideouts or tunnels as there were, either were crushed or their exits bulldozed shut, for in many cases the adversary (as well as civilians) hiding in the tunnels disappeared in their deepest recesses rather than surrender. "Tunnel rats," American soldiers specially picked for their small size and equipped with gas projectors and what looked like flamethrowers, sometimes penetrated for hundreds of meters into the burrows, looking for what was said to be a veritable "subway" crossing the whole Triangle. It was never found and perhaps never existed.

Inexorably, the bulldozers bit into the countryside, cutting huge swaths of cleared land right across the Triangle. They were followed by flamethrower tanks and teams on foot, destroying the felled trees with fire. And not only the trees: every human inhabitation within the beaten zone, be it an isolated hut which may have been used by the Viet Cong, or a whole little hamlet inhabited for years by charcoal kilners—non-white Saigon cooks with charcoal almost exclusively—went up in flames. There was one day toward the end of the week in which the air was totally still and the sky as transparently fresh and pure as on a spring day in America. Yet as I joined a new unit within the Triangle by helicopter, the whole sky, literally in a 360° circle, was framed in by perfectly straight black columns: the earth was being scorched on the whole perimeter of the Iron Triangle. And the town of Ben-Suc was among them.

Ben-Suc had been occupied in less than two minutes by two battalions of the 28th Infantry, followed by Vietnamese troops, while overhead loudspeaker helicopters instructed the population to stay put, for "anyone seen running away will be considered a Viet Cong." The 3500 women, children and old men (there was not one able-bodied man in the lot) stayed put as Vietnamese Navy landing craft beached in front of the village and began to take aboard the population for a 10-mile ride downstream to a temporary refugee camp at Phu-Cuong. They went without offering resistance, believing that they would merely be taken away temporarily until the operation was over. But Operation "Cedar Falls" (the code name for the whole undertaking) was, in the words of a briefing officer, an "operation with a real difference"—there would be no coming back, because Ben-Suc would be put to the torch and then razed with bulldozers, just like the forest and part of the rubber plantation. A clamor arose as the women begged to be allowed to return long enough to dig up their meager treasures, for as in Europe during the Thirty Years' War, the peasants of Viet-Nam have long resorted to burying their money and jewelry in earthenware jars to keep them from being pilfered by government troops or taxed away by the Viet Cong. The respite was granted and the American troops even made arrangements to evacuate the most precious movable belongings of the villagers, their buffaloes and wagons.

"Make damn' sure the buffaloes stay with the refugees and don't end up in the market place," I overheard the earnest young major in charge of the evacuation say to one of his subordinates escorting the landing craft.

As the burning houses began to collapse and the bulldozers methodically bit into the remaining standing walls, a new town seemed to emerge altogether from the debris. Ben-Suc was honeycombed with tunnels, trenches, and stone-lined bunkers, and every house was built atop huge rice caches carefully lined with wicker mats. There were hundreds of tons there (the total "take" in the Triangle was 3170 tons), far in excess of what Ben-Suc could have produced, let alone saved from previous crops.

"You see," said the young major, "Ben-Suc was a major transit point of supplies both for War Zone 'C' and probably the VC's central headquarters. The stuff would come up here by motor sampan and the population then transfers it on its buffalo carts and off it goes into the deep jungle in escorted convoys.

"Look at the rice," he said, picking up a handful which he carried in the breastpocket of his combat jacket, "there are at least 20 different brands here from all over South Viet-Nam and probably from the U.S., too. I've sent a batch down to Intelligence. They'll find out where it came from."

He looked back on smoking Ben-Suc with real affection as he held its rice in his hand.

"Would you believe that we offered the women that they could take the rice with them as their own if they told us where the rice caches were? *Not one* of them spoke up. Now *that's* loyalty."

As he spoke, he opened his hand to let the golden rice grains fall on the ground, stopped in mid-gesture, and put the rice back into his pocket. I scooped up a handful from the smoldering heap to my right and put it in one of my pockets. That much of Ben-Suc would stay alive. Later, what was left of Ben-Suc would be obliterated by Air Force bombers in order to destroy whatever underground caches and depots had been missed by the bulldozers.

In the evening at the mess tent, the day's doings were toted up as officers from nearby units came in for briefing and for a hasty bite to eat. There were over 400 dead by "body count," 62 prisoners, 18 machineguns (including three brand-new American M-60's), more than 200 individual weapons (there would be close to 400 by the end of the operation, along with 508 enemy dead and 6000 displaced civilians), and miles and miles of destroyed tunnels.

A whole jungle hospital, with two levels below ground and one above ground, had been captured.

"You should have seen the equipment," said the G-2. "Some of the stuff was good enough to be used in our hospital. West German surgical scissors at $45 apiece by the trunkful; French antibiotics."

Now, according to an order issued by General Westmoreland, on September 20, 1966, in compliance with Article 33 of the 1949 Geneva Convention, "captured or abandoned medical supplies or facilities will not be destroyed intentionally." I was told, however, how the head hospital had been disposed of.

"Well," said an eyewitness, "we removed all the medical equipment, and then all there was left was just another empty bunker and tunnel system. So we destroyed it like everything else." The same also happened to a smaller VC aid station.

251

An NBC television crew with a neighboring outfit witnessed and photographed the mutilation of a dead enemy soldier, but the NBC hierarchy in New York, mindful of the uproar created more than a year ago when an enterprising CBS cameraman filmed the burning of a village with cigarette lighters, "killed" the sequence. Conversely, a reporter for a Texas newspaper was wounded that day by a VC sniper while he was flying about in a med-evac helicopter clearly marked with large red crosses. It is this kind of mutual barbarization, the needless cruelties inflicted far beyond military necessity, which will make the Viet-Nam war stand out in modern history.

"You should see 'em," said the burly prison camp commander. "Unrepentant, unyielding. The only thing they're sorry for is that they got taken alive."

Like Green-Clad Desert Arabs

He was referring to Professor Vinh Long and Middle-Level Teacher Tran Van Tan, captured in the Iron Triangle, and probably the highest-ranking Liberation Front cadres thus far to fall into American hands. Both were native Southerners, Vinh Long being born in Danang, and Tan in the province of the Iron Triangle. Both had gone to North Viet-Nam in 1954 when the country was partitioned, and both had gone on to higher studies. Long got his AB in physics and mathematics in 1963, Tan an AB in education in 1962. Both were "finds" in their own right, since they were involved in running the general education department of MR 4. [*For security reasons, we have substituted fictitious names for the real names of the prisoners interviewed by Mr. Fall.*—THE EDITORS]

The prisoner-of-war enclosure of the 1st Division was a small clearing in the rubber tree forest, surrounded by concertina barbed wire in which two squad tents had been erected. Within the enclosure was an even smaller enclosure, housing three captive women, one of them a pretty 19-year-old Eurasian girl with long red hair and freckles, but almond-shaped eyes. "She was a cook in the outfit," explained an escort.

Viet-Nam can be bitingly cold in January and we were shivering in our jungle combat uniforms, particularly after a night spent rolled in a poncho liner. The prisoners were lying on normal Army cots

252

and had been issued three woolen blankets each, and each of them seemed to have his share of C-rations. Courteously sitting up on their cots as we approached, they looked, wrapped in their blankets, like green-clad desert Arabs. Intelligent, ascetic faces with deep-burning eyes, showing no fear—just curiosity as to what next. I first sat down with Vinh Long, flanked by a Vietnamese sergeant acting as an interpreter and an American captain. The captain was showing signs of a very bad cold, sneezing and fumbling through his pockets for an absent handkerchief. The Vietnamese prisoner picked up the C-ration box, searched around in it and came up with the tiny roll of toilet paper it contains, which he handed to the captain.

"We'll Win, Anyway"

Long said that he spoke no French, but he spoke Russian. I explained to him in Russian that I was a college professor myself, not a soldier, and that I was not interested in military information. I also apologized for my bad Vietnamese and for the fact that I'd have to use an interpreter. That's all right he said, now clearly relaxed. Who had ordered him to return South?

"The party. But I would have gone in any case because I wanted to. I was happy. I visited Hanoi before I left."

He had left the North in December 1963 for the Duong Minh Chau area—the headquarters area of the Liberation Front. Before his departure from the North, where he had been stationed with the 338th Division at Xuan-Mai (he offered no information on units except those already known from papers captured with him), he had been briefed on the war here.

"We were given an accurate picture of what was going on in the South and told that victory would be easy. Of course, with the Americans here, it's not so easy." He picked up a cigarette in the C-ration carton, offered the others around, and then looked straight at me.

"But we'll win, anyway. Every country in the world helps us. Look at the American, Morrison, who committed suicide because he disagreed with American policies."

True, I said. But how about the other 200 million Americans who don't kill themselves?

"The Liberation Front forces will win in any case, because all

253

the Vietnamese people help us. This war can only be settled among the Vietnamese themselves. The Americans and their allies must go."

But he had seen the Americans, now. Realistically, could they be made to go?

"Lots of American soldiers do get killed in battles. Look at Chulai, Pleiku, Tayninh. We can do it."

To the Viet Cong, those battles, which we either claim as having won ourselves (Chulai), or as having suffered only minor losses (Pleiku), represent major victories. I said that I feared he was confusing the Americans with the French. The French weren't one-tenth as powerful as the Americans.

"Oh, I know the French were weaker than the U.S. is, but we'll still win because our cause is right. Do the Americans think they can stay with this kind of war for 30, 40 years? Because that is what this is going to take."

The members of the Front are known to practice self-criticism. If he were to criticize himself for his activities over the past year, would he do something differently? There was a momentary lowering of the head, and a great deal of pride in the short answer: "I wouldn't change a thing."

And what would he do after all this was over?

"When I get out of this a free man, I will again work for the Liberation Front."

There was a poem, in wartime France, about a resistance member who had given exactly that answer to a German military court:

> *Et si c était à refaire*
> *Je referais ce chemin . . .*

Yes, but that was 23 years ago, and the Nazis were the bad guys, and here the Free World is fighting the good fight with billions of dollars' worth of firepower against bad guys like Long and the freckle-faced cook.

"I told you," said the captain. "Unrepentant. Unyielding."

Tan was less tense than Vinh Long; perhaps because we had switched from a Veitnamese interpreter to an American GI (one of the few real side-benefits of this whole mess is that the U. S. Armed Forces are going to have more Vietnamese linguists than all the

254

universities of the whole world taken together; and that is *not* a figure of speech). Tan, in addition to education, had minored in anatomy and physiology and had been the inspector of the VC's educational system for the military zone. Though having fought in the Viet-Minh against the French since 1950, he only joined the Communist Party here in South Viet-Nam in 1966, and like Vinh Long, he was sure that his side was winning.

"It's only natural that we should receive help from North Viet-Nam. After all, we're all Vietnamese, aren't we? Just as the Saigon government gets American help, the Front gets help from the socialist countries." There was a pause, and Tan said with great emphasis: "And it will never stop. *Never.* Even if their help does not rise above the present level, we'll win."

How did he feel he was being considered in the movement, being an intellectual, I asked. Wasn't he treated with a certain amount of suspicion?

"Oh, there is a certain amount of suspicion against intellectuals, but that is understandable. After all, being intellectuals, they are divorced from the masses and the working class, in particular.

"We Southern cadres are not discriminated against by the Northerners, although it did happen that some of the 'regroupees' [Southerners who went to the North in 1954 and then were reinfiltrated. B.F.] would desert from homesickness once they came South again. It doesn't affect our status at all."

But as a man trained in dialectical materialism, how could he dismiss American power so lightly in his estimates of the outcome of the war? That, to him, was no problem at all:

"After all, the Front is fighting a just war, as a true representative of the South Vietnamese people. This being a just war, we shall win."

But other "just wars" were lost in other places . . .

"Indonesia?" he interjected helpfully.

No, I said, but Greece, Malaya, and the Philippines for example. As an intellectual, he could not dismiss these defeats lightly, unless he felt that these wars weren't "just wars."

"Not at all. They were just wars, to be sure, and the people were defeated, but only temporarily. The will to fight on remained in their hearts and they surely will rise again. But here, there won't

255

be even such a temporary setback. The party has been active in South Viet-Nam for 36 years and thus defeat of its organization is impossible now.

"Here, the guerrillas will become stronger and stronger with the help of the socialist countries."

Yes, but did not the Sino-Soviet split introduce a weakening factor in this aid effort? Now he was on the defensive for the first time.

"Those struggles for greater socialist unity no more affect the socialist camp's effort in Viet-Nam than the French-American dispute affects power relationships in the West."

Come now, I said, if you read *Pravda* and the *Peking Reveiw* and the incredibly severe mutual accusations between Peking and Moscow, you wouldn't describe this as a "struggle for greater unity."

"Let's not get into this. We'll win in any case."

Even if South Viet-Nam is totally destroyed in the process by American artillery and bombers? He had seen what happened here. It's happening all over the country. There was a hurt look in his eyes as the implication sunk in: "If South Viet-Nam is lost, we have got nothing left to live for. We would rather be dead than live as slaves. Have *you* ever seen anybody who wants to live as a slave?"

No, I had never seen anybody who wanted to, but I'd seen plenty of cases where people *had* to because they were given no choice. And I cited, on his side of the fence, the Budapest uprisings, and on our side, the Dominican Republic operation.

"These are small things," was his reply. And what did he think of how this whole war got started, I asked.

"Ah, the Americans are sly and clever," said Tan, whereupon the Americans present broke out in uncontrolled laughter. The interpreter explained to Tan that the Americans themselves never thought of themselves as either sly or clever. He nodded pensively, as if this were an important revelation.

"You know, they never smile," said the captain to me. I told him that considering their position and what was in store for them— transfer to the far-from-tender South Vietnamese—I wouldn't smile, either.

"The Americans," Tan went on, "took over military planning for the Saigon government. Their economic experts forced the South

Vietnamese to work for them and Diem persecuted everybody. He would have killed us all, and that is why we revolted."

Tan, who had been silent for a moment, looked up and asked the interpreter if he, too, could ask me a few questions since I was a professor. Of course, he could.

"Do you know whether we will be treated as prisoners according to the Geneva Convention?"

Obviously, word must have gotten around among the Viet Cong about how badly most of the prisoners are still treated on this side, all promises of improvement notwithstanding, with the Americans reluctant to intervene once the prisoners have been transferred. All that I could say lamely was that he was being treated according to the Convention right now.

"Do American families approve of their soldiers here killing innocent people?"

Most of them weren't aware of innocent people being killed here, I said. As for the soldiers themselves, they were carrying out orders just as he was.

"Yes, but I'm here as a Vietnamese, in my own country. Why are the Americans all over the place, in Greece, in Laos?"

Well, they were helping their own allies, just as he expected the socialist camp to help him. But the socialist camp's aid was "political," he retorted. To which I answered that the Chinese weapons we had captured yesterday did not look "political" to me. A quick fleeting smile conceded the point to me.

"You may be right on that, but after all, it is the Americans who are the aggressors."

"Victory by Fade-Out"

Why were the North Vietnamese so difficult about negotiations? I asked. On this, he was probably to the left (or was it right?) of official Front and North Vietnamese policy. Like Ambassador Henry Cabot Lodge here, who feels that negotiations are pointless if "victory by fade-out" can be achieved—a point which he has repeatedly made ever since September 1965—Tan felt that there was little to negotiate since his side was winning and since Viet-Nam was "one country."

257

Contrary to the Front's and Hanoi's avowed programs, he felt that reunification would come rapidly if the Americans were to leave. In fact, he did not believe that a divided Viet-Nam would "work." I told him that, for the sake of world peace, both Germany and Korea had accepted more or less permanent division.

"That's all right for them. But we rose up and fought for our own independence. We don't want to stay divided."

Yet, when asked what he would have done differently, Tan said that he would have negotiated last year, before the massive input of American troops, and he came through with a small truth which confirmed what intelligence specialists here had been wondering about for quite a while:

"You know, this is no longer the 'Special War' General Taylor talked about, but a new type of war [here the interpreter was faced with one of those party neologisms for which there was no acceptable single word] where outside forces became primary.

"The decision that the character of the war had changed was made late last year here in the South, either by the People's Revolutionary [i.e., South Vietnamese Communist] Party, or by the Central Committee of the Liberation Front. But when I was captured I did not yet know what this decision entailed."

As far as is known, the decision entails the maintenance of large units in reserve at more or less secure bases, while small forward units inflict heavy losses on the allied forces. How well this tactic works was shown this week, when the U.S. suffered the highest casualties of the war (1200 in one week)—all as a result of dozens of pinprick attacks.

But Tan knew that he was on the right path. As I was getting up to leave, he said earnestly: "We are not fighting here to have a cease-fire and prolonged division. It is the Americans who sent their troops here. They will have to make the decision to leave. Nobody can make it for them."

As I walked out, after he had ceremoniously shaken hands with the captain, the interpreter and me, Tan said something very rapidly.

"He's asking you to thank the American people and Lord Russell for what they are doing."

Back at Division, reports were still filtering in. Ben-Suc was now totally evacuated. A herd of 61 reluctant buffaloes which proved

258

intractable to adult Americans—it seems to be true that buffaloes find the white man's smell offensive—had required the re-airlifting in of 10 Vietnamese buffalo-boys aged six to 10 who rounded up the two-ton beasts without much difficulty. The town was now bulldozed flat and awaited its final air strike.

Standing in his map tent, the brigade commander was going through the details of the pull-out, for after all the blood and the firepower spent here, the Iron Triangle would not be held.

"We just haven't got the troops to stay here, and the Arvins simply won't."

"In other words," I said, "the VC will move right back in again."

"Sure," said the general. "But they'll find their dugouts smashed, huge open lanes in the forest, and at least we'll have helicopter LZ's [landing zones] all over the place. Next time's going to be easier to get back in."

As I walked out of the command post, a short, whitewashed obelisk caught my eye, standing at the entrance to Lai-Khé. It was a monument to the dead of the 2nd Moroccan Spahi Regiment, the 2nd Cambodian Mobile Battalion, the 3rd and 25th Algerian Rifle Battalions, and 3rd Battalion, 4th Tunisian Rifles; who had died for the Iron Triangle between 1946 and 1954.

Street Without Joy
Revisited

꧁꧂

THE WORDS "Street Without Joy" ring very familiar to anyone concerned with the struggle in Viet-Nam. It was in this coastal area, between the cities of Quang Tri and Hué, that one of the most frustrating operations of the Indochina War took place. A study of what happened there, in contrast with what is taking place there today, reveals the very definite progress that has been made toward defeating the insurgents who have long infested the area.

The French Effort—1953

On 28 July 1953 the French Army in Indochina had assembled a great number of troops for what they hoped would be a decisive victory along the Street Without Joy. The area had long been a haven for the Viet-Minh 95th Regiment, whose harassing actions along Highway 1 severely hampered operations of the French Army in the area.

An impressive force of over 30 battalions; including the equivalent of two armored regiments and two artillery regiments, were utilized in the operation. Equipment varied from the Crab (an

Unpublished piece, written in late 1966.—*Ed.*

amphibious cargo carrier), and the Alligator (Tracked Landing Vehicle) to 155mm howitzers and M-24 tanks.

The basic plan was a four-pronged thrust into the area, with the goal being an encirclement and gradual closing of the ring to trap the enemy force. Groups A and D were to land on the coast while B and C proceeded overland from secure bases along Highway 1. Two airborne battalions remained in reserve.

The bulk of the enemy resistance was concentrated in the "Street" itself, a long, narrow strip of villages very thick with undergrowth and heavily fortified. To the southwest of this strip are rice paddies and tidal swampland. To the coastal side many graves hidden among sand dunes appear first, followed by a 2–3 kilometer wide stretch of sand that is very trafficable. The coast itself is characterized by another row of scattered fishing villages, lightly populated but ideal for the hiding of insurgent forces. The French hoped to overcome these many obstacles by an overwhelming superiority in numbers and the use of armored vehicles.

The Landing—28 July 1953

The operation began with the landing of the 3rd Amphibious Group at 0600 on 28 July, between the coastal villages of Tan An and My Thuy. The operation was plagued by the many problems inherent in a large-scale effort—lack of coordination, vehicle breakdowns and communication difficulties. But by 0830 all units had reached their lines of departure and the methodical process of finding the Viet-Minh began. Village after village was first surrounded and then searched thoroughly, with most of the young men being detained as suspects.

Around 1100, in the village of Dong Que, a vicious fire-fight erupted at very close range between the Viet-Minh defenders and the Moroccan tanks and infantry. The infantry spread in an arc around the village while the tanks took up positions off the road. Artillery was on target within minutes and soon the village began to disintegrate, climaxed by a secondary explosion. The Viet-Minh, using civilians as a shield, tried to break out but the infantry had done its encircling job well, and by 1300, the 2nd Company, 310th Battalion, 95th Regiment, Viet-Nam People's Army, had been defeated. But not before its heroic stand had allowed the bulk of the 95th to withdraw to the south.

As the ring of French troops closed in, contact was gained at Phu An, in the southeast, and finally overcome by 1730. During the day both airborne battalions had been committed, with a great deal of men and equipment lost due to high surface winds.

The Results—1953

After an uneventful night, the French shut the jaws on the trap. Except for suspects, very little enemy contact occurred, and by 1300, Groups A and D, along with parts of Group B, had pushed into the Van Trinh canal to link up with Group C coming in from Highway 1. Human chains, mine detectors, and bloodhounds had found 51 rifles, 8 sub-machineguns, 2 mortars and 5 BAR's. The French suffered 17 KIA and 100 WIA, while the enemy lost 182 KIA and 387 captured. It will never be known how many of the enemy losses were hard-core Viet-Minh or simply local guerrillas and innocent civilian victims of Communist indoctrination and occupation. Once again, the numerically inferior Viet-Minh had slipped away from their pursuers to fight again.

The Vietnamese Effort—1966

Today, The Street Without Joy remains a haven for the insurgent, who now calls himself the Viet Cong. The terrain is unchanged. What has changed is the approach to the problem of insurgency, and the employment of modern equipment in counterinsurgency operations, particularly the use of the firepower and mobility of armored units. The operation described below is typical of operations that A.R.V.N. now conducts in the coastal area on a continuing basis.

The Plan

Headquarters, 1st A.R.V.N. Division, began planning for Operation on the night of D Day minus 2, and on D Day minus 1 at 1500, orders were issued to the commanders involved. The basic plan was to split an area of VC activity into 3 zones of action, with a task force in each zone conducting a search and destroy operation. VC contacts with local Popular Force units occur almost daily in the area and a VC battalion was suspected to be in the area. Each task force was assigned and observation aircraft and FAC's were airborne to handle air strike requests.

Contact Gained—Contact Lost

At 0545 on D Day, Task Force 41, consisting of 2 A.R.V.N. Marine battalions trucked into the area, and 1 APC Troop, moved toward the ID. Their objectives were fishing villages on the coast. The TF CO decided to move the 2 Marine battalions through the villages while the APC troop, carrying 1 company of marines, would move parallel to the villages on the open sandy terrain.

Crossing the ID at 0830, the task force searched methodically, finding nothing but a few peasant villagers. At 1630, both battalions became pinned down by fire from the village of Gia Dang. The APC troop immediately swung to the left and approached the village from the west flank. Two hundred meters from the treeline boundary of the village, the VC opened up with a heavy volume of 57mm recoilless rifle, 30 and 50 caliber machinegun fire, and also 60 and 82mm mortars. The troop closed to 100 meters, taking two direct hits from the recoilless rifle fire. They pulled back 300 meters for the air strikes and artillery that soon followed. The Marines were still pinned down and although an attempt was made to link up with the APC's for an assault, darkness set in and the task force had to settle for a stand-off.

During the hours of darkness, the VC pulled out as only one-third of the area was encircled. Task Force 11, with an infantry battalion and another APC troop, had progressed to Objective 13 only 3 kilometers away, but were not employed in the encirclement. A search of the village at dawn showed evidence of many VC casualties and a few confirmed KIA, but the bulk of the enemy force had slipped away, just as they had done so many times before. Just as all units were preparing to end the operation, local intelligence produced information that was soon to spell disaster for more than a battalion of hard-core VC.

Contact Regained—Forces Shift

A Popular Forces soldier was going home to his village of Phu Lieu, just 8 kilometers northeast of Quang Tri, when he contacted civilians coming out of the village saying that a strong force of VC had entered the village during the night. Division HQ reacted immediately. An RF company was moved into a blocking position to the west. The 2 VN Marine battalions were helilifted to an LZ south of the objective, and the APC troop from Task Force 41 linked up with the helilifted troops. From 1500 to 1600, air strikes and artillery covered the objective, and then the attack commenced. The VC again opened fire at close range, pinning down the Marines and forcing the APC's to assault three times before the VC defenders started to fall back.

While the VC were falling back and reorganizing, Task Force 11 was ordered to attack from the north, encircling the VC force. The attack was so quickly executed that the defenders were killed or captured while trying to reorient their weapons. The battle continued throughout the night with the aid of flare ships, the only escape being the river. Many tried other routes of escape but were stopped by the encircling forces.

The Results—1966

At dawn the mopping up began. The final A.R.V.N. losses were 37 KIA, 6 from the APC troops, and 104 WIA, 33 from the APC troops. The VC lost 154 KIA, 38 captured, 60 suspects, 58 individual weapons, 12 automatic weapons, 2 mortars, and 2 antitank weapons. These were confirmed losses, with the actual total undoubtedly much higher. An A.R.V.N. force of 4 battalions and 2 APC troops, aided by artillery and air strikes, had dealt this VC force a severe blow, and yet remained ready to react against the enemy again if necessary.

The above example is not an isolated one, as operations such as this are taking place constantly in the coastal area. It demonstrates what can be accomplished during operations characterized by minimum planning time, minimum reaction time, immediate use of current intelligence and maximum use of mobile forces.

Of special interest is the employment of armor in this area. The M-113 was utilized in areas where it could move and employ its firepower and shock action. The APC's were positioned to allow maximum visibility, and thus cover a wide area without physically occupying the terrain. The committing of Task Force 11, with its APC troop, was a striking example of shock action, catching the enemy completely by surprise.

The Difference

What has changed in The Street Without Joy? Certainly not the enemy or the terrain he operates in. And no one can deny that the French had many superior fighting units in the area. But a definite change has occurred.

The first reason for the change is modern combat equipment. The M-113 APC can negotiate terrain that the Crabs and Alligators couldn't. And there is no comparison in either airpower or air mobility. Also, due to increasing government influence in some areas, intelligence has improved. However, the biggest factor in the change has been the realization that counterinsurgency is a full-time operation, that one big sweep will be only a temporary success at best. Frequent small sized operations, utilizing all the firepower and mobility available, are keeping the VC off balance and constantly on the move. Peace is still not a reality in this area. However, government forces are headed in the right direction toward their goal of eliminating the insurgent, the first step in the making of a better life for the war-weary people of The Street Without Joy.

The Last Tape

ᕼᕼᕼ

FEBRUARY 19, 1967. This is Bernard Fall in The Street Without
Joy, the old area where the French fought in 1953.

I am lying right now in a small stone hut near a big church
in a small village with part of the 1st Battalion, 9th Marine Infantry
Regiment, and we just walked across something like 12 kilometers
of sand dunes and tomorrow morning we're going to push Southeastward where supposedly there is part of a Viet Cong battalion,
Viet Cong Battalion 800 . . .

. . . the voice in the background is that of a Vietnamese lieutenant who is talking to the A.R.V.N. 1st Division and next door
we got the switchboard of the battalion that's now installed in
the rectory of the church. And there's still only about two companies
at the present moment . . . there's two more companies coming
up the road. Route was just normal march—few shots one side,
had to cross four blown up bridges climbing over girders. One
Marine lost his footing on the last one and fell through. In fact,
the whole operation was supposed to be a heliborne assault and
the helicopters couldn't make it because of the weather so we landed

Bernard B. Fall was reporting the war, as he saw it, at the time of his death.
This transcription from his tape recorder covers February 19, 20, and 21, 1967.
—*Ed.*

up marching on foot just as it happened with the French in 1953 and, well, we hope it's going to be a good night without mortar fire.

There were punji stakes on the road, also, and at least one mine but so far—so good.

[*Pause here. . . . . .*]

Now, on The Street Without Joy, this is the morning and we are patrolling down with Charlie Company.

[*Other conversation here. . . .*]

". . . driving the buffalo back and the priest (?) should be back pretty soon . . . he's got a lot of them with him, too . . ."

FALL: What happened to the 14 VC's that were supposed to have walked out of Alpha Company? Who's seen them since?

ANS.: No one, I guess.

[*Radio instructions can be heard here . .*]

"resupply requests must be submitted on time . . . You have that time in your stat folder. We request no late editions if they can be avoided . . . supply will be delivered to you in afternoon. All resupply requests should come through your HST . . . over . . ."

Just slushing through the water now.

[*Instructions can be heard in background . . .*]

". . . pick up your squads and come around this way . . . get around this little river here . . ."

Now we're in a fire fight!

[*Gunfire here on tape*]

VOICE: Continue to phase line . . . Tango . . . Oscar . . . Tangerine . . .

FALL: Well, that was that for a while. It didn't look very good but we made it. They ran and since the sky was too dark for air support, we just kept on going and then we came to a church and it was a big church and was constructed in 1963 and—oh, very beautiful. I decided to walk into it and the Vietnamese passed ahead of us and then our own Marine point.

I walked behind a fellow, thought I walked pretty well in his traces. Apparently I stepped slightly aside and all of a sudden the ground gave way under me and this was one of these punji stake traps that the VC sets with very sharp points and if you fall on this you pierce your foot and go to the hospital. I was very lucky because when I felt the ground yield under my feet I threw myself forward so that my whole body weight shifted to my knees and hands and so the trap gave way and nothing happened to me but it . . . ah, shakes you up a bit and now we are sitting in a deserted farm destroyed by gunfire. But the floor is still good and we've got about two companies of Marines and a small detachment of about ten Vietnamese Regional and Popular forces— some of them are former Communist guerrillas from this area. They don't look like they're worth a damn. But here they are and a very nice Army captain who commands them from the sector here.

So now the chopper which can be heard in the background is probably our supply chopper—it's coming in—we have had no supplies since yesterday and no water since yesterday and after a second day of march everybody much is pretty short—I kept my water down to the end so I've still got some water left and part of a C-ration and tomorrow we're going to get resupplied. So—everybody now cleans his weapons and Captain files his report via radio and another day has gone by on The Street Without Joy.

[*Voice over radio can be heard at this point*]

". . . going to come down to your location and conduct a little business and then return so expect them starting out . . . to pick up your positions . . ."
". . . Roger . . ." "Thank you . . . Out"

That was the company commander being advised that the Vietnamese are going to come into our area.

[*Silence . . . and sound of crickets can be
heard on tape at this point*]

Well, we're moving out again on The Street Without Joy—it's the third day now and what you heard before were the noises of the crickets and the frogs next to us where we were sleeping out in the open. It started to drizzle afterward and now we've got thick-packed fog at 9 o'clock in the morning—supply chopper couldn't come in but we had enough food for this morning and on we go now.

Charlie Company picked up two Viet Cong suspects which within a few seconds were confirmed to be Viet Cong supply carriers. Yesterday evening also we captured two of them—a little girl about twenty—strapping girl—and a boy about sixteen, in the village. By the time the Vietnamese had left us they were already beating them and, of course, it's no small wonder no civilians stay behind except a few old women.

We have been walking now for two and a half days in a virtual desert. Now we're with Able Company on the road and Able has found a mine. Charlie Company already exploded a mine with a trip wire and apparently one fellow is hurt.

[Instructions can be heard in background of
tape at this point]

". . . This is Alpha . . . to Bravo . . . to Bravo . . . I want you to move on . . . move down . . . bring 'em up, bring your squad up and start moving down to the South along that tree line, along that tree line . . . we'll . . . a spot for you . . ."

[Sound of chopper can be heard on tape]

Now we are near Lai-Ha and one of the Vietnamese who was with us . . .

VOICE: . . . a little bit too late.

FALL: A little bit too late, you think?

VOICE: Yeah.

FALL: Well, if they were only three or four minutes away from that village, they should be only about 22 meters from the road.

FALL: They have a mortar, don't they?

VOICE: Two mortars.

FALL: Two mortars?

VOICE: 2-60's. They can drop one in here any time they want. They can stop—set it up in about . . .

FALL: VC got the mortars?

VOICE: Yeah, VC got the mortars.

FALL: VC got the mortars!— Sorry about that—I thought you were talking about our mortars.

VOICE: Oh, no—we've got 16 60's 80 1's

FALL: Well, it's an almost equal fight. (Both chuckle here)

VOICE: We have 3(?) times as many as they do.

[Sound of gunfire on tape at this time]

Still on The Street Without Joy. (Sound of gunfire) That's Charlie Company firing.

[Voices can be heard in background on tape]

"beef steak, potatoes and gravy, Sarge . . ."

That's the appeal now for the Viet Cong to surrender.

[Inaudiable sounds in background here on tape]

Afternoon of the third day. Still on the street. Now bunker system out there they're going to blow up. The weather is finally cleared and we have an observation plane over our heads, turning around shepherding us. But Charlie Company has fallen very badly behind now there's a big hole in our left flank and there's some people running away from us obviously getting out of the way . . . Trying to move across . . . we've got to start firing if they move . . .

[Sound of gunfire and plane here on tape . . .

A lot of gunfire here . . . much excitement . . .

Shouting of instructions, etc. . . .]

FALL: There's our machine gun firing! They're running!

VOICE: Advance word—they're moving off to the left.

"Moving off to the left . . . running"

FALL: There's our mortar!

VOICE: What are they shooting at?

FALL: What do you mean—they're shooting at the buffalo boys! —Oh, for Christ's sake! Those Vietnamese? . . . Oh, my God!

[A lot of rapid gunfire here]

FALL: There they go.

FALL: They're shooting at some buffalos apparently

[Gunfire]

FALL: How does he know?

VOICE: See that guy right in the center? You can hardly see— move across—got on a white jacket—see that hat? Set up about 1100 meters—open up with burst of 20 . . .

FALL: It's impossible at 1100 meters to distinguish with . . .

[Gunfire]

270

VOICE: Very good.

FALL: There's no return fire whatever but the Chieu Hois who are with us—there are former Viet Cong returned to the government side and are fighting now with the government forces—well, they assured us that Charlie Company is moving right through the area and by tonight we will know whether what we killed were genuine VC with weapons or simply people. I personally looked through binoculars of the platoon leader from the machine gun platoon and I saw people fleeing to the boats and waving the Vietnamese government flag with three red stripes on a yellow background. Find out more about this later . . . This is Bernard Fall on The Street Without Joy.

[*Silence here on tape*]

. . . . first in the afternoon about 4:30—shadows are lengthening and we've reached one of our phase lines after the fire fight and it smells bad—meaning it's a little bit suspicious . . . Could be an amb . . .

[*End of tape*]

PART III

"There Is Going to Be a Silence..."
A Way to End Revolutionary Wars

AT FIRST, the insurgency had been conducted entirely by native revolutionaries against their own government, and it stayed that way for almost four years, with minor operations see-sawing all over the country. The government, while making some concessions (mostly to appease its critics at home), also continued to throw more and more troops into the fight. But the insurgents also now were joined by the regulars of an outside power: in fact, as the war went on the outside regulars began to assume an ever-increasing share of the military burden, thanks to their superior armament and tactics. Their generals and technicians could be seen everywhere, advising the insurgent leaders, but finally commanding more and more their own and the native forces in the field.

The home government was, of course, not fooled by that foreign-abetted insurgency. The highest officials of the government proclaimed loudly that the whole insurrection was little else but a foreign plot and the insurgents nothing but the stooges of the foreign power. Negotiating with them was not only impossible, but uncalled for. And perhaps the government's best argument was the number of loyal local citizens who continued to fight on *its* side against the rebels, and who, to the end of the conflict,

An unpublished piece.—*Ed.*

275

far exceeded anything the insurgents could muster. The insurgents (and who could blame them) made much of the fact that the government also began to use foreign troops from other nations who were indebted to it. But the historical record shows that those "mercenaries," as they were promptly dubbed by the insurgents, were far less numerous than the foreign troops who now were backing the insurgents. In fact, the leaders of the insurgency had entered into a formal agreement with them and had sent ambassadors abroad as if they were a legal government.

Little wonder, then, that when British general Cornwallis surrendered at Yorktown to the combined French and American forces almost 185 years ago to the day, his aide, General O'Hara, made a slight (and, perhaps, intentional) error in etiquette as he tried to surrender his commander's sword to French general Rochambeau rather than to one of the American generals present, while the British military band played a ditty with the appropriate title "The World Turned Upside Down." Count Rochambeau, well styled in the role of military advisermanship ("You take all the blame, and the advisee gets all the credit," as they say in Viet-Nam today), turned down the honor, and the sword was finally handed to General Benjamin Lincoln, who had been defeated by the British at Charleston, S.C., three years earlier.

There is no question but that the American Revolutionary War, when considered as a "normal" insurgency, entirely fits the bill of the many revolutionary wars which afflict the middle of the twentieth century. Shorn of almost two centuries of 4th-of-July oratory, it was a military operation fought by a very small armed minority—at almost no time did Washington's forces exceed 8000 men in a country which had at least 300,000 able-bodied males—and backed by a force of 31,897 French ground troops and 12,660 sailors and Marines manning sixty-one major vessels. The total cost of the campaign to the French (almost $2 billion) drove the French monarchy into bankruptcy and subsequent revolution. But politically, the French had achieved exactly what they had intended to do: they had temporarily shattered Britain's position of pre-eminence not only in America but in Europe as well. But Britain, even in the short run, had realized that a completely intransigent position toward the American revolutionaries would

276

only further drive them into French hands and could also drag other powers (notably Russia) into what was rapidly becoming a world war. Soon, Britain and the young United States were negotiating on two levels—directly, in London, and within the Franco-American alliance, in Paris. (The same was true for the French, as came to light recently, who, at one point were willing to settle the war with Britain even at the expense of America's independence.)

To be sure, the present Viet-Nam War is not a colonial war in the same sense as the American Revolutionary War was, but, unless one accepts the Marxian concept of "just" and "unjust" wars, this has absolutely no bearing on the central problem: *When* is it in the interest of the legitimate government of a country to deal with insurgents (foreign-backed or not) on the basis of negotiations? And once the decision has been made to negotiate, *how* can such negotiations be initiated and *what* can they achieve?

As will be seen, colonial and non-colonial situations are hopelessly intermingled in the various categories of situations in which most insurgencies fall; but it is extremely difficult even to define what exactly constitutes an "insurgency." In his much-noted speech at Montreal in the spring of 1966, Secretary of Defense McNamara spoke of 167 different insurgencies said to have taken place since World War II. A closer examination of those insurgencies shows that they include one-shot uprisings such as East Berlin's on June 17, 1953, and various Latin American coups involving a handful of junta generals. More conservative—in terms of setting up certain qualifications of duration, number of participants, and size and type of military engagements—estimates bring down the list to about fifty, ranging alphabetically from Algeria and Angola, to Viet-Nam, West Irian, Yugoslavia and Zanzibar.

On a straight statistical basis, the cases which involved direct negotiations between the insurgents and the "counterinsurgent" (legitimate or foreign invader, as in World War II) outweigh the others by about thirty to twenty. There is not one guerrilla movement in World War II—even the heroic Jews who fought to the death in the Warsaw Ghetto—who did not at one time or another enter into contact with the Nazis, or was not contacted by them: in Yugoslavia, the anti-Communist general Mihailovich secured several truces from the Germans (they were to cost him his life at the hands of a Tito Yugoslav tribunal later); in Greece, the 11th ELAS (Communist) guerrilla division traded free passage in its area against German weapons; in Warsaw, SS-*Brigadeführer* Jürgen Stroop asked the Jews for a short truce to remove his own wounded; and the negotiated surrender of the German garrison of Paris to the French Forces of the Interior (FFI) has become a part of world history. The same, of course, has held true ever since for almost all the post-World War II insurgencies.

In general, however, the end of insurgency situations falls into three categories: the counterinsurgent wins; the insurgent wins; or there is a stand-off. In turn, each of the three categories can be neatly divided into "talk" and "no-talk" subcategories.

Some examples in each category come readily to mind. Others, however, are somewhat startling. Thus, the category of "no-talk" victories by government forces is surprisingly slim. The most outstanding example is perhaps Greece's fight against Communist guerrillas between 1946 and 1949. Indeed, at the price of a no-holds-barred military campaign and with the help of a bitter quarrel between two major backers of the guerrillas—Stalin and Tito—Greece defeated the insurgents decisively. The Greek government, however, in fact accepted a political compromise in the form of letting pro-Communist elements run fairly overtly for parliament. As early as March 1950, 18 members of the "Democratic Group" won legislative seats in an assembly of 250. The Philippines' case is another one of an outright government victory without any concessions to the rebels. However, even the Filipino Communists admit that their defeat was as much due to their own extremely serious mistakes, notably in the field of political organization; as to the government's effective counteroperations. The fact that the Huks have recently begun to reappear either means that the Huks have learned something in the meantime; or that Manila may well have forgotten something—mostly its promises to its own peasantry. More primitive or spontaneous movements are likely to be annihilated without negotiations: an Algerian uprising against the French in 1945 was so swiftly and ruthlessly crushed as to be well-nigh forgotten today. A similar anti-French uprising in Madagascar in 1947 also got short shrift, although it tied down for a crucial six months most of the reinforcements the French had meant to send to Viet-Nam to crush another "minor" rebellion there—that of Ho Chi Minh. The Mau-Mau in Kenya were never given much of a chance of negotiating with Britain, until they had been crushed militarily. But their cause prevailed in the end, nevertheless, just as those of Algeria and of the Malagasy Republic. A more tragic case of last-ditch destruction of guerrillas were those of the various anti-Russian Ukrainian and Latvian groups. Some of the *Banderovci*—as the Ukrainians were called, after their leader Bandera—lasted until 1949 in the Carpathians.

The list of "government" victories after talks with the insurgents is longer and more variegated: in 1944, the recently-deceased Polish general Bor-Komorowski negotiated the capitulation of the Warsaw Resistance fighters with a distant cousin of his—SS general von dem Bach-Zelewski. In 1956 in Hungary, the Russians negotiated for a time with a Hungarian general, Peter Maleter, who led the Freedom Fighters. They broke their promise of safe-conduct to him and killed him later. In other places the amenities are observed: in Malaya, for instance, Prime Minister Tunku Abdul Rahman in 1960 met the leader of the Communist terrorist organization, Chin Peng (a British-trained commando leader decorated for his bravery in behalf of Britain during World War II) under a safe-conduct. Chin Peng insisted upon total political freedom and complete amnisty for all his associates. The Tunku considered this as giving Chin all that he had failed to gain in twelve years of jungle fighting, and refused. Whereupon Chin Peng once more shouldered his American carbine and walked back into the jungle. He is still there.

In 1946 in Azerbaijan, which lies astride the Soviet-Iranian border, pro-Russian elements had proclaimed an "Autonomous Republic of Gilan" in the Iranian part which bid fair to become either an integral part of the U.S.S.R. or the cornerstone of an altogether Communist Iran. In that particular case, the settlement went from the local insurgents and government to the two outside backers: the Russians and the Americans. President Truman's stern views of the matter were clearly conveyed to the Kremlin, and the Gilan Republic disappeared into limbo. The various Congo pacification campaigns of 1960–65, with their U.N. forces, white mercenaries, CIA-financed Cubans, Belgian paratroopers, Egyptian agents and Chinese arms shipments; interspersed with interminable palavers in ex-Leopoldville, ex-Elisabethville, ex-Stanleyville, and the sometimes-United Nations; are an excellent example of the fact that on-and-off negotiations with rebels do not necessarily have to disadvantage the counterinsurgent. This, in fact, is even clearer in the stand-off situations, of course.

In case of ultimate victory going to the insurgent, there also seems to be a marked preference to talks between the opponents as against the no-holds-barred extermination of the enemy, regardless of how favorable (or unfavorable) events seem to turn. In only three major cases in recent decades do we find examples of last-ditch fights: Franco in Spain, Mao in China, and Castro in Cuba. All three, to be sure, offered the individual combatants on the other side a chance to surrender and *join* the guerrillas— but they did not offer the other side a chance at surviving as a political entity. That intransigence was not necessarily unilateral: only too often, the regime in power, by turning down initially modest demands of the revolutionaries, finally corners them into a position where nothing else matters except (as one of them once said, and he was an American) liberty or death.

In the case of ultimate insurgent victories as well as long-drawn stand-offs, the general tendency seems to be, on the part of the government side or its foreign backers, to first refuse to talk to the local insurgent: The French in Indochina for a long time believed that either Russia or Red China could call off the Viet-Minh's war against France; and later, in Algeria, they also hoped that Nasser's defeat at Suez could influence the outcome of the war in their North African possession. In the case of the Yemen stand-off, negotiations go on on all levels at once—between the two Yemeni factions alone, their foreign backers alone, and between the Yemeni-Egyptian and the Yemeni-Saudian coalitions. In fact, the Yemen case has more than one strange resemblance to the Viet-Nam situation precisely because it is non-colonial and because both Yemen factions have solid claims to legitimacy and are in fact recognized by outside powers. The United States, for example, recognizes the Egyptian-backed Sana's regime, and thus finds itself at diplomatic opposites with its own British ally and, above all, the pro-American Saudi Arabians.

The same also held true of the two separate Cyprus insurgencies; the first being an anti-colonial liberation war from Britain; the second a civil war between two Cypriot groups. What makes the Cyprus situation so interesting is that it started out, as its military leader, Greek General George Grivas, clearly points out in his memoirs; as a totally external-fomented attempt at "reunification" [*Enosis*] between Greece and Cyprus. Begun in a sidewalk café in Athens on May 1, 1951, and culminating in overt warfare in Cyprus on March 31, 1955, the Cyprus insurgency finally saw the deployment of 40,000 British troops in an area one-third the size of New Jersey—to deal with 385 guerrillas. Here also, the British commander, Field Marshal Sir John Harding, proclaimed at one point that there could be "no bargaining with violence." But bargaining there was, in a most beautiful Byzantine way, inside Cyprus with the political head of the "liberation movement," Archbishop Makarios; the guerrillas themselves; then with their foreign backers in Athens; and the key foreign opponents of the foreign backers—the Turks (to whom Cyprus once belonged). Other negotiations took place in London, and others yet in the United Nations. One cease-fire was negotiated in 1957, but warfare resumed once more, and when a final settlement was achieved in February, 1959, in Zurich, Switzerland, there was a great deal of fear that neither the Greek outside backers nor the Cypriot political leaders could win the assent of General Grivas and his guerrillas.

What the British overwhelming and terribly expensive military posture on Cyprus achieved was that Cyprus, instead of being unified with Greece, remained as a pro-Greek but independent state studded with British, Greek, and Turkish garrisons. Here again, a comparison with a possible South Viet-Nam settlement is not entirely far-fetched: North Viet-Nam fails in its original plan of reunification—a failure the North Vietnamese have in fact repeatedly conceded since 1956—but the government emerging in Saigon from the war is not unfriendly to Hanoi and gets saddled with American bases at Danang and Cam Ranh, two North Vietnamese garrisons in Camau Peninsula and north of Kontum, plus a stronger Indian-Canadian-Polish International Control Commission (ICC) force in the North-South demilitarized zone.

The second phase of the Cypriot struggle perhaps has even

more bearing on the Viet-Nam case, as the precarious equilibrium of Zurich broke down under the stress of communal strife between the Greek ethnic majority and the Turkish minority, comprising about one-fifth of the total population. A mixed U.N. force, by keeping the roads open and the two ethnic communities apart (along with their foreign military backers), dampened down the war hawks and re-established an equilibrium which has lasted over two years by now, as both sides realized that needless escalation of the Greek and Turkish military presence would only broaden the war without changing political realities.

In the case of Viet-Nam, the French negotiated directly with Ho Chi Minh twice in 1946, once in 1947, and another time in 1952; and there can be no question but that it was the French side which, in every case, caused the contacts to abort by either failing to carry out what was agreed upon (in 1946); by posing totally unacceptable conditions (in 1947); or by withdrawing from the negotiation (in neutral Burma, in 1952) because of American pressures to stay in the war 'till victory—or at least until a cease-fire was achieved in Korea. When the negotiations were finally internationalized at Geneva in 1954 [cf. this writer's "How the French Got Out of Viet-Nam," *NYT Magazine,* May 2, 1965], the internationalization turned out to have added a great deal more power to the Communist side in the form of strong Russian and Chinese delegations than to the French side, with Britain determined to settle the war at almost any price and with the United States unwilling to commit herself to the dire alternatives to settlement. And the French themselves, with the Dien Bien Phu disaster now on their shoulders, had lost all the bargaining power they still had at Rangoon two years earlier, or when Ho in turn made a peace offer to them via a Swedish journalist late in 1953.

In the case of Algeria, the French were in a militarily unlosable position. Hence, the political bargaining that went on was conducted on a great variety of levels and mostly face-to-face with the main opponent, the insurgents themselves. In fact, this seems to emerge as a sort of theorem on how to end an insurgency: when the counterinsurgent is fairly unsure of himself politically, he either tends not to talk at all or prefers the multinational negotiation

282

where middlemen acceptable to both sides can save him from what he considers the "humiliation" of talking to the "rebels." On the other hand, if the counterinsurgent feels fairly sure of himself politically but believes that the military conflict may drag on for a long time, he will attempt to talk—as quietly as possible—with the insurgents themselves. For the latter, too, being relatively weak, might be unable to resist the pressure of some of their own friends to come to terms with the opponent, should the negotiation reach a multinational conference table. The losses which the Viet-Minh needlessly suffered at Geneva in 1954 under the pressure of both Moscow and Peking probably contribute to a large extent to Hanoi's present stubbornness.

Indonesia all by itself is a laboratory for just about every category of how to end undeclared revolutionary wars: the independence war against Holland from 1945 until 1949, assorted with various negotiated cease-fires with the help of the good offices of third parties and of the U.N.; the 1948 Communist rebellion of Madiun, and the one of 1965, both ruthlessly crushed with military force; the 1958 right-wing rebellion, liquidated with the help of a great many multi-level maneuvers and fighting; the *Konfrontasi* with Holland over Western New Guinea which the Dutch won militarily on points but preferred to settle with the help of both the U.N. and Mr. "Good Offices" himself, the infatigable American Ambassador Ellsworth Bunker; and the "Crush Malaya" campaign of the past four years which was recently settled by face-to-face diplomatic negotiations between Indonesia and Malaya. The on-again-off-again fighting in Laos, which was finally frozen into a highly volatile equilibrium, would fall into the same category as the Indonesian situation. Here also, the face-to-face negotiations of 1957 were those that were most successful, and perhaps the best contribution which the 1962 Geneva Conference made to the Laos crisis was that it compelled the three Laotian factions (Right, Left, and Neutral) to come to the conference with at least a semblance of a viable unity program between them. That the whole scheme finally failed can be blamed a great deal more on the various foreign friends of all the Laotian factions than on the Laotians themselves. Almost the same could be said for the Palestine-Israel situation, in which international pressure was barely sufficient (and willing) to bring about an end to open war, but unable (and largely unwilling) to bring about normalization.

That leaves the stand-off situations. Stand-offs can occur anywhere, and not only when the counterinsurgent is militarily stalemated. In fact, most of the time the internal or international political climate simply does not permit him to liquidate the opposition to his heart's content or the best of his military ability. Such stand-offs then occur in many unlikely places: the German-speaking South Tyroleans fight an irredentist guerrilla against Italy since 1918 with at least the quiet and sometimes active sympathy of the neighboring Austrians. To be sure, Italy could muster the military strength and the required police-state measures to jugulate the insurgents, but in a Western Europe still terribly sensitive to the horrors of Nazism and fascism, this is simply not possible. The same goes for the pinpricks of the *Front de Libération Jurassien* in the Bern canton of Switzerland, which fights for a French-speaking Jura canton [state]; for the *Front de Libération Québecois* and other French-speaking nationalist groups in Canada; the Basques in Spain and the Welsh in Britain. In a world where a handful of barely literate fishermen in the Indian Ocean can aspire to, and obtain, full independence, the possibilities for mischief on the part of larger and better-organized communities elsewhere, is almost unlimited. In such cases, stand-off is achieved through the granting of most of what the insurgents want in the way of political and cultural autonomy in the hope (which indeed then often materializes) that the moderate elements will prevail over the hotheads.

In such cases where the government either misses that opportunity or fails to realize in time how dangerous the situation is, it may well find itself embroiled in a real shooting war before it realizes what has happened. The case of the Nagas and Mizos in easternmost India is a case in point: after almost a decade of guerrilla warfare, India now is willing to grant statehood to the Nagas, and direct negotiations have taken place. But with the suffering caused by the war, the demands of some of the Nagas also have escalated, as some of them are now willing to carry on the fight until full independence is attained. The fact that the Indians are 470 million and the Nagas at the most a half-million, does not seem to faze them. A similar stand-off has been reached by the Kurds in their also decades-long struggle with Iraq. Every successive Iraqi government alternately promises the Kurds national equality and local self-government, and a quick military liquidation of the insurgents when the talks break down. That also seems to have been the fate of most Latin American rebellions, even in the face of American military intervention in behalf of one side, as illustrated most recently in the Dominican Republic, or in the past in such places as Guatemala and Nicaragua.

In an article by General V. E. Megee, U. S. Marine Corps (Ret.), published by the *Marine Corps Gazette* at the very moment the Dominican Republic operation was under way, and dealing with the American operations in Nicaragua from 1926 to 1933, General Megee, after having described the unsuccessful attempts of the Marines to catch up with the guerrillas, then told the story of the political outcome: The Marines who had landed to preserve a pro-American Conservative regime in power (an operation which was as unpopular on American campuses in 1927 as the Viet-Nam war was 40 years later) stayed to control the fairness of an election which brought the Liberals of José María Moncado to power. This led General Megee to conclude:

> "There appears to be a lesson here to guide possible future [American] intervention in the domestic politics of occupied countries. If we must intervene, favor the side of the electoral majority."

What all this may mean in terms of settling the Viet-Nam problem is obviously open to divergent interpretations. There is no question, however, but that—all semantic papering-over to the contrary notwithstanding—there is an extremely serious divergence of views between Washington and Air Vice-Marshal Ky's government in Saigon as to how to proceed from here, now that to all appearances military "unlosability" has been established inside South Viet-Nam. At least Washington has, in various ways, gone on record that some sort of direct contact with the Viet Cong is not excluded altogether. Saigon has, with equal consistency, never since the days of the late Ngo Dinh Diem deviated from its view that the only solution to the insurgency was, at the very least, the unconditional surrender of all Viet Cong elements, or their outright extermination.

285

And both the regimes of General Khanh and Ky are on record as being in favor of "liberating" North Viet-Nam as well.

In less extreme terms, Ambassador Henry Cabot Lodge explained that view to an American correspondent in the following exact terms:

> "I think that among the Vietnamese that I know there is a feeling that once the Viet Cong and once Hanoi have been convinced that their attempt at aggression is doomed to failure, that they will stop. They don't visualize a Geneva-type meeting with a lot of people sitting around a table with little signs in front of them, and paper coming out with seals and ribbons on it; that's not how they think it's going to happen."
>
> "I think they [the South Vietnamese] think that once these aggressors are convinced this aggression isn't going to work, the thing is there is going to be a silence, the way there was in the Philippines twelve years ago and the way there was in Malaya . . ."
>
> ". . . I say we know we've won when one morning the young man who's been in the Viet-Cong wakes up and says 'I'm not going back today, and the reason I'm not going back is (a) I think I'll get killed; and (b) . . . American aid is coming in and life looks pretty good right here.' So, he just stops . . ."

There are not only many Vietnamese in Saigon, but also a great many Americans who see the solution to the Viet-Nam problem exactly in those terms, which are also those of Greece and of the Philippines. The only trouble with this reasoning is that the situation in Viet-Nam at the end of 1966 simply is *not* that of Greece in 1949, either politically, militarily, or in terms of the international situation. Too much depends not on the intrinsic strength of South Viet-Nam, but on such uncontrollable contingencies as that China will simply keep mouthing its threats but do nothing; and that the Soviet Union will limit its efforts to keep North Viet-Nam from collapsing but will do no more for the Viet Cong than she did for the Communist guerrillas in Greece or in Azerbaijan. Too much also rests on the assumption that Hanoi can *really* "turn off" 250,000 South Vietnamese guerrillas —she can, of course, "turn off" her 50-odd thousand infiltrated regulars and the logistical support for the VC—like an old water faucet. But, as the Cypriot example has shown, or that of the

Irgun and Stern extremist guerrilla groups in Israel; to name but a few, guerrillas simply don't operate that way.

If Hanoi, after a cease-fire were to go into effect, were to be held directly accountable for every incident in South Viet-Nam (does anyone at all know how many *armed bandits* there are in South Viet-Nam?), then the war will go on forever. After all, the mighty United States, with all the electronic gear at her disposal in the Florida area, is still incapable of keeping airborne or seaborne Cuban exile raiders from attacking Cuba.

But if both Hanoi and Saigon—and the latter is, in that case, far more important than Washington—are willing to accept a peace-making machinery which involves a measure of international "buf-fering" between the two parties, then all is not lost. I would envisage a mix of the Palestine and Cypriot peacemaking structure as being most applicable to Viet-Nam. To be sure, Hanoi has thus far been strongly opposed to a United Nations intervention. However, it is willing to accept a revitalized ICC with its Indians, Canadians, and Poles—and those three nations are U.N. members and could well accept a U.N. "presence" in their midst or attached to them in some capacity. After all, the Communist nations (China included) did not object to such a presence a few years ago in Laos. And, perhaps most noteworthy of all, the National Liberation Front—the political arm of the Viet Cong—has, in some of its statements in the past, shown that it would not be opposed to some sort of international presence in a settlement of the Viet-Nam conflict. This, by the way, is again an occasion where differences of view between the N.L.F. and Hanoi would work in favor of the West, if only there were some willingness to recognize that such differences exist.

The ultimate problem, then, seems to be whether Saigon and Washington can see any usefulness not only in talking to the Viet Cong, but in making it the more important of the interlocutors on the other side; or whether the immense arsenals of American weapons and the vast reinforcements of American troops bound for Viet-Nam in the months to come, are precisely designed to make such negotiations totally groundless by reason of extermina-tion, surrender, or evacuation of the enemy. If the latter is true, then the whole present peace effort, like (as is now apparent) that of last year, is merely to have everybody "hold still" long enough to make the next military round possible.

But if, as was the case in some other revolutionary wars before, the insurgent again manages to survive this new huge effort just as he survived the 1965–66 bomber offensive and "spoiling operations"; then the next round of negotiation attempts may well involve an enemy now fully backed by an aroused Soviet Union, if one is to believe the news of the arrival of significantly larger amounts of Soviet military advisers and matériel in North Viet-Nam.

And *that* would make a "silent" ending of the Viet-Nam war rather unlikely.

288

141